T0329989

Human Capital, Inter-firm Mobility and Organizational Evolution

To Eva and Matilde,
our very loyal supporters

Human Capital, Inter-firm Mobility and Organizational Evolution

Johannes M. Pennings

Department of Management, Wharton School, University of Pennsylvania, US and Faculty of Economics and Business Administration, University of Tilburg, The Netherlands

Filippo Carlo Wezel

Faculty of Communication Sciences, University of Lugano, Switzerland

Edward Elgar
Cheltenham, UK • Northampton, MA, USA

Published by
Edward Elgar Publishing Limited
Glensanda House
Montpellier Parade
Cheltenham
Glos GL50 1UA
UK

Edward Elgar Publishing, Inc.
William Pratt House
9 Dewey Court
Northampton
Massachusetts 01060
USA

A catalogue record for this book
is available from the British Library

Library of Congress Cataloguing in Publication Data
Pennings, Johannes M.
  Human capital, inter-firm mobility and organizational evolution / Johannes M. Pennings and Filippo Carlo Wezel.
      p.   cm.
  Includes bibliographical references and index.
  1. Human capital.   2. Personnel management.   3. Career development.
4. Corporations—Valuation.   I. Wezel, Filippo Carlo, 1973–   II. Title.
  HD4904 7.P49 2007
  331.11—dc22

                                                                    2007017580

ISBN 978 1 84542 757 3

Printed and bound in Great Britain by MPG Books Ltd, Bodmin, Cornwall

Contents

Figures

Tables

Preface

This volume is the fruit of various collaborative efforts to trace the evolution of firms in a professional service sector that happens to be located in the Netherlands but which could be viewed as paradigmatic of the evolution of organizations and their sectors over a wide range of fields and geographies.

This monograph comprises both previously published and unpublished chapters. Chapters that appeared as edited articles in refereed journals have been refashioned in such a way to coherently and thoroughly conform with the topic of the book. We have added two introductory chapters (Part I) to theoretically position the studies reported here and to provide a more integrative perspective on an important class of organizations, namely single proprietorships and partnerships. The completion of this book has been possible thanks to the invaluable collaboration of an evolving network of authors who, at one time or another, were conducting empirical research regarding the Dutch audit industry. They represent several disciplines, including industrial economics, strategic management, human resources management and, above all, organization theory.

Chapters on the single proprietorships and partnerships that constitute the players in the Dutch accounting sector are presented in two groups. The book builds upon recent developments within macro organizational theory to investigate the role of individuals in shaping firm-level and sector-level processes of mutualism and competition. Theoretically, the book deals with two main subjects: human (and social) capital and inter-firm mobility in relation to firm evolution, change and performance. We theorize about the contribution of people (that is, human and social capital) into macro-organizational theories with specific reference to ecological and institutional theory. Moreover, taking into account the fact that geographical proximity increases social interaction and the circulation of knowledge and information via personal contacts, in several of the following chapters we consider the role of geography in an examination of the institutional and ecological mechanisms under investigation. Part II provides conceptual and factual background on professional services firms to set the stage for people in organizational behavior and decision-making. Part III elaborates on Part II: as people matter for organizational behavior, the consequences related to their individual conduct, such as mobility between firms and their demographic, are further explored.

Much of the original data used in these chapters was collected as part of a research project conducted by Willem Bujink, Steven Maijoor, Arjen van Witteloostuijn, and Maurice Zinken, NIBOR, Department of Economics, Maastricht University, the Netherlands. The investigation was launched by these colleagues at the University of Maastricht who converted hard copies of membership directories into a spreadsheet that comprised bi-annual data from the inception of the sector into the year 1992. Johannes Pennings was a part-time faculty member at Maastricht University and soon joined the team to probe deeper into what proved to be a very rich data set.

Maurice Zinken, in collaboration with Ilja Gottfried, was critical in the conversion of the data from hard copy to electronic format – a truly gargantuan task. Kyungmook Lee also played a major role in the data management, cleaning the entries, which were fraught with inconsistencies. He eliminated many false duplicates that inevitably surfaced when sourcing and transmitting names from paper to the keyboard. Eliminating the numerous errors in the directories was an equally gargantuan task. To reduce the workload of data entry, it was decided to skip every other year during the most recent decades, up to the beginning of the 1990s. The entry of the hard copy data was financed by the Limpberg Institute in Amsterdam, an organization created for the advancement of accounting research in the Netherlands.

The membership directories of successive Dutch accounting associations were available in book format for transfer to electronic files. The directories provided extensive information on various demographic attributes of members, for example gender, educational level, location, private address, office and firm affiliation, and rank within the firm. The individual data could be aggregated to firm, regional and national level, thus also producing sector or market information. The longitudinal data permitted a further culling of false duplicates, and even more so the construction of information on career progression, firm size and firm growth. The multi-level nature of the data was also a major advantage. While the data permitted the creation of 'frequency-related' analyses, much deeper and more interesting analyses could be performed on a remarkable sample of firms with their members in an emerging and evolving industry showing a wide range of events including entrepreneurship, merger and acquisition, splits, bankruptcy and mobility. All this could be examined at the firm level, but as firms comprise a membership, the analysis was extended to phenomena such as career steps, turnover, mobility between competitors and organizational demography. The data used in these chapters permitted a longitudinal examination of demographic profiles within and between firms. Such inquiries are quite unique in the literature to date where demographic studies are often approached via a cross-sectional design.

Many colleagues have been involved in the production of the chapters that are included in this volume. Foremost are those who co-authored papers. Arjen van Witteloostuijn from Antwerpen University, formerly at the University of Groningen and at Maastricht University, was a major instigator of the research reported here and co-authored Chapter 4. He was the catalyst for moving the inquiry beyond a study of the accounting sector into a study of accounting as a market, comprising firms endowed with human assets and connected via personnel mobility.

Kyungmook Lee, now at Seoul National University in Korea, formerly a doctoral student at the Wharton School, not only provided major clerical input, such as the cleaning of the data, but was also a major architect of the data files, and performed significant econometric analysis on the data. Most importantly, he co-authored chapters 3, 4, 5 and 6. Later, Gino Cattani, then at the Wharton School of the University of Pennsylvania, and Filippo Carlo Wezel jointly developed an interest in the strategic aspects of partnerships by exploiting the multi-level nature of the data. Revisiting the data revealed the potential to exploit the individual level of analysis for understanding strategic and sector-level inquiries, drawing on implications from evolutionary economics and biology. Our collaboration on chapters 7 and 8 was fun, enhancing and very fruitful. Thank you very much Gino for all that. In Philadelphia, Rahul Patel of Drexel University provided magnificent data management assistance.

Many people have commented on various components that are included in this volume or have sustained our effort. We would like to mention Paul Allison, Harry Barkema, Jos Becker, Josef Bruderl, Christophe Van den Bulte, Christophe Boone, Anne Cummings, Henrich Greve, Mauro Guillen, Ben Hoetjes, Peter Kamper, Cornelis Lammers, Mark Lazerson, Jackson Nickerson, Jan de Pree, Joel Waldfogel, Udo Zander, Paul Almeida, Sigal Barsade, Timothy Devinney, Bernard Forgues, Donald Hambrick, Bruce Kogut, Gianni Lorenzoni, John Lafkas, Daniel Levinthal, Alessandro Lomi, Xavier Martin, Tammy Masden, Phanish Puranam, Ayse Saka, Gabriel Szulanski, Gordon Walker, and Sidney Winter. We greatly appreciate the generous financial support of several institutions whose grants made possible the research presented in this book as well as the time required for its writing. We would like to mention the Wharton School at the University of Pennsylvania, the University of Lugano (Switzerland), Tilburg University (the Netherlands), and the Universities of Groningen (the Netherlands), Bologna (Italy), and Antwerpen (Belgium). Needless to say, all errors remain our responsibility.

We thank the following publishers for permission to adapt portions of the following copyrighted articles:

Pennings, J.M., K. Lee and A. van Witteloostuijn (1998), 'Human and Social Capital and Organizational Dissolution', *Academy of Management Journal*, **41**(4): 425–40.

Pennings, J.M. and K. Lee (2002), 'Mimicry and the Market: Adoption of a New Organizational Form', *Academy of Management Journal*, **45**(1): 144–62.

Pennings, J.M. and K. Lee (1999), 'Social Capital of Organizations: Conceptualization, Level of Analysis and Performance Implications', in *Corporate Social Capital*, ed. S. Gabbay and R. Leenders (Norwell, MA: Kluwer Academic).

Cattani, G., J.M. Pennings and F.C. Wezel (2003), 'Spatial and Temporal of Heterogeneity in Founding Patterns', *Organization Science*, **14**(6): 670–85.

Wezel, F.C., G. Cattani and J.M. Pennings (2006), 'Competitive Implications of Inter-firm Mobility', *Organization Science*, **17**(6): 691–709.

Philadelphia and Lugano,
January 2007

PART I

Theoretical and empirical foundations

1. The role of individual conduct in macro-organizational theory

INTRODUCTION

The main idea of this book centers on the relationship between sets of organizations and their members. The intuition behind it is simple: organizational evolutionary processes take place simultaneously at multiple 'Russian-doll-like' hierarchical levels of analysis (Campbell, 1974). Industries are composed by organizations, which are composed by groups of people. The elements of these hierarchies interact, influencing organizational evolution. Such mutualistic and competitive interactions take place both within and across levels of analysis. Literature on strategic management, for instance, studies the competitive interactions among the firms that compose a sector. Yet, the interactions within one level provide a limited view of the evolutionary process under investigation. Cross-level interactions influence organizational evolution as well. Consider, for instance, the role of managers in shaping organizational outcomes. As individual members are essential components of organizations, their decisions and actions (notwithstanding inertia) affect organizational behavior, which in turn conditions the interactions among the firms in a sector. While there is a relative autonomy within each evolutionary level, cross-level interactions may well be responsible for processes of upward and downward causation (Singh and Lumsden, 1990).

Hierarchical thinking has a long history in organizational studies (March and Simon, 1958; Thompson, 1967). However, in much of the existing macro-organizational literature, the individual level is often disregarded (at least when formulating empirical predictions) with the result that firms are treated as black boxes. This approach remains rooted in sociological principles that assume organizations to be 'imperatively coordinated associations' (Weber, 1947) and relatively independent from their members, ultimately stressing elements of similarity and the competitive pressures for resources or normative legitimacy they face. Organization ecologists, for instance, relying heavily on the concept of organizational inertia (Hannan and Freeman, 1984), have focused on cycles of variation, selection and retention at the population level, often making abstractions from the processes taking place within organizations (see Carroll and Hannan, 2000). Institutional theory has dug a bit deeper into organizational processes and decision-making by considering the ways in which structures, rules, norms, or routines, become established as authoritative guidelines for organizational behavior. A great deal of empirical research has concentrated on how these elements are created and diffused over space and time; or how they may fall into decline and disuse.

When adopting a more micro point of view, a different picture emerges (see also Boone et al., 2006). Other theoretical fragments suggest that people should feature more prominently in theories of organizations as they are the essence of organizations (see Stinchcombe, 1997). Building on the insights of March and his colleagues (March and Simon, 1958; Cyert and March, 1963), Pfeffer (1983) and Hambrick and Mason (1984) have underscored how organizations are, to a certain extent, a reflection of the characteristics of their upper echelons and of the distribution of their demographic traits. Because individuals enact routines, it becomes central to study managers' demographic profiles since their characteristics are presumed to be associated with specific psychological dispositions and subsequent strategic choices.

This book aims at bridging these seemingly diverging perspectives. Building on micro-level research, we argue that individual characteristics such as career progression, tenure or length of service in the industry, and personnel mobility may inform us not only about organizational behavior and performance, but also about cross-level effects, such as the competitive positioning that becomes shaped by individual actions. Consider, for example, the case of inter-firm mobility. Organizational members are free to migrate in and out of firms as well as of the sector. Typically job mobility has been studied using vacancy chain models (White, 1970). The basic assumption of these models is that mobility depends on both the availability of empty positions within a given job system and the interdependence among jobs to be filled. In other words, when one person gets a new job or leave his/her current job, a vacancy is then created. If another person gets that job, his/her previous position becomes vacant and so on. A person entering the system to take a job ends the chain of vacancies. In growing industries the demand for labor increases. However, the emergence of new firms creates new job opportunities (Hachen, 1992). In his study of the US economy over the 1974–76 period, Birch (1981) found that organizational foundings increased the pool of all jobs by 6.7 per cent. By the same token, a study by the Brookings Institution examining the years between 1978 and 1980 found that new enterprises added 7.7 million jobs to the pool (Carroll and Hannan, 2000).

While some scholars (Hannan, 1988; Carroll et al., 1992; Haveman and Cohen, 1994; Greve, 1994) have acknowledged that variations in new job opportunities reflect the evolution of populations of organizations, little attention has been devoted to the study of the consequences of inter-firm mobility, both for the donor and for the recipient (but see some notable exceptions discussed below). Individuals constitute the repositories of the skills and the knowledge accumulated by the firm over time. As individuals move, not only are such skills and knowledge transferred spatially and temporally (Argote, 1999), but also pre-existing relations with clients may follow analogous migratory patterns. Loss of (key members) is likely to alter the firm's human and social capital and affect the functioning of its routines and structure. We elaborate on this logic by moving from two simple assumptions: (i) members (especially those belonging to the upper echelons) critically shape organizational behavior and (ii) they tend to replicate their behavior and choices across firms (see, for example, Fligstein, 1990). When these two conditions hold, inter-firm migration may inform us on the way in which mutualism and competition unfolds among organizations. Managers are carriers of firm knowledge that becomes diffused through their migration among firms, and can condition the intensity of competition as well as the diffusion of prevailing institutional arrangements. Members' departure or entry incurs significant additions or losses of firm knowledge which might embellish or erode a firm's competitive advantage. We believe that by invoking members' conduct (that is, inferred from their demographic profiles and their mobility) we learn a great deal about firm behavior and its changes over time, especially long-term changes that entail ecological and institutional patterns.

Empirically, the book will deal with two main subjects: (i) human and social capital and (ii) inter-firm mobility. We will primarily theorize about the contribution of people to macro-organizational theories (that is, ecology and institutional theory). The discussion of these two dimensions will be further anchored into geographical space which is especially interesting because it roots firms back into spatial environments. Taking the spatial reach of industries into account is important to a consideration of the social and institutional contexts within which firm decisions are embedded. Geography can be regarded as a source of opportunities and constraints for entrepreneurs. Geographical differences across markets, in fact, often mirror differences in social structures and conduciveness to innovation (Almeida and Kogut, 1999; Jaffe et al., 1993; Saxenian, 1994). Geographical proximity induces more frequent interactions and information exchange (Teece, 1994; Levinthal and March, 1993; Peteraf and Shanley, 1997) and stimulates the circulation of knowledge through personal contacts (Scherer, 1984) and spillover effects (see Saxenian, 1994). Consider the decision of entrepreneurs to enter a specific industry. As Aldrich and Fiol remark, the standard theory implies that 'founders of new ventures appear to be fools, for they are navigating, at best, in an institutional vacuum of indifferent munificence' (1994: 645). Entrepreneurs – as boundedly rational actors – are more likely to seek new investment opportunities locally (Lomi, 1995; Sorenson and Audia, 2000; Wezel, 2005). Any entrepreneurial decision is in fact embedded in a geographical space characterized by heterogeneous characteristics.

The geographical dimension becomes especially important when considering that the book deals with professional services organizations in law, accounting, consulting, medicine and architecture – all heavily rooted in their geographical environment. The empirical setting draws heavily on a set of empirical studies of the Dutch accounting industry, analyzing data including firm- (thousands of firms) and individual-level information (that is, regarding the careers of thousands of partners). Partnerships differ in many respects from other classes of organizations, whether by governance, ownership, legal liability, staffing and operations and have not received the same level of attention as for example industrial corporations, NGOs or small and medium-sized enterprises (SMEs). Chapter 2 will review partnerships from their inception and explores such phenomena as sector evolution, regulations, mergers and acquisitions, connections with competing firms, turnover, recruitment and poaching. Altogether, therefore, this book provides insights into members, their mobility in and out of firms, the shifts in human and social capital and the associated organizational demographics in order to shed light on organizational and inter-organizational changes over time, including renewal and dissolution.

Before moving to the discussion of specific empirical issues, we would like to briefly review the state of the art of the two major theoretical building blocks we discuss throughout the book: the ecological (Hannan and Freeman, 1977) and the neo-institutional (Meyer and Rowan, 1977) theories of organizations. First, we will stress the sociological nature of these theories and their relative obliviousness to the role of human agency in organizational behavior and performance; later we will review more recent developments that have helped to move the field beyond the early approach and to shed light on the role of individual action in the aggregate patterns observed.

ORGANIZATIONAL ECOLOGY AND INSTITUTIONALISM

Organization ecology developed as a paradigm for the description of markets and the firms which comprise them. The original question that inspired Michael Hannan and John Freeman to launch their organizational ecology research program, relates to the genesis of organizational diversity: 'Why are there so many kinds of organization and why are there no more?' (Freeman and Hannan, 1983: 1116). Translating insights from human ecology (Hawley, 1950) and biology (Levins, 1968) to an organizational context, Hannan and Freeman's key to answering this question was to be found in the environmental resource space. Organizations exhibiting a comparable set of skills and routines to transform inputs into output (that is, a similar blueprint) will depend on similar resources (Hannan and Freeman, 1977). Organizational forms, like biological species, come and go in close relation with shifts in their environmental fitness. Hannan and Freeman (1977 and 1984) believe that long-term change in the diversity of organizational forms within a population occurs through selection rather than via adaptation. A central pillar of their logic is that organizational theories often fail to acknowledge the inertial forces that kept firms frozen in their structure and tend to embrace too readily the possibility of fundamental change. In their 1984 article, Hannan and Freeman argued that organizations strive towards consistency of replication and high levels of reliability and accountability to reach a low variance in the quality of their performance, including its timeliness. As organizations evolve over time, and enhance their practices, routines become well established and acquire further consistency. The institutionalization of organizational structures, processes, and routines renders them taken for granted and widespread, thus conferring legitimacy. Stable and reproducible routines are in fact the foundation of reliable performance (Hannan and Freeman, 1984). Since the ability to reproduce a structure with high fidelity strengthens resistance to change, structural inertia is the end result of selection. Organizations face economic (previous investments), social (internal conflict) and evolutionary constraints (strategic legacy, path-dependence in learning, information filters), which often hinder them from adapting (Hannan and Freeman, 1977: 931). In a related way, Nelson and Winter (1982) have elaborated on routines as the genes of organizational existence and evolution. They have highlighted, for instance, the disruptive effects triggered by organizational turnover. In particular, they maintain, 'the memories of individual organization members are a primary repository of the operational knowledge of the organization. Some part of the information thus stored may be readily replaced if the particular member storing it leaves the organization' (1982: 115). As knowledge is often tacit the 'loss of an employee with such important idiosyncratic knowledge poses a major threat to the continuity of routine – indeed, if the departure is unanticipated, continuity is necessarily broken' (1982: 115). The continuity of routines then is seriously undermined when, as in the case of personnel turnover, established patterns of activity are disrupted and an organization is unable to keep things under control.

But how does a form gets defined? Identifying an organizational form is not an easy task, and commonsense categorizations – for example, on the basis of catalogues and locations – have been applied to define them (Rao, 2002). An emerging line of research has challenged the idea of industries as homogeneous entities and underscored the existence of geographical boundaries responsible for spatial heterogeneity (Cattani et al., 2003; Greve, 2002; Lomi, 1995; Sorenson and Audia, 2000). More recently, Pólos et al. (2002) have adopted a more cognitive approach and argued that organizational forms (the genes of populations) are defined on the basis of a set of codes, shared interrelated rules, assumptions, beliefs, and premises that lead to prescribed patterns of behavior. In other words, the members of a population may be conceived as involved in the production and reproduction of symbols, rituals, and myths that develop and sustain the existence of an identity. Whatever the rationale adopted for setting the relevant boundaries, when one (or more) of the dimensions sustaining the existence of the form is modified through an environmental change, organizations face adaptation constraints and selection is likely to unfold. A vast array of findings in related fields of research provides support to this logic. Levinthal and March (1993), for instance, have demonstrated how decision-makers are unable to recognize and consider alternative and potentially more rewarding courses of action due to cognitive inertia. This evidence builds on the behavioral principle of threat-rigidity (Staw et al., 1981), according to which an event interpreted as a threat (that is, a change in the status quo) distorts rational information-processing and leads to the adoption of conservative interpretation schemes. Similarly, Tripsas and Gavetti (2000) attributed Polaroid's failure in the digital camera market to top managers' inability to recognize the paradigm shift in photography, sharply distant from the deeply-held beliefs crystallized in their historical business of analog photography. This type of cognitive inertia has been shown to render an organization more rigid in the face of disruptions (Christensen, 1997). Given the limited ability of human beings to cope with change, and given that environmental change routinely shapes economies and markets, population-level selection can be meaningfully considered a critical driver of industrial evolution.

Subsequent studies have built on these insights and focused on the evolutionary dynamics of certain forms – on the ways in which new types of organizations arise, compete, and vanish over long periods of time (Hannan and Freeman, 1989). In this respect, the theory of density-dependence has taken center stage in the last two decades. According to this theory organizational entries and exits from a population are affected by density-dependence phenomena (Hannan, 1986). In particular, the forces of legitimation and competition are the main drivers that shape the vital rates of a population and these processes are proxied by the density of incumbent organizations. An organizational form obtains *legitimation* the very moment it is considered to possess a socially recognized genetic code (Meyer and Rowan, 1977). According to the original formulation, increments of density during this phase improve the social acknowledgement of the form, increasing the entries in the population and diminishing the chance of mortality of the incumbent organizations. However, marginal increments of organizations above the level of capacity of the system generate competitive pressures that act in the opposite direction of legitimation, with the result of declining entries and increasing mortality rates. As ecological theories view organizations essentially as consumers of resources, the presence of competitors reduces the population's carrying capacity. As Hannan and Freeman put it: 'High density implies strong competitive interaction within populations dependent on limited resources for organizing [. . .] As density grows relative to the current level of the carrying capacity, supplies of potential organizers, members, patrons and resources become exhausted' (1989: 132). At a population level, then, the overall growth is constrained by a limited set of resources available. With respect to the classical formulation of the theory, legitimation and competition are supposed to counterbalance one another (Baum, 1995).

Recent developments have stressed the role of geography in moderating the forces of density-dependence. In an attempt to clarify the unit of analysis of density-dependence, the study by Carroll and Wade (1991) marked a period of renewed attention to the spatial dynamics of organizational populations. Other researchers have studied smaller geographical areas (regions, states, provinces) and compared the effects of local, neighboring, and national density-dependent legitimation and competition. Recent empirical findings seem to suggest that legitimation and competition affect entries along a geographical gradient, with a primacy of local processes over both neighboring and national ones (Lomi, 1995; Greve, 2002; Wezel, 2005). However improved, the theory of density-dependence remains silent on the role of individual actions (for example, managerial mobility) for diffusion of an organizational form and its associated level of competition, ultimately stressing the sociological, blind component behind the aggregate changes taking place within industries.

Institutional theorists, albeit starting from a more micro-level perspective, have concentrated on those processes of 'pluralistic ignorance' and conformity that sustain organizational homogeneity. Meyer and Rowan (1977) and DiMaggio and Powell (1983) 'propose that isomorphism is the master bridging process in institutional environments: by incorporating institutional rules within their own structures, organizations become more homogeneous, more similar in structure, over time' (Scott, 1981, p. 209). It has been argued that social upheaval, technological disruption, competitive discontinuities, and regulatory change (Meyer et al., 1990; Powell, 1991) destabilize established rules and practices, redefining the values and the assumptions to which organizational behavior is anchored. With the emergence of new structures of meaning, stability is reduced. Under such conditions, organizations cannot rely on performance feedbacks to make sense of their behavior. That is because, in uncertain environments, 'the application of old routines can produce experiences that are not easy to explain within the current interpretative schema of the organization' (Lant et al., 1992: 588). Consequently, organizational rules that act as templates for action no longer serve as an effective guide for future action. Under conditions of institutional instability, organizations model themselves after other similar organizations (DiMaggio and Powell, 1983; Tolbert and Zucker, 1983). Misalignments with the institutional context create pressures in terms of social expectations to imitate popular routines for success. In a recent review Ingram (2002: 658) remarked that under uncertainty, it may be appropriate to mimic others' behavior, for 'as long as there is some chance that others have better information than the focal decision maker, it may be rational to do what those others do'. The advantage of such mimetic behavior is that, in the face of uncertainty, an organization can carry out the search for a viable solution more conveniently by utilizing the experience of similar others (DiMaggio and Powell, 1983). Building on the work of Berger and Luckmann (1967) and Selznick (1957), these scholars suggest that organizations consider not only their technical environment but also their 'institutional' environment: coercive, normative, and cultural-cognitive features that define 'social fitness' (Meyer and Rowan, 1977; DiMaggio and Powell, 1983). By and large Meyer and Rowan (1977) advance the idea that formal organizational structures have rather symbolic properties. Through coercive, mimetic and normative isomorphism, new rules and practices are legitimated.

'Neo'-institutionalists thus called attention to the role of symbolic elements – routines and scripts that perform a critical role in shaping individual and collective behavior (Scott, 2001). Legitimacy is a central concept in institutional theory (Meyer and Rowan, 1977; Zucker, 1977; DiMaggio and Powell, 1983) and has been widely used by various other organizational theorists (for example, Hannan and Freeman, 1989; Aldrich and Fiol, 1994). As Suchman (1995: 574) puts it, legitimacy is 'a generalized perception or assumption that the actions of an entity are desirable, proper, or appropriate within some socially constructed system of norms, values, beliefs, and definitions'. A key feature of legitimacy is the positive feedback behind its reproduction. As actors take collective action in the direction of a common purpose, legitimated activities become routinized. Selznick (1957: 17) observed that practices become connoted with social meanings, 'infused with value beyond the technical requirements of the task at hand'. As Colyvas and Powell (2006) have stressed, the extant literature highlights multiple aspects of legitimacy, which may well be – according to several authors (see Baum and Powell, 1995; Aldrich and Fiol, 1994) – separable. A central feature of legitimacy, however, whatever its conception and main components, is that it exists as a shared presumption.

The legitimacy of the new rule or practice depends on the nature of the taken-for-grantedness (see Colyvas and Powell, 2006). Taken-for-grantedness has been central to institutionalism, providing the cognitive pillar of the existing social order (Zucker, 1977). In this respect, organizations have to exhibit some kind of social fitness to survive. As Selznick put it, there are two very distinct approaches to studying organizations: as economies on the one hand, and as components of social structure on the other. As he explains:

> [C]onsidered as an economy, organization is a system of relationships which define the availability of scarce resources and which may be manipulated in terms of efficiency and effectiveness . . . Organization as an economy is, however, necessarily conditioned by the organic states of the concrete structure, outside of the systematics of delegation and control . . . Unfortunately for the adequacy of formal systems of coordination, the needs of individuals do not permit a single-minded attention to the stated goals of the system within which they have been assigned. (Selznick, 1948: 25–26)

Therefore, the social fitness of the organization matters as much as the economic fitness. As previously mentioned, institutional theory primarily emphasizes the role of social factors (for example, external conformity pressures from regulatory bodies, social pressures and collective, social construction processes) in driving organizational action. As a result of such an emphasis on social fitness, most of the empirical research in institutional theory has analyzed adoption as a conformance model. Conformance models of adoption propose that new procedures are imitated owing to their popularity rather than their performance. This view holds that organizations are embedded in a web of values, norms, rules, beliefs and taken-for-granted assumptions through relational connectedness. Conformity pressures stem from emotional and cognitive needs such as the affirmation of social identity and reduction of cognitive dissonance. Therefore, new ideas diffuse and become taken for granted in social contexts (Meyer and Rowan, 1977) creating imperatives for conformity for organizations to gain legitimacy (Meyer and Scott, 1983).

RECENT DEVELOPMENTS IN ECOLOGY AND INSTITUTIONAL THEORY

Ecological research has centered around the concept of structural inertia. Entering new markets, for instance, implies a strategic repositioning of the company that is likely to generate a cascade of associated changes – both inside and outside the organization. Different products may require different production processes, logistic procedures, pricing policies, marketing campaigns, and the like (see, for example, Wezel and van Witteloostuijn, 2006). Given that significantly modifying organizations threatens their performance, ecologists have analyzed the vital (that is, founding, change and mortality) rates of organizations as the main drivers of change and of diversity within organizational populations, often abstracting from individual conduct. Similarly, neo-institutionalism views firms and managers as being superseded by prevailing standards, socially constructed codes or 'myths' to which they subscribe and conform in the quest for legitimacy and, ultimately, for survival. Yet, recently we have witnessed some cracks in this sociological bulwark with both ecology and institutional theory becoming informed by the role of human agency for inter-firm competition and for the institutionalism of organizational fields.

With a few recent exceptions, both perspectives have remained oblivious of the significance of individual action and decision-making in triggering mutualistic and competitive relations among organizations. We remain convinced that to advance research on organizations we need to develop theories in which micro processes (individual choice) are integrated into macro (population) ones and *vice versa* (see also Baum and Singh, 1994). Several prominent scholars have investigated the process through which individual decisions influence collective behaviors and *vice versa*. Adopting a backward approach – from macro to micro – sociologists like Durkheim (1897) have shown how suicide rates can be interpreted in the light of macro-structural forces, such as, for example, the decline of mechanical solidarity and rise of organic solidarity due to industrialization. By the same token, embracing a forward-looking perspective – from micro to macro – economists like Schelling (1978) have illustrated how local interactions among agents following simple behavioral rules give rise to aggregate regularities. Consider the way Campbell (1994) discusses the issues related to executive incentives. He sees executives as 'parasites', whose efforts to maximize their benefits are at odds with the fitness of the firm. The critique of Campbell concerns the fact that organizational ecologists work on the wrong level of analysis: it is not the firm (or the population) that has to be studied but rather the executive

– and his/her mobility. Driven by strong incentives for clique selfishness (Campbell, 1994), migration into and out of top management teams does contribute to modifying the behavior of companies, their choices and outcomes. Building on these insights, this book underscores how the actions of individual members shape organizational outcomes whether these ought to be framed ecologically or institutionally, or as mutualism and competition.

How much discretion or 'freedom' do members enjoy in a social context whose structure is a phenomenon in its own right, what the sociologists call '*sui generis*'? These emerging organizational properties on the one hand constrain individual behavior and endow it with meanings while, on the other, providing it with opportunities for deviance and innovation (see Granovetter, 1985; Emirbayer, 1998). The rationale is that individual actions, including motivated or premeditated behavior, are embedded in social relations and cannot be assumed to be independent. Granovetter (1985) famously indicated that an economics based methodological individualism and social reductionism are paradoxically similar in their neglect of social structures. The under-socialized concept, which prevails in neoclassical economics abstracts away from the social context in which people engage in exchanges and conceptualizes markets as comprising atomistic behavior of price-taking anonymous buyers and sellers supplied with perfect information. Similarly, the over-socialized concept of man treats human agency as being subject to the inducement of consensually shared norms and values, absorbed through socialization such that compliance is not perceived as an imposition. As Granovetter indicates, 'both have in common a conception of action and decision carried out by atomized actors. In the under socialized account, atomization results from narrow utilitarian pursuit of self interest; in the oversocialized one, from the fact that behavioral patterns have been internalized and ongoing social relations thus have only peripheral effects on behavior' (1985: 485). Granovetter then proceeds with the concept of 'embeddedness' and argues that individuals are at once the beneficiaries of a normative impact of their networks of relationships (trust, mutuality, and so on) and the very authors of the networks that sustain the order that we observe among them. This echoes Giddens's (1971) views that social structures are both constituted by human agency and at the same time are the very medium of this constitution. Both authors would therefore suggest that the prominence of human agency is paramount when individuals are well embedded, while in the opposite case, where individuals behave atomistically, the impact of their actions remains small scale, inconsequential and episodic. For example, fraudulent behavior and unpremeditated actions are particularly harmful and large-scale when leveraged through connected individuals – compare Leeson at Baring with, for instance, the Unabomber who operated as a loner from the state of Montana.

This train of thought is implicit in many of the inquiries in this volume. Members associated with a firm might engage in behaviors that have important repercussions on their firm or even their firm's sector or niche. In Chapter 8, for example, it is observed that two firms become similar demographically through the movement of members between the top echelons of two competing firms, while Chapter 9 explores the movement of key members who start a competing, entrepreneurial firm and greatly impact the long-term outlook of the firm from which they defected. Leaving a firm as a group is disproportionately harmful, and its effect is further amplified when the members have kept company for a long time. Such findings demonstrate the importance of human agency in conditioning ecological and institutional processes. McPherson is one of the first scholars to investigate the role of individual choice and action for ecological competition.[1] He started by noticing that social groups (including top management teams and organizations) are not random samples of people (McPherson et al., 1992). Instead, people are systematically sorted into groups whose members have similar sociodemographic characteristics. Blau (1977) convincingly argued that demographic characteristics influence social interaction: social interaction is more likely to occur between people who are similar with respect to demographic features (McPherson et al., 1992; 2001). Indeed, evidence shows that 'distances along sociodemographic dimensions translate into probability of contact between individuals for almost all kinds of messages passing through the system, whether the messages are money, socialization, attitudes, group formation, or the like' (McPherson et al., 1992: 155). This self-reinforcing relationship is also known as the 'homophily principle'. The tendency of social groups to reproduce themselves by the selective recruitment of similar others and by facilitating the turnover of dissimilar ones, has also been labeled as 'homosocial reproduction' by Kanter (1977) – see also Schneider's (1987) attraction-selection-attrition (ASA) model. McPherson and colleagues (McPherson, 1983; McPherson and Smith-Lovin, 1987; McPherson et al., 1992; McPherson and Rotolo, 1996) systematically studied a large variety of voluntary organizations, ranging from sports clubs to churches in the US. They found that in the course of competition for members, these organizations specialize in specific local regions of sociodemographic space (McPherson et al., 1992). When mapping voluntary organizations onto the demographic dimensions of the member's occupation and education level, they observe that the means in both dimensions differ between organizations and that the within-firm standard deviations are much smaller than a random sample of individuals would produce. In McPherson's (macro-) sociological theory, social structure, via its impact on network ties, drives the selective entry and exit of members into and out of groups. As people tend to develop network ties with other people sharing similar sociodemographic characteristics, individuals coming together to form groups are relatively similar. This similarity is perpetuated due to conservative, selective recruitment of new members (McPherson et al., 1992; Popielarz and McPherson, 1995). The putative reason is that demographic dissimilarity from group members acts as a centrifugal force because homophily implies that atypical members have more external ties to non-members and are less closely tied to fellow group members (Popielarz and McPherson, 1995). Empirical research on voluntary organizations indeed shows (1) that entry and exit of groups members depend upon the number and strength of social network ties that connect group members to each other and to non-members (McPherson et al., 1992), and (2) that atypical members will leave the group first (Popielarz and McPherson, 1995). Group formation is determined by general constraints in the social network with respect to logically possible choices, rather than by 'individual utilities or imputed production functions' that guide our choices to join and stay in groups (McPherson and Ranger-Moore, 1991: 38).

Boone et al. (2006) have pushed this multi-level logic which stresses the role of individual actions as the foundations of aggregate ecological diversity even further. The logic of their argument comes in three steps. First, social groups follow rules of reproduction based on the principle of homophily. In most cases (for example, in organizations) they also compete with other groups for resources or are nested in higher-order groupings. It is well established that inter-group competition alters the behavior of members in important ways. For instance, people are more likely to cooperate in a social dilemma when it is embedded in the context of inter-group conflict (Bornstein and Ben-Yossef, 1994). The reason for this is that from the standpoint of the individual such behavior increases the survival chances of the group. However, within-group cooperation is only sustainable when people trust each other and/or deviance from reciprocity can easily be monitored and sanctioned (Campbell, 1994). It is likely that group homogeneity facilitates trust and reciprocal altruism in face-to-face groups (Ruef et al., 2003; Boone et al., 2004). Moreover, group homogeneity might also enhance group survival for sociopolitical reasons. That is, homogeneity is likely to increase a group's power to control competition between groups in nested settings. For instance, top managers might prefer to hire and promote people in the top management team who are similar – for example, having the same functional background and sharing the same strategic preferences – to perpetuate and institutionalize their managerial power. At the same time, similarity facilitates communication within a team, and diminishes the likelihood of conflict and within-team power struggles (see, for example, Pfeffer, 1983). Second, as organizational features, such as routines and strategies, can partly be considered to be a reflection of top management team composition (Hambrick and Mason, 1984), these homosocial reproduction processes have an impact on the higher-level selection entities – that is, organizations that compete for growth and survival in the marketplace. The upper echelon research tradition has indeed demonstrated that organizational routines and strategies do not exist independently of the characteristics of individual human beings (Miner, 1994). Third, as the degree of heterogeneity in demographic characteristics amounts to a 'proxy for cognitive heterogeneity, representing innovativeness, problem-solving abilities, creativity, diversity of information sources and perspectives, openness to change and willingness to challenge and be challenged' (Finkelstein and Hambrick, 1996: 125), the unfolding of homosocial processes will inevitably reduce the spectrum of opportunities available to the organization. The result is that organizations gradually carve out a specialized niche in resource space. As these processes apply to all organizations within a given population, Boone et al. (2006) argue that, under specific conditions, homosocial team-reproduction goes hand in hand with between-firm differentiation in top management team composition and capabilities (as inferred from the demographic characteristics of the managers), reducing niche overlap among organizations. Their conclusion is that, paradoxically, team homogenization may trigger population-level organizational diversity (see also Boyd and Richerson, 1985; Campbell, 1994).

Several issues remain however unresolved. As Williams (1999: 549) observed '[W]hile thousands of studies have investigated why employees choose to leave their jobs, very little research has directly examined the organizational consequences associated with voluntary employee turnover.' Boone et al. (2006) heed Williams's lament but do not provide any empirical evidence on how turnover may or may not be harmful, especially when considering that member exit may lead to joining competing firms. Sorensen (1999a, 1999b) elaborates on these issues and provides some empirical evidence concerning how demographical managerial characteristics affect competition between organizations in products markets in studies of the growth of commercial television stations. His main finding is that the distance of a focal firm's top management team's mean tenure to the mean tenure of competitors increases a focal firm's growth rate. The putative reason is that overlap in tenure indicates overlap in managerial capabilities, which leads to greater competition for resources since managers shape a firm's pattern of resource utilization. In so doing,

Sorensen provides path-breaking empirical evidence on the inter-firm consequences of top management team diversity. However it remains silent on where specific demographic team distributions come from in the first place, as conversely stressed by the models of McPherson and colleagues and by Boone et al. (2006).

Other scholars have followed this line of inquiry and explored the consequences of members' exits to competing firms. Phillips (2002) goes beyond the findings of Sorensen (1999b) by examining the impact of spin-offs on the donor firm survival. Members might exit because of death or retirement, or because they join a non-rival such as a client firm. Such departures differ markedly from those that involve the founding of a new company. The reallocation of members among new firms takes on extra weight because personnel migration triggers the transfer of routines and resources across organizations (see Pfeffer and Leblebici, 1973; Aldrich and Pfeffer, 1976). Unlike intentionally formed ties such as joint ventures, ties based on inter-organizational mobility are essentially an ecological phenomenon because they cannot be construed as a premeditated attempt at establishing relationships between organizations. Inter-firm mobility results in involuntary experience spillovers. Personnel outflows occasion the transfer of routines (and resources) from parent to progeny (Phillips, 2002). Because managers as boundedly rational actors replicate their actions across firms, such personnel outflows produce a growing similarity of behaviors/competences across organizations (see, for example, Boeker, 1997). Identifying the mobility implications among rivals requires us to delve more deeply into the aspects that render them competitively interdependent. Phillips provides evidence on how the movement of individuals is a critical mechanism of ecological competition via the transmission of organizational practices and skills among firms.

Other studies have adopted a different perspective and connected the micro level to the macro one by studying the influence of organizational entries and exits on employee mobility. Organizational ecology provides theory and evidence on how organizational populations affect labor mobility (Carroll et al., 1992; Hannan, 1988). Hannan (1988) proposed that diverse organizational populations improve mobility. As careers do take place in organizations, the distribution of career opportunities depends on the distribution of organizational forms. When considering organizational populations in ethnic enclaves, Hannan stressed that a diverse population would allow immigrants to develop protected career paths, but a lack of diversity would leave the group exposed to discrimination. Hannan's (1988) insights have been used to predict how diversity of organizational sizes facilitates mobility (Greve, 1994) and how size inequality increases intra-industry mobility (Fujiwara-Greve and Greve, 2000). Further research has investigated the effects of organizational founding, failure, and growth (Haveman, 1995; Haveman and Cohen, 1994) on employee mobility. The dynamic branch takes as its starting point that a substantial portion of job mobility is due to organizational foundation and failure causing jobs to appear and disappear (Carroll et al., 1992). As Carroll and Hannan claim, 'job shifts caused by demographic processes constitute between 25% and 55% of all the individual mobility' (2000: 431). Haveman and Cohen's (1994) study of the California savings and loan industry provided an empirical test of this claim. Their findings show that the effects of demographic factors are 'directly responsible for a large proportion of managerial job shifts in the industry and affect directly a large fraction of the industry's managerial employees' (1994: 146). If a new organization is created, new job opportunities emerge which tend to be filled with employees from other firms within the same industry. The most important source of new employees is in fact the industry where such vacancies are created. Thus, 'individuals will move out of established organizations and into start-ups' (1994: 111). By contrast, exits reduce mobility. As Haveman and Cohen (1994: 113) put it 'after controlling for the positive direct effect on inter-organizational mobility (out of dissolved organizations into surviving organizations) the indirect effect [of failures] on inter-organizational mobility will be negative, as the closure of vacancy chains diminishes the chances of employees moving across organizational boundaries.'

Likewise within the institutional area of inquiry we witness efforts to bring individuals back into firms' decision-making of whether or not to adopt specific practices. Building on the insights of the old institutional school (Selznick, 1957), we see a healthy flurry of efforts to spell out the micro-mechanisms behind the formation and diffusion of institutional norms and practices. Proponents of heterogeneous diffusion models have contributed to underscoring how firms vary in their rates of adopting new practices owing fundamentally to adopters' characteristics, characteristics of innovations and the environmental contexts (see, for example, Strang and Tuma, 1993; Davis and Greve, 1997). The main critique provided by these authors is that institutional theory does not give sufficient attention to the social embeddedness of the decision to adopt a new rule or practice. These models have provided a significant advance in institutional theory by empirically disentangling three different multi-level components of diffusion processes: the susceptibility of the focal organization (that is, how much the organization is likely to be affected by the information concerning the new practice), its infectiousness (how it is likely to affect other organizations), and the social proximity between the source and the destination (that is, the ease of transfer). Such an approach allows a recognition of the importance of examining both economic and social forces leading to the adoption of a new practice (Young et al., 2001; Palmer et al., 1993; Davis, 1991; Westphal et al., 1997). This adoption pressure can also be viewed from a more rational standpoint: empirical evidence suggests that early adopters are moved by economic reasoning (Tolbert and Zucker, 1983), that poorly performing organizations (that is, those below their aspiration levels) are quicker in adopting a new practice (Saka and Wezel, 2006), and that the post-adoption performance is used by competitors (Lee and Pennings, 2002). By the same token, 'internal and external sources often play different roles in a diffusion analysis and imply different adoption trajectories' (Strang and Soule, 1998: 271). Moreover, besides the adopters' characteristics, the processes of actor-to-actor transmission and the pressures exerted by exogenous actors also influence the adoption (see also Coleman et al., 1966). The adoption of new practices occurs within a social system, denoting a flow or movement via communication and influence (Strang and Soule, 1998). Communication and influence are grounded in social relations ranging from face-to-face interaction to perceived similarity. Frequent interaction promotes exchange of information about the motivations and effects of diffusing practices. This is especially necessary in the context of risky and uncertain new practices where adopters carefully weigh the experience of others before acting (Strang and Soule, 1998).

This logic suggests that the flow of a new practice is assumed to move in a grapevine-like form from prior to potential adopters. This process emphasizes interaction networks as the conduits of diffusion, where ongoing relationships between organizations, or what social network theorists call direct ties, play an important role in determining whether observed behavior will be learned and adopted (Kraatz, 1998). Exchange relations or direct ties lead actors to take the perspective of the other and to exert powerful pressures for conformity beyond economic reasons. Direct ties facilitate the flow of information, which promotes mutual understanding of each organization's distinctive capabilities and needs, and increases the quality and relevance of advice (Westphal et al., 1997). They allow new institutional rules to be encoded in actors' interpretive schemes, resources, and norms, and come to influence how people communicate and enact power (Barley and Tolbert, 1997). They not only forge a sense of personal belonging, but also create and sustain a clear normative framework which shapes their decisions (Podolny and Baron, 1997). In other words, organizations tied to new institutional rule adopters are likely to experience conformity pressure. Direct ties within a network can also serve as sources of reliable information, facilitating adoption. Galaskiewicz and Wasserman (1989), for instance, have found that personal ties among corporate officers already involved in charitable contributions was a powerful force influencing the decision to donate money to non-profit organizations. In a similar vein, Palmer et al. (1993) demonstrate how interlocks with firms that have already adopted an M-form structure increase the propensity of contagious behavior by the focal firm. Furthermore, Davis and Greve (1997), in their study of poison pill and golden parachute responses to the threat of hostile mergers, show that the pill diffused primarily via board interlocks. In a similar vein, Rao and Drazin (2002) explain the mechanisms by which similarity among organizations may unfold due to inter-firm mobility. Rao and Drazin (2002) suggest that the migration of managerial personnel from one mutual fund organization with an international stock fund to a second organization with no such fund increases the internal propensity of the latter to create a new international fund on its own.

Last, but not least, a new emerging area of research concerns 'institutional entrepreneurship'. An increasing number of studies are currently exploring where new institutional rules come from in the first place – not only how they diffuse. This body of research focuses attention on the way in which specific actors shape their institutional contexts. Within this sub-field, the relationship between individual interests and institutions becomes central. Building on DiMaggio (1988) and Fligstein (1997), these authors stress that '[N]ew institutions arise when organized actors with sufficient resources see in them an opportunity to realize interests that they value highly' (DiMaggio, 1988: 14). Institutional entrepreneurs act as champions to a new rule or practice and deploy their social skills to stimulate cooperation within the field between other actors with common interests and goals. Institutional change then is seen as a political process which involves the power and interests of actors such as the institutional entrepreneur. As Rao et al. (2000: 240) put it:

> the construction of new organizational forms is a political process in which social movements play a double-edged role: They de-institutionalize existing beliefs, norms, and values embodied in extant forms, and establish new forms that instantiate new beliefs, norms and values. Crucial in these processes are institutional entrepreneurs who lead efforts to identify political opportunities, frame issues and problems, and mobilize constituencies. By so doing, they spearhead collective attempts to infuse new beliefs, norms, and values into social structures, thus creating discontinuities in the world of organizations.

THE CONTENTS OF THIS BOOK

This book builds on the recent developments within organizational ecology and institutional theory to investigate the role of human capital and individual decisions in shaping processes of mutualism and competition among organizations. Theoretically, the book will deal with two main subjects: the role of human (and social) capital and that of inter-firm mobility for firm behavior and performance. We will theorize about the contribution of people (that is, human and social capital) to macro-organizational theories with specific reference to organizational ecology and institutional theory. Moreover, as geographical proximity increases social interaction and the circulation of knowledge and information via personal contacts, in several of the following chapters, we will emphasize the role of geography in examining the institutional and ecological mechanisms under investigation.

Chapter 2 will introduce the reader to the empirical setting. Although the book generally deals with partnerships as a major form of organization in professional services such as law, accounting, consulting, medicine and architecture, this chapter presents a series of works that focus on the Dutch accounting sector during the period 1880–1990. Partnerships differ in many respects from other classes of organizations, whether by governance, ownership, legal liability, staffing and operations and have not received the same level of attention as for example industrial corporations, NGOs or small and medium-sized enterprises (SMEs). Chapter 2 will review the meaning and the essence of partnerships, their history, incentive systems and socialization practices, focusing specifically on the Dutch accounting industry and providing a comparison with corporations and the like.

In Chapter 3 we explore the benefits of social capital and the harmful affects of social liabilities. Following Allison (1971), two *theoretical* models of organizations are juxtaposed: those of the Rational and Political Actors, pointing to the inherent tension between economic principles of organization and social fitness. The issues of social capital require different perspectives when its implications for performance are addressed. The mediation through individuals takes a prominent place in the Political Actor, and moves to the background in the Rational Actor. The issue of aggregation from the member to the organization is primarily relevant when we view the organization as a Political Actor in which the members' social capital aggregates to that of their organization. Two illustrative cases that fit the two models are then presented, the industrial business groups in Japan and Korea on the one hand, and the population of professional services firms in the Netherlands on the other. In the case of business groups we point to both the benefits of social capital and the drawbacks of social liability. The implications for social capital and liability are thereby exposed and reviewed.

Chapter 4 enriches this discussion by *empirically* focusing on the impact of human capital upon firm dissolution. Human capital was captured by firm-level proxies for firm tenure, industry experience, and graduate education. The social capital proxy was professionals' ties to potential clients.

Human and social capital strongly predicted firm dissolution and effects depended on their specificity and nonappropriability. A micro–macro model linking individual attributes to aggregate competitive phenomena is introduced and empirically investigated. The findings obtained suggest an integration of the resource-based view of the firm (micro level) and organizational ecology (macro level) and a concomitant stimulant for the future along these lines.

Chapter 5 investigates the economic and normative drivers behind the diffusion of the PA-form during the period 1925–90. While all firms were composed of partners only before 1925, some among them began to partition professional accountants into partners and associates (PA-form) and the PA-form became a dominant form. We suggest that the institutional change was the result of an interaction between selection at the population level and mimicry at the firm level. In the empirical part, we focus on the effect of negative selection on imitation behavior, and propose that market feedback favoring the PA-form enhanced its legitimacy, which in turn fostered imitative adoptions. We also hypothesize on the spillovers between firms: that the market feedback differentially affects the adoption of PA-form on the basis of firm-idiosyncratic filters such as network embeddedness, percentage of adopters among similar sized firms and geographically proximate firms. The analysis produces results that are supportive of our hypotheses. We conclude with a discussion of diffusion in the private sector as a legitimization process, unfolding both at the industry-level and the firm-level of analysis.

Chapter 6 offers a bridge between the first part, focused on human and social capital, and on the role of agency in institutional theory, and the second more clearly ecologically inspired. Mergers and acquisitions involve the bundling of two firms which are more or less equal on relevant attributes. Chapter 6 explores the interactive effects of human assets compatibility (that is, the matching of the demographic attributes of the two firms) and complementarity (that is, combining people whose human capital might complement each other) on organizational dissolution upon an M&A. We examine the two firms' resource complementarity and organizational compatibility. We control for previous M&A experiences as acquisitive learning suspends some of the M&A risks. Employing a multinomial logit model for repeated-event history analysis that reflects the dynamics of organizational evolution, we analyze 461 M&As in the accounting industry. Our results show that *compatibility* is not associated with firm dissolution. Resource *complementarity* is negatively associated with the likelihood of dissolution.

The impact of managerial mobility for organizational evolution and, more specifically, for the diffusion of a new organizational form, is introduced in Chapter 7. A growing body of literature suggests that populations of organizations are not homogeneous entities, but they rather comprise distinct sub-entities. Firms are in fact highly dependent on their immediate institutional and competitive environments. Chapter 7 advances this line of inquiry, proposing a new perspective on organizational entries by focusing on the spatial and temporal sources of heterogeneity within a population of organizations. The goal of this research is threefold. First, we explore entrepreneurial activity as a function of spatial density, arguing that local, rather than national, density-dependence processes help explain industry evolution. Second, we show how multiple, heterogeneous local clocks shape such entrepreneurial activity in different geographical areas. Our empirical findings provide support for the existence of spatial and temporal dimensions of heterogeneity and on the role of mobility for the spread of organizational forms across geographical locales.

Chapter 8 builds on this ecologically inspired logic to discuss the multilevel consequences of within-team diversity for organizational survival. In particular, we concentrate on inter-firm mobility as a key driver of demographic variations. Existing literature suggests that heterogeneity taxes the collective decision-making of members, undermines the firm's *esprit de corps* and impedes its effective functioning. Demographic diversity also has performance implications that transcend group functioning. Inter-firm mobility involving key members offers attractive opportunities for detecting the intra and inter-firm implications of demographic diversity on performance – which we measure in terms of hazard of organizational dissolution. At the organizational level we do not find seemingly symmetrical effects, in that an increase in heterogeneity is harmful, while a reduction is not. The result does not hold true at the inter-firm level of analysis: a reduction in competitive overlap due to mobility is beneficial, while increased overlap impairs survival. These findings are derived from data on the recruitment of partners between competitively interdependent firms.

Chapter 9 examines the competitive consequences of inter-firm mobility, elaborating on the micro drivers of (macro) ecological competition. Given that the loss of key members (defined as top decision-makers) to competing firms amounts to a diffusion of a firm's routines, we examine whether the consequences of losing such assets is amplified under certain conditions: (1) when inter-firm mobility entails groups rather than single individuals, (2) when members found a new enterprise rather than joining an existing competitor, and (3) when members' new destination is in the local domain of their prior firm. We exploit information on membership migration and on the competitive saliency of the destination firm as inferred from the recipient status (incumbent vs. start-up) and its geographic proximity (local vs. non-local). We find the dissolution risk to be highest when inter-firm mobility results in a new venture within the same province.

Finally, Chapter 10 provides a tentative discussion of some of the volume's contributions, shedding light on new avenues of further research. Without downplaying the editors' categorization, it is fair to argue that the chapters could have been easily allocated in a different way. As a result, the variety of material does not necessarily need to be read sequentially. Apart from Chapter 2, which provides the foundations of the empirical setting and, in our judgment, should be read before the others, the order can easily be determined according to specific interest (human, social capital and firm survival (chs 3 and 4), the adoption of new practices (Ch. 5) or the diffusion of new organizational forms (Ch. 7), recruitment, poaching and competition (chs 8 and 9), and the impact of the demographic make up of partnerships on performance (Ch. 8)).

NOTE

1.   This paragraph and the next one are adapted from Boone et al. (2006).

2. Partnership as a major type of organization form

INTRODUCTION

This chapter provides an overview of partnerships as a special class of organizations. A distinction is made between ownership-derived governance and organization structure to articulate their distinctive features. Partnerships are highly human asset-intensive which means that they govern the firms' strategic capabilities but also face major challenges in attracting, specializing and advancing their members. Here we delineate the properties of partnerships and contrast them with other classes of organizations.

The ownership-governance and organizational structure in human asset-intensive firms assume each other. In other words, the creation and upgrading of strategic capabilities by the corporate leadership are very much a function of the authority and control structure that surrounds the organizational strategists. Ownership structure deals mainly with the relationship between owners and managers around the firm as a bundle of strategic assets – in knowledge-intensive firms mostly carried by people – while organization structure deals with managers and employees, the stratification of people into various echelons and positioned in different departments.

The governance structure is central to the building and upgrading of strategic capabilities. The firm comprises a bundle of routines – both lower order routines such as sales, marketing, finance and production and higher order or meta-routines that govern the organization of lower order routines. In Chapter 4, for instance, results are presented on a firm's superior human and social capital and the performance advantages that are associated with such non-financial capital. Chapter 6 describes mergers and acquisitions between professional services firms and explores their relative success based upon the combination of strategic assets that are more or less compatible and complementary. In Chapter 9 empirical findings are presented on the role of strategic assets and their spillover to peer firms when key members migrate to rivals.

Partnerships are unique among various classes of organizations which include not only single proprietorships but also private and public corporations, as well as cooperatives, professional associations, and sub-contractors. Unlike other classes of organizations, in partnerships owners, managers and employees often comprise the same person. The implication is that the boundary between ownership structure and organization structure becomes less clear cut compared with boundaries in corporations, particularly public corporations. We can therefore argue that partnerships display governance and employment conditions that render them distinct from corporations.

Partnerships are different from corporations in the drivers of strategic posturing and performance. Like any organization, partnerships need to manage their platform of strategic capabilities, but being human asset-intensive they are even more compelled to attend to their human resources. Management involves the creation, retention and upgrading of strategic assets which the firm accomplishes through its own internal systems (compare Coff, 1997). On the other hand, the partners, as owners, need to motivate the members of their firm, whether they are other partners or future partners (that is, associates). As we indicate in chapters 8 and 9 the firms in this volume's empirical studies faced multifaceted challenges in building and retaining their human and social capital – suggesting that partnerships should be focused strategically while motivating their members to achieve long-term results.

We distinguish between corporations and partnerships, recognizing many different gradations in governance and organization. Foremost, they differ in ownership arrangements (for example, private single proprietorships, limited liability firms, family companies, including patrimonial corporations, and so on) where these forms are mostly defined in terms of liability in that corporations are owned, and (by implication 'controlled') by owners who have more or less limited liability – typically confined to that which has been invested in the organizations. Partners are fully liable, but some partnerships have adopted clauses which limit their partners' liability. The ownership, control and liability aspect is therefore somewhat deficient as a defining characteristic, in that some partnership forms have assumed limited liability, but not necessarily limited control, while some corporations have features resembling partnerships with limited liability, such as the German form, GmbH (literally 'company with limited liability') not to mention so called 'family businesses' which function under the shield of corporate liability. Various jurisdictions exhibit subtle differences in the legal framing of ownership and its ramifications. Apart from the legal framing, the firm might assume governance practices that seem at odds with what one would expect within the institutional mold of that firm.

Google, for example is now a public corporation, but its two founders possess a controlling stake in the firm through holdings of disproportionate numbers of voting shares and act managerially as if they are partners (Batelle, 2005). In that respect Google resembles a 'patrimonial firm' in which the corporate ownership overlaps with corporate control: owners are also involved in management and governance in general (compare Reeb and Anderson, 2003). This example would indicate that private and public corporations can resemble partnerships in overlap of ownership and governance practices. Tax-sheltered firms and private equity corporations represent still another array of organizational forms, with often highly convoluted and non-transparent liability arrangements. And as we indicated, the structure of accounting firms might not as readily map onto these different classes of organizations, except in the case of partnerships without associates, where partners are owners, managers and employees. If the partnership employs associates, then the firm membership bifurcates into owners and non-owners, further complicating classification efforts. Additionally, structural departures from the original partnership form, such as incentive regimes might blur the distinction with private and even public corporations. In fact, an extensive literature is emerging on different governance arrangements under various ownership conditions that include partnerships. While this volume dwells primarily on partnerships in which the role of owner and manager is often united, at least until recently, it should be emphasized that public and private corporations as well as recent governance innovations such as hedge funds have introduced myriad control modalities. While that literature has mostly a finance and accounting origin, newer contributions also surface in the strategic and organizational literature (for example, Schultze et al., 2001), challenging financial perspectives (for example, Jensen and Meckling, 1976) that maintain that private corporations as well as patrimonial or family firms are comparatively free of agency hazards; perhaps because like partnerships they might hire lower quality managers compared with more accountable, public corporations as they are comparatively insulated from the discipline of the market and might behave altruistically towards relatives and other confidants. In professional services sectors such as the accounting sector, the single proprietorship and 'family-style' governance are prominent as will be shown in the next chapters. Interestingly this new literature also includes contributions which contrast the Anglo-Saxon with the continental, European context (for example, Burkhard et al., 2003) in which private corporations, family-controlled firms and presumably partnerships in continental Europe are more susceptible to agency hazards such as expropriation by outside stakeholders. Privately (incomplete or otherwise) held firms and partnerships face the trade-off between superior management by outsiders and discretion to favor personal or family-based interests. Stakeholder protection is strong in UK-like cultures, including the US, while in continental countries such as the Netherlands, from where the organizational findings in this volume derive, it is comparatively weak. It would be beyond the scope of this volume to further elaborate on these issues. In the next paragraphs, such ownership and control issues are not explicitly addressed but they need to be acknowledged when contrasting partnerships with other governance forms.

The next section reviews the history of the partnership versus other organization forms, through its evolution into the present day. A contrast is drawn between partnerships and corporations – whether private or public. Next we review the two above-mentioned versions of structure: governance structure and strategic management to cultivate, preserve and upgrade capabilities and management and organization structure to assure the motivation and performance of people. We then elaborate on these structural aspects of accounting firms as professional service organizations and ask whether this form is most appropriate for these knowledge-intensive firms, and whence a structure that should serve as a template for many firms outside the service sector in which this form emerged. We conclude with a historical account of the Dutch accounting sector and describe the empirical setting of the studies reported here.

HISTORY OF THE PARTNERSHIP VERSUS OTHER ORGANIZATION FORMS

Typically, partnerships are very limited in separating ownership and control – as is common among many public or private corporations. Unlike public corporations, private corporations might seemingly appear equivalent to single or partner-controlled firms, and differ primarily in that the owners are liable only for assets that they have committed to the firm. Conversely, the distinction between private corporations and single and partnership-owned organizations, most notably the so-called limited liability partnership (LLP), is difficult to draw in that the former limit the owners to only those obligations that have been made for their firm. Since the early nineteenth century, various countries have witnessed interesting developments in legally defined forms of organizations such that many different gradations of ownership and associated liability have surfaced. These developments can be partly attributed to legal precedents that further blurred the liability distinction among classes of organization – compare a partnership case of French jurisprudence, curtailing liability, occurring as early as 1807, documented by Porter (1937).

Such developments challenge the notion of liability as primary or sole basis of defining partnerships. In the US, some firms that transitioned from partnerships to public corporations – for example the investment bank Goldman Sachs – continue to have a governance legacy of partnership-like arrangements even though the legal foundation of the firm as partnership has been disbanded. Greenwood and Empson (2003) have shown that at the beginning of the twenty-first century formal partnerships continued to dominate accounting and law while firms in sectors such as advertising and management consulting have altered their liability status and are more commonly organized as either private or public corporations (compare Lowendahl, 1997). Such differences suggest that liability arrangements are not the sole attribute of organizations, but merely an important attribute that combines with structural differentiation, culture, organizational demography and various 'fifth dimensions' such knowledge arrangements (for example, Nonaka and Takeuchi, 1995; Senge, 1990). These differences also call for an inquiry into the 'intelligence' of various governance arrangements where such intelligence might hinge on the nature of the market, the prevailing work practices, the firm–client interfaces, the oversight by public sector agencies such as FDIC, bar and trade associations, non-government organizations and SEC, Federal Reserve Board, European Central Bank or European Commissioners. For example why do some classes of firms show episodic negative selection propensities such as investment versus commercial banks, mutual versus stock ownership savings banks and investor-owned versus public utilities companies? Why did cooperatives decline as governance form in the European dairy sector after the Second World War, while they thrived prior to that war? Likewise, the savings bank sector in Italy and Raifeissen banks in the Netherlands and Germany declined during the most recent decades but not so the so-called 'Krankenkassen' and 'Sparkassen' in Germany. Unfortunately these examples of sectors with 'peculiar' governance arrangements amount to a very fruitful domain of research and so far are typically left to marginal research realms (but compare Moore and Kraatz, 2007).

Apart from asking why firms shift their liability form, we might also ask what other aspects define a (partnership) firm and why firms exist in the first place – a question that has surfaced repeatedly since writers began to reflect on the rise of complex organizations. Certainly the industrial revolution of the nineteenth century, with the concomitant rise of many types of organizations, has triggered many inquiries about form, membership, governance, and functioning. Organizations were not only differentiated from other forms of human aggregates but also were examined on their optimal form – beginning with the likes of Max Weber and Frederick Taylor. The rationale for creating organizations and reflections on their viability was argued by authors such as Coase (1937) and by numerous writers who followed in his footsteps – Barnard (1939), Simon (1947), Thompson (1967), Williamson

(1975), and Roberts (2004) to just name a few. Organizational forms have varied over time (for example, Brown, 2003) as well as geographically (see North, 1997).

The initial debates revolved around single proprietorships, corporations (private and public) and partnerships, with two aspects standing out: liability and autonomy – particularly when the firm grew to involve two or more individuals. The matter of liability pertained to the question of owners' liability beyond the level of their financial commitment to the firm, while the aspect of autonomy concerned matters such as the existence of the firm as a (legal) entity beyond its members (for example, Horwitz, 1977). Much of the later discussion of various organizational forms has revolved around ownership and the attendant issue of governance. Partnerships have unique qualities of governance allowing them to deal with so-called 'organizational failures', such as adverse selection and free-ridership. In the present day, partnership is also seen as symptomatic for prevailing forms of organizing in the twenty-first century (Hindle, 2006). Some writers go so far as to claim that the partnership is well suited to knowledge-intensive firms and could figure prominently as organizational form in the 'knowledge economy' as some have begun to characterize post-industrial societies (for example, Ghoshal and Bartlett, 1997).

Many forms or types of organizations have evolved beyond the range that existed prior to the industrial revolution in Europe and North America. It would be wrong to assume that partnerships are a recent phenomenon largely characteristic of contemporary professional services sectors. The partnership as an organizational form was widespread before the arrival of the corporation and other classes of limited liability public firms and even prior to that by several centuries as documented by Lamoreaux (1995, 1998). Even in some 'younger' societies, like the US, the corporation as an organizational form emerged only around the 1850s and was pre-dated by the partnership (Kim, 2007). Kim reports that as much of 40 per cent of US manufacturing took place in partnerships during the early part of the nineteenth century. In Europe, the corporation, in the form of a military or monastic organization, emerged much earlier, particularly monasteries in the Middle Ages. Trading companies such as the East India Company and VOC (Dutch East India Company) as limited liability organizations emerged during the Enlightenment, although in some respects they varied from those corporations that surfaced during the industrial revolution – for example dividends could be paid in kind, for example, as spices. As societies evolved through agricultural to industrial and more recently knowledge or service-oriented societies, writers on organizations followed suit and sought to document, analyze or prescribe certain templates for organizing. With the arrival of the so called 'knowledge

economy' at the end of the twentieth century, forms that purport to facilitate the creation and dispersion of knowledge and the building of organizational capabilities have gained prominence. Furthermore, a preference
for an organizational structure that fosters empowerment, motivation, creativity, and innovation has clearly established itself. Organizational forms
differ in the processes they utilize to furnish employees with greater discretion, influence and other resources and foster employee engagement. The
major quality of partnerships – as of other organizations – is that of building a distinctive competitive advantage through the ongoing accumulation
of strategic assets such as reputation and unique skills. Today, the partnership form has become associated with knowledge-intensive or professional
services sectors such as health care, education, law, consulting, merchant or
investment banking, and architecture.

Highlighting salient attributes of firms and their various trade-offs has
been a preoccupation of many authors since the onset of theories of organizational governance and structure. While earlier framing attempts, such as
those by Weber (1968), revolved around horizontal and vertical differentiation and were illustrated by division of labor and distribution of
power and authority, other and more recent attempts have stressed attributes such as control and incentive arrangements (for example, Milgrom and
Roberts, 1992). Both types of ownership arrangements have undergone
important institutional changes. The corporation began to show a separation between ownership and control, as has been well documented by such
early writers as Berle and Means (1932). In the nineteenth century, during
the onset of the industrial revolution such separation was uncommon and
owners were heavily involved in the management of their firms. As has
been amply documented, management became increasingly a function of
manager-employees with owners becoming increasingly anonymous and
absent. The rise of manager-employees led to significant changes in governance and management, documented and investigated by strands of literature under the headings of strategic capabilities (for example, Barney,
1991), agency theory (for example, Fama and Jensen, 1980), the market
for corporate control (Jensen, 1994) and incentive regimes (for example,
Milgrom and Roberts, 1992). For sure, the emergence of complex organizations in general and of the corporation in particular after the industrial
revolution contributed to diminishing the significance of this partnership
form.

What advantages and disadvantages do single proprietorships and partnerships have in comparison with corporations? Several empirical studies
show the elimination of partnerships in favor of corporations during the
early stages of the industrial revolution, mostly due to the transactional disadvantages of such forms of organization (Lamoureaux, 1998). Lamoreaux

(1998) views partnerships as much more susceptible to the 'hold-up' problem, rendering them less of a 'firm' than corporations. The assets, particularly those having an intangible nature such as routines and reputation, are tied up in the membership and cannot easily become separated from firm owners as legal owners. She argues that corporations, due to their higher degree of 'firmness', are much better equipped for the accumulation of intangible assets such as knowledge because they constitute a shield against that hold-up threat when employees have invested specific human capital in firms or when they seek to protect their stock of intangible assets against unwanted spillovers.

For example the rise of the multi-divisional form has been attributed to corporate growth which imposes limits on the size of the functional form and favors the adoption of the divisional form (compare Williamson, 1975). Larger firms break themselves up into component units, thereby alleviating the cognitive stress on top decision-makers, the senior management or a group of partners. It could likewise be surmised that the emergence of the public corporation in the nineteenth century favored the corporation over the single proprietorship, the private corporation and the partnership. The near total absence of partnerships among the Fortune 500 companies could be attributed to the limited capacity of partnerships to attend to the control that is required in larger firms.

GOVERNANCE AND STRATEGIC MANAGEMENT

The organizational structure or template of many non-corporate firms, broadly corresponding to 'partnership', varies with the idiosyncrasies of the firm. Such idiosyncrasies inform us about variations in strategic capabilities that set partnerships apart from corporations. The competitive advantage of different partnership firms is very much apparent in Chapter 4 in which we review the competitive advantages of human and social capital and show that firm-specific human capital stands out in shaping partnership performance. In the sea of structural sameness profound differences in organizational skills and practices are encountered. Similarly, in Chapter 9 the idiosyncrasies of partnerships that make up the Dutch accounting sector document the limits of transferring governance routines across partnerships. When well-calibrated routines of a higher order, including governance routines, become replicated in other firms their integrity becomes compromised if certain conditions are not met.

A case study by Lazega (2001) on a prestigious New York law firm, ATC, illustrates the subtle implementation of a strategic governance arrangement within the grounds of a partnership. A number of routines have evolved in this firm towards a bundle of practices that renders it rather distinct, even though it still corresponds to the tenets of partnership. Lazega (2001) also contrasts partnerships with corporations and dwells on the dilemma of how peer groups resolve the tension between competition and cooperation, or what he calls 'social discipline'. Peer groups face a paradox in which members differentiate themselves, thus suspending the peer quality of a peer group. From a cozy partnership the firm had evolved towards 36 partners and 35 associates in three offices on the US eastern seaboard. While most peer firms had adopted an aggressive incentive compensation scheme, ATC maintained lock-step remuneration during the first 13 years and an equal share for those having more seniority – even less productive partners whom other firms would have discharged. With one exception, it employed no life-time associates or processional managers – a practice that has become increasingly common among legal partnerships. The finders and minders collaborated in a way that suspended the need for protecting a partner's social capital whereas the absence of incentive compensation made the allocation of cases much less contentious. Although shirking could surface as a major dysfunction in such an incentive regime, while there were major disparities in workload among the partners aberrations in shirking were kept to a minimum by maintaining a position 'where we have just a bit too few' partners (2001: 81). This case study makes it clear that in spite of being a partnership, with little contention among its senior members and a well-calibrated up or out promotion system, important departures from processes in peer firms could be observed. These included not only egalitarian pay practices but also the creation of task forces properly to accommodate the variable and intricate nature of the law firm's workload. Membership on such task forces entailed an intrinsic reward, including professional prestige and status. Such a reward system also highlights the collective nature of knowledge labor – whether in R&D or professional services. The performative ties among the partners at ATC likewise signaled the social character of knowledge creation and knowledge sharing and points to ATC as a possible knowledge-intensive firm.

The above-mentioned case study makes clear how tight the link between strategic management and human resource management is. Unlike the strategic assets of corporations which can become alienated, traded or transferred to other corporate owners, the transfer of capabilities in partnerships is more problematic. The skills that confer advantages to a partnership are embedded in the owners who are at once also managers and guardians of the firm's strategic assets. In most instances, the partnership is human asset-intensive (Coff, 1997) and its asset carriers therefore exhibit comparatively low exit barriers. The partnership epitomizes therefore the major dilemma of such human asset-intensive firms in that the ownership claims of strategic capabilities are tenuous and reside in what Teece (1996) calls a weak appropriability regime: firm-specific knowledge is difficult to protect against unwanted spillovers. Partners may leave, join a rival or start their own firm, and thus inflict considerable damage to the firm from which they defect.

In this respect, knowledge-intensive firms should be considered as organic rather than mechanistic. This distinction goes back to early writers such as Burns and Stalker (1962) who suggested that organic firms are endowed with a high capacity for information processing and knowledge management as demonstrated by decentralization of decision-making, empowerment, collective and dispersed ownership of strategy and professional orientation to clients. Because partners combine ownership and governance in the same individuals, they enjoy intelligence advantages regarding their proprietary know-how. Such firms are highly dependent on their members as carriers of knowledge whose buy-in is required for successful performance. Being proximate to peer partners, protected by anti-competition claims and endowed with an elaborate socialization apparatus (such as described by Lazega, 2001) partnerships are much better informed about their unique capabilities – even if that intelligence is more tacit than explicit. From Chapter 9 it is apparent that the loss of certain routines is harmful to the firm that witnesses its loss to rivals, but it is equally apparent that firm owners know quite well what those routines are. In corporations where the person of manager and owner are separated we often encounter a diminished engagement on the part of strategists – most notably executives, who might behave more opportunistically than their equivalents in partnerships.

Important in the structure of knowledge-intensive firms such as accounting partnerships is the distinction between partners and associates. Partners as managers are surrounded by other partners and by associates who participate in tournaments towards partnerships. The tournament revolves around the screening and subsequent evaluation of absorbing firm culture and other routines by the advancing membership. The key to long-term success hinges on the ability to recruit, develop and retain their membership. A major strategic capability for partnerships resides therefore in the domain of human resources. The human resources in knowledge-intensive firms are thus the basis of their competitive advantage and require them to induce their employees to invest themselves into the firm and as partners fully to share in the ownership rights of intangible assets such as knowledge and routines. The rewards are commensurate with the firm-specific investments they make (Hart and Moore, 1990). Many CPA firms might have evolved towards greater routinization, thus diminishing the need for collegial governance, greater emphasis on hierarchy, formalization and central-ization, thereby evoking internal agency problems. Here we need to con-sider the management of strategic capabilities and the management of human resources. Perhaps we are entering a new phase in sectors such as accountancy where we encounter a pendulum swing towards corporate forms of governance with associated trends towards larger audit firms leaning towards private corporations and LLP forms of partnership. Similarly, we encounter a stronger emphasis on knowledge-management issues, with many knowledge-intensive firms making heavy investments in tacit as well as explicit knowledge-management systems? For example, many consulting firms have not only established intranet-based informa-tion contexts, but have also tried to infuse themselves with organic design features such as networking, teams and 'spaghetti' structures (compare Foss, 2003) that confer a high degree of empowerment and decentralization in decision-making.

MANAGEMENT AND ORGANIZATION STRUCTURE

The structure that organizations exhibit can be reviewed through various conceptual lenses. Economists gravitate either to transaction cost econom-ics (for example, Williamson, 1975) or to agency theory (Fama and Jensen, 1980). The transaction cost approach would suggest that organizations forestall problems of governance and, compared to markets, are much less susceptible to the hold-up threat. Principal-agent theory has also been a compelling frame for depicting a major advantage for corporations – for example, committing and retrieving equity and debt – and even control, as in the discussions around the 'market for corporate control' (Jensen, 1998).

By contrast, as we saw in the previous chapter, sociologists have assumed an ecological or institutional perspective, as illustrated by Hannan and Freeman (1984) and DiMaggio and Powell (1983) respectively. In such a treatment of the firm, the emphasis is on enduring and well-entrenched structures together with prevailing patterns of interactions and routines rather than on the discretion of managers or decision-makers to shape and control the firm's choices. When applied to partnerships, economists would focus on their transaction or agency problems, while sociologists might focus on the relative prominence of this structural form over other forms such as public versus private corporations, or generalist versus specialist firms defining sector-specific strategic profiles. Adaptations to shortcomings in economic treatments would dwell on structures or practices geared towards governance and control – for example alternative incentive arrangements – while sociologists would identify changes in some prevailing form – for example the gradual shift from firms exclusively comprising partners to a bifurcation of partners and employees. Likewise, we have encountered the drift from accountancy to IT consultancy, while Greenwood and Empson (2003) observed that in sectors such as advertising the partnership form has vanished altogether.

In Chapter 5, for instance, the creation and spread of governance innovation among Dutch accounting firms is spelled out. The partnership, which pre-dates the corporation, became subject to various adaptations, mostly revolving around ownership distribution, employment and other contractual arrangements and governance. In fact, in the very early days of accountancy, firms expanded from single proprietorships to partnerships.

In contrast to corporations, as mentioned before, many contemporary partnerships are dual in their stratification or vertical differentiation. While often viewed as inherently collegial in their decision-making arrangements, they might also appear very hierarchical, exhibiting a putative pecking order. Perhaps the employment relationship is among the most salient attribute which distinguish the partnership from the corporation, since in the former, owners typically manifest a strong involvement. Owners of corporations are often anonymous, their counterparts in partnerships are not, although the involvement of corporate owners is occasionally strong, while partners might become 'limited' or 'passive'.

Since the mid-1920s partnerships have displayed a significant bifurcation between owners and employees – commonly called partners and associates. This development has also contributed to the evolution of partners as not only owners but also managers of firms that have become increasing differentiated vertically, and eventually also horizontally – for example when partnership-based firms diversify into discrete lines of business such as accounting and consulting. Yet, partnerships provide a unique solution to employment, setting them apart from most other organizations. Partners as managers continue to display a much more profound involvement in the governance of their firm compared with so-called activist capitalists, hedge fund managers or private investors and family dynasties in so-called 'patrimonial firms' (Blondel et al., 2002). Promotion ladders are usually cast in the form of a tournament in which a small subset of recruits moves into the ranks of partners and become owners of the firm (Galanter and Palay, 1992). The firms recruit far more individuals than they expect to become owners and advancement will only follow a probationary period of between five and fifteen years. Most begin their career as employees, but some members enter 'laterally' as partners and do not participate in a tournament. The compensation of employees, called associates, is tied to the rate that the firm charges its clients – often expressed in so-called 'billable' hours. The hourly rate matches the employees' marginal productivity and when it falls short, the associates exit the firm; conversely if it exceeds productivity they enter into the partnership group of owners. Whence the expression 'up or out'. During their tournament, partners bear the costs of retaining associates with an ongoing process of churning older associates in favor of younger ones.

Partnerships permit the adoption of high-powered incentive arrangements with an 'eat what you kill scheme'. A large proportion of partnerships' revenues are distributed to the partners, assuring the collegial group of professionals of a near perfect correlation between performance and compensation. Therefore, it should not surprise us that partnerships are deemed most attractive in resolving internal agency issues (at least up to a certain size, or leverage), including free-ridership and shirking. Goldman Sachs, a partnership which became a semi-official public corporation but continued to rely on its traditional incentive regime enjoyed an $11 billion bonus pool to pay its members on average $500,000–700,000. Nearly 50 per cent of net revenue is earmarked for its bonus pool (McDonald, 2005). Interestingly, this firm changed its ownership structure from partnership to public corporation, thus challenging the practice of splitting their profits among themselves, and contending with other stakeholders such as shareholders. The history and its associated legacy at Goldman Sachs suggest that the implications of actual ownership might not be as dramatic when comparing partnerships with other forms of organization. After going public, the 'partners' still controlled the distribution of 'excess' revenue – about 50 per cent, diverting a disproportionate share to themselves. Partners became senior managing directors 'PMDs' (for partner managing directors) and junior managing directors or 'EMDs' (for executive managing directors) or 'MD Lite' (McDonald, 2005). The PMDs slice off a large portion of the bonus pool, about 15 per cent, with the result that approximately 250 EMDs split $1.65 billion. The stratification in compensation mirrors the hierarchy of partnerships into several discrete categories (for example senior partner, managing partners, partners, principals and associates).

The partitioning of partnerships into partners and associates is particularly important for the governance of organizations in which each and every owner is fully responsible for all services rendered by a partnership. Mentoring in partnerships is far more critical than in corporations. Partners are commonly mentors or sponsors of certain associates and recruitment; retention and promotion of valuable associates is one of the three pillars that shape the competitive advantage of a partnership (Maister, 1993). The partners can leverage their human and social capital by adding associates but are constrained by resources such as time and energy from mentoring many employees, such that the leverage ratio in many sectors rarely exceeds 1 to five or ten. Prestigious Wall Street law firms might have a leverage ratio of less than one. The firm, as internal labor market, thus presents an arena in which partners vie for the best associates while the latter have incentives to invest in a partner's human and social capital, thus maneuvering into a relationship of mutuality and support. As associates become vested in certain partners, partners become more committed to certain associates – otherwise the associate's option value outside the firm will draw them towards competitors (Groysberg and Nanda, 2002). The external inducements often overcome the incompleteness of the employment contract and alleviate the bounded rationality of the owners (compare Coff, 1997). Coff suggests that in human asset-intensive firms the actual productivity of an employee is difficult to ascertain – the external labor market becomes an important component in the evaluation of its human capital. In partnership firms or organizations, however, the partner-managers do not face the same level of information asymmetry towards employees (that is, associates) since the lengthy tournament assures a high level of familiarity with the employees' skills and appropriate fit with the firm's culture.

Inter-firm mobility is comparatively rare (see Chapter 9) but might provide additional information about the human and social capital of partnership employees. McDonald (2005) describes what looks like an auction system after Wall Street professional services firms have paid out bonuses to their members based on their annual performance evaluation. The bonus often constitutes a signal to peer firms about the perceived value of particular professionals and might trigger a bidding war, resulting in either the retention or defection of the partner/employee. Financial incentives represent an important means to buy the loyalty of partners, although non-financial factors also play a role in binding members to the firm, as was amply demonstrated in the case study mentioned above (Lazega, 2001). Such non-financial factors include camaraderie among partners which can be a strong glue holding the firm together – for example the symbiosis between those who brought in clients and those who serviced their needs (the so-called finders and minders), resulting in strong bonds between the partners. Altogether, the benefits of superior information about human assets that comes with partnership forms of organizations is largely internal.

Agency Problems and Organizational Failure

Agency has both internal and external ramifications. The governance arrangements of partnerships (and particularly the partnership with partners and associates, the so-called PA structure) reduces some of the internal agency problems that are prevalent in public and private corporations but might exacerbate external agency problems. Compared to corporations, partnerships empower the partners to participate in strategic decision-making as well as strategy implementation. Unlike corporations, the managers are both owners and managers and are therefore the beneficiaries of a governance arrangement that assures their stake as the primary beneficiaries. They own job rights and decision rights. It is therefore plausible to assume that the governance structure in the auditing sector favors its specific performance aspects and elevates the members as the primary constituency. Individuals in this sector are plausibly endowed to greatly affect the competitive conditions of their firm and enjoy disproportionately strong leverage in aligning their interests with that of their firm. The role of the individuals in these organizations should therefore be paramount. In short, partnerships face comparatively low external agency costs.

The prevalence of the partnership in auditing is not only beneficial to the owners (that is, partners) but also to other constituencies, including recruits and customers. Corporations have advantages that outweigh some agency costs, mostly related to scale economies and diminished hold-up problems in capital-intensive but knowledge-extensive firms and therefore these predominate in capital-intensive sectors such as telecommunication, mining, chemical and transportation equipment. Compared to partnerships, public corporations are fraught with external agency problems, especially when ownership and control become separated and the owners, as dispersed and fragmented principals, become misinformed about the efforts and skills of their agents, the executives. Internal agency costs are often dealt with in large diversified firms as such organizations become decomposable into smaller divisional units to cope with information overload, monitoring costs and the alignment of lower-level decision-makers with those in the top management team (Williamson, 1975). Partnerships produce limited scale advantages as internal agency problems grow proportionally to their size which explains why partnerships are considerably smaller than corporations.

Size-induced changes away from the partnership form have been dramatically illustrated by well-known firms such as Goldman Sachs and McKinsey which altered or eliminated their partnership structure to alleviate internal agency costs. The partitioning between managing and regular partners is said to result in a corruption of the interest of the latter, triggering pressures either to break up the partnership or to revert to a corporate form (Bhide, 1992; van Lent, 1999). Large size and a disproportionate prevalence of intangible assets also renders asset portioning less than feasible. As we have seen, in a partnership the personal assets cannot be isolated from the members so that the firm does not exist independently of its owners. In a public corporation the assets can be fully partitioned and are therefore tradable and perfectly separable from the owners, regardless of size. One owner is unlikely to be held up by a fellow owner, and owners can separate themselves from the managers either by selling their investment in the firm or entering the market for corporate control and ousting the unwanted managers.

A comparison of internal agency costs by contrast, often favors the partnership over the corporation, partly because the role of manager and owner are united in the same individuals. Note that unlike the corporation, a partnership does not exist independently of its members. Customers and other stakeholders who put claims on the firm have complete access to the resources of each and every partner. The rise of the limited partnership in sectors such as advertising, architecture and investment banking might be motivated by the need for risk exposure reduction. Likewise, the replacement of partnerships by private corporations might be due to internal agency problems such that partners shield themselves from the non-performance of fellow partners. Such considerations are particularly plausible when partnerships grow in size and stratification among partners is unavoidable, with some partners becoming elevated to the status of managing partner. Such stratification leads inevitably to further centralization, in line with the infamous *Iron Law of Oligarchy* (Michels, 1915) while at the same time marginalizing many of the remaining partners, particularly in larger partnerships, and in spite of measures to forestall such centralization through the creation of annual retreats and the limit in tenure of the senior managing partner. In other words, while internal agency problems can be met by the partnership form of organization, growth put limits on partnership's governance. And paradoxically, knowledge intensity, which favors partnerships over corporations, creates agency problems that are unique to human asset-intensive firms which is what professional service companies are. In partnerships the confluence of agency and knowledge management is perhaps their most distinguishing trait and might explain why partnerships are so attractive among knowledge-intensive firms. The template is merely an overarching descriptor for organizational arrangements that can vary widely across firms.

Partnership and Organization: The Economic Sociology of Partnerships

We should, therefore, try to complement an efficiency or economic-oriented review of partnership in all its varieties; ultimately a synthesis of an economic and sociological frame of reference is desirable. The comparative analysis of organizations, combined with case studies and computer simulations might inform us about the relative merits of various organizational forms, including that of partnerships and its range of structural arrangements. As institutional theory argues, a great deal of causal ambiguity exists among various organizational templates and an unequivocal link between partnership, knowledge sharing, governance, and performance is still a remote ideal. Organizational ecologists have remained even more oblivious of the practices that exist within a firm.

Ecologists, beginning with Hannan and Freeman (1977, 1984) take as a starting point the 'core attributes' of organizational form and examine the density of firms corresponding to the preponderance of certain attributes. For example, the relative frequency of partnerships versus private or public corporations that has been reported by Greenwood and Empson (2003) signals the relative fitness of this form in accounting and law, but apparently not in advertising or management consulting. Likewise, the emergence of accounting firms in general and the rise of certain types of structures – as we document in Chapter 5 when discussing the rise and proliferation of the partner–associate structure – benefits from an institutional theory of organizational forms but remains relatively coarse in fully documenting the negative selection of certain governance arrangements.

Unlike economists, sociologists have been largely absent from the inquiry into governance as a core attribute of organizations in general and partnerships in particular. Governance pertains very much to the internal functioning and structure of the firm, while ecologists have centered their theory and analysis on readily available data that are irrelevant for governance. The bulk of research has focused on products or services providers, ranging from restaurants, newspapers, automobiles, disk drives to wineries, and has been confined to the (addition and deletion) of firms that comprise a sector or industry number. Thus far, no study has explored the mortality and creation of firms having certain ideographic governance characteristics, perhaps because a longitudinal database that includes information on both governance and performance is hard to secure. Implicit in the summary statistics of Greenwood and Empson (2003) is the relative viability of partnerships and their fitness value across different sectors. The present volume partly alleviates this dearth of studies through an investigation of the audit firms, and references ecological factors such as density (number of firms) of the sector with classes of firms such as single proprietorships and partnerships, and elaborates on governance that help us to move beyond this approach, providing complements to it.

By contrast, institutional studies on governance have been more common but typically also fail to reach the depth of observations that we encounter in a study like that of Lazega (2001). The diffusion from 'peer groups' to hierarchy has included hybrid organizational structures, such as functional, divisional or matrix structure (Fligstein, 1990; Wholey and

Burns, 1993). A second set of studies has examined agency related practices such as those by Davis and Greve (1997) and Rao et al. (2001) on the diffusion of the poison pill. These studies have moved the adoption of organization structures beyond the 'mere' diffusion, as Armour and Teece (1978) did in their study of the M-form among petrochemical firms, to the issue of whether governance changes reflect a rational as distinct from an imitative motivation, perhaps because a firm's governance structure confers legitimacy. In general, these institutional studies demonstrate a strong propensity for firms to mimic each others' structures – for example firms tied to each other through interlocking directorates have a higher propensity to share a divisional as opposed to a functional form of organization structure (Davis and Greve, 1997). Such studies also inform us about the limits of a strict agency or transaction economics framing of partnerships. The studies on ecological versus institutional aspects of accounting firms that are presented in chapters 5 and 7 should suggest ways in which to advance the economic and social understanding of partnerships and other organizational forms. The findings in Chapter 8 suggest that when contrasting external ecological conditions with internal membership-related aspects, such as cumulative human and social capital, the former tends to drop out of the equation.

THE AUDIT INDUSTRY IN THE NETHERLANDS

The first accounting firms emerged at the onset of the industrial revolution in the late 1800s. Since then they have evolved considerably and significant developments in the constituent firms and their classes can be traced by using either an economic or sociological perspective. Thus, observations on their mergers and acquisitions, splits and member defections are food for agency theorists who attempt to document issues of strategic capabilities, control, incentives and scale. Sociologists might identify the causal ambiguity of the partnership and major or peripheral changes in its form to understand the propensity of professionals to endorse some dominant form of organization. The creation and dissolution of partnerships could likewise signal their fitness as distinct to other forms or organization in the accounting sector.

Associations in this sector protecting the interests and regulating the standards of its professionals mirror occupational groups such as medieval craft guilds and scientific associations, which have had a long history in Europe and display sophisticated administrative governance. However well-bounded sectors, with associated governance templates for its providers such as law, medicine and architecture emerged during and after the industrial revolution. Due to their control of membership (including documentation), it has been possible to garner comprehensive information on the structure, growth, evolution and internationalization of the accounting industry. The chapters with empirical results in this volume have been based on data obtained from membership directories of Dutch accounting associations which eventually converged into a single professional entity.

While the Dutch audit 'industry' might display some unique patterns of sector evolution, it also resembles developments that took place in other industrialized societies. In the same way, the audit industry shows many similarities with other professional services such as law, consulting and advertising, although it shares with the legal sector an almost complete attachment to partnership as the dominant form of organizing (Greenwood and Empson, 2003). Initially, the sector comprised single proprietorships but soon professionals began to band together into small partnerships and by the 1920s we see a further significant development when partnerships began to employ professionals who were not (yet) partners. Later still, this form of organization permitted the rise of the multinational confederate professional services firm. Subsequently, the audit sector has become increasingly concentrated, with stratification into large global organizations, an intermediate section with large, but more local firms and a complement of numerous small firms including the ubiquitous single proprietorship. Nowadays, the four largest firms account for 60 per cent of the Dutch audit market revenues (Langedijk and Deetman, 1992). The high concentration rate notwithstanding, this sector is also characterized by a very large number of single proprietorships. The partnership form entails either limited or full liability with larger firms such as KPMG representing a limited liability form. Such concentration ratios are likewise prevalent in other countries within the European Union (for example, NERA, 1992). Mozier and Turley (1989) and Tomzyck and Read (1989) show that concentration is equally high in the UK and the US respectively. The implication is that the size distribution of this service sector has undergone important transformations. Similar observations have been made for other components of the service sector. The five largest global advertising firms operate in many countries via numerous local units. Several law firms have also evolved into 'legal factories' (for example, Spangler, 1986) and some of them have become veritable multinational firms with clients across the globe.

At the start of this chapter, it was indicated that information on professional service sectors has been made accessible because professional service associations go to great length in certifying individuals as bona fide members of the profession. The presence of membership directories which constitute a byproduct of membership oversight by professional associations have made it possible to track the emergence and growth of the industry as well as the creation, dissolution, mergers and acquisitions of firms that comprise the industry. The information allows access to individuals who constitute the membership and whose career trajectories can be mapped both within and across firms.

The members of professional associations who created either single proprietorships or partnerships provide a window on the structure of the industry. The story of the industry can be traced to the creation of the very first firms that provided auditing and other financial control services. These emerged in 1880 and, not surprisingly, they were single proprietorships. However, the first entrants were soon joined by firms that constituted partnerships and by 1890, the number of accounting firms in the Netherlands had grown to sixteen, with an average size of two professionals per firm. By the end of the First World War the sector had grown to more than 150 firms and the largest firm counted eight members. In 1990 the number of firms exceeded 500 and the largest firm employed a thousand individuals.

Throughout its history the audit sector has been affected by exogenous trends such as the transition from an industrial to a service-oriented economy and numerous regulatory interventions, especially those that were implemented in response to demands for greater transparency of corporate performance and financial health. Significant restrictions were introduced in the Netherlands with at least two major regulatory changes. The Act on Annual Financial Statements of Enterprises was approved in 1970 and took effect in 1971. It required annual audits for the first time and increased the amount of financial information to be reported by companies (Zeff et al., 1992). From 1984 onwards, definitive guidelines for auditing were promulgated and enforced by the NIvRA (the exclusive professional association) in collaboration with the Justice Ministry (Zeff et al., 1992). Besides establishing disciplinary rules, the organization granted the Registered Accountant (RA) license on condition that a prospective auditor acquired 'knowledge of complicated audit techniques (such as statistical sampling, risk analysis and analytical review) and extensive knowledge of financial accounting (measurement methods, regulations and standards)' (Maijoor and van Witteloostuijn, 1996: 555). In 1925 the Dutch audit sector witnessed the very first firm with dual membership in that some professionals were owners while others were employees and were called 'associates'. This important innovation triggered a great deal of mimicking and contributed to the growth of the market share of firms with a bifurcation of owners and employee-professionals. The empirical results in Chapter 5 elaborate on the adoption and diffusion of this organization form in the Netherlands accounting sector.

Regulations increasing the complexity of accounting procedures and specifying the companies that should be externally audited significantly heightened the demand for audit services. As such, they could be seen to increase the demand for large accounting firms and perhaps to influence adoption propensity. Changes in audit technology which had possible scale implications included statistical sampling techniques, risk management, and control and auditing innovations ranging from activity-based accounting to the balanced score card (see Kaplan and Norton, 1992). Finally, client concentration and globalization have affected the accounting sector in all western economies (Benston, 1985). In the evolution towards internationalization, larger and global clients can only be serviced by large accounting firms, especially if the client operates in multiple societies. Larger audit firms can also diversify their service delivery over a broader and more heterogeneous roster of clients thus preserving their professional independence. Unlike smaller firms, these larger audit firms also signal their professional quality through their visibility, implied integrity and international reputation. Therefore, accounting firms enjoy scale advantages that are impossible to command for their smaller and more local competitors. The bifurcation is further accentuated by internationalization. Apart from the changes within the Dutch audit sector, significant networking between large Dutch and foreign players has been paramount. This networking has resulted in some full mergers or other forms of strategic alliance. In some cases worldwide consolidation did not incorporate the Netherlands. For example, the Dutch component of Deloitte did not consent to an international merger and abandoned the network (Sluyterman, 1993). Altogether, it should be noted that the growth in concentration during the 1970s was independent of internationalization. Rather the increase in the concentration ratio was due to large accounting firms affiliating with a global network and absorbing smaller firms (Maijoor and van Witteloostuijn, 1996). Figure 2.1 shows the concentration ratio during this period covered by our study.

Notwithstanding such trends, the preponderance of numerous small and medium-sized firms points to competitive advantages that accrue to these classes of firms. The accounting sector is, in fact, very much a local and regional industry, the globalization and growing market share of the very large firms notwithstanding, and buyer–seller relationships are very common. The localness of the sector in fact permits us to evaluate the importance of geography in mapping out competitive pressures as we do in several chapters. When considering geography, we should ask not only whether 'mere' distance matters, but also, and more importantly, whether 'borders' matter. It is not, in fact, mere proximity that determines the spatial heterogeneity of organizational founding rates. Entrepreneurs are embedded in geographic entities that have more or less well-defined

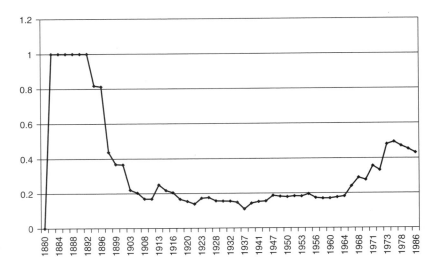

Figure 2.1   Concentration index of the four biggest firms in the Netherlands

boundaries, comprise institutional and socioeconomic identities, and are endowed with distinct bundles of resources. Geographic entities within a country include Standard Metropolitan Statistical Areas (SMSAs), provinces or states, counties, industrial districts, and autonomous regions. They are distinct for historical as well as developmental and administrative reasons. The study by Pennings (1982) found sharp differences among SMSAs in entrepreneurial activity within specific four-digit SIC codes because SMSAs vary considerably in relevant resource endowments. Other studies show the existence of significant geographical differences, as illustrated by Putman's (1996) classic study on social capital (for example, with some exaggeration, Alabama is a world of loners, while Minnesotans are well endowed with social capital), and by the famous paper on Spain by Linz and de Miguel (1966), in which they identify the existence of eight Spains. Over the period presented in the empirical studies of this book – 1880–1986 – the Netherlands comprised eleven provinces: North Holland, South Holland, Fryslan, Groningen, Drenthe, Overijssel, Gelderland, Utrecht, North Brabant, Zeeland and Limburg. The seven northern provinces in the seventeenth century constituted autonomous regions held together through a confederation called the Republic of the United Provinces. Perhaps it was the extraordinary degree of autonomy and home rule that accounted for the disinclination of provinces to secede. Such autonomy might also have further engendered their unique socioeconomic identity. Two of the three

Figure 2.2   Map of the Netherlands and its 12 provinces

southern provinces – located below the Rhine and the Meuse rivers – were ruled partly by the republic, partly by Spain and Austria, and showed much-delayed economic development. Figure 2.2 provides a map of the Netherlands, with its twelve provinces. Flevoland, the twelfth province, is a recent addition due to land reclamation, but is not pertinent to this study and its examination of provinces as local ecologies. The map also hints at geographic distance as a conditioning variable in shaping diffusion and legitimation. For example, let us consider Utrecht. The first founding event followed similar events in the neighboring provinces Noord and Zuid Holland. Gelderland experienced the same event only after its neighboring province Utrecht. Apart from history, the eleven provinces vary in soil structure, geology, religion, economic development, urbanization, and language or dialect (Frysk is an officially recognized language, spoken in Fryslan, a Northern province of the Netherlands, while other provinces, such as Groningen, Zeeland and Limburg, speak a sub-language or dialect). Two of the three provinces located south of the Rhine are Roman Catholic rather than Calvinist. The provinces are thus not merely administrative units but are also historically, culturally, institutionally, and economically distinct. Even if their significance is declining, they have been critical in determining the current administrative structure of the Netherlands (Centraal Bureau Statistiek, 2002). Such observations drive home the point that scale enlargements notwithstanding, spatial considerations are also significant for delivery of services and recruitment of professionals. The paradox of partnership – with its internal and external agency problems – further exacerbates the local constraints of national and global firms.

The data used in the following empirical chapters cover the entire population of Dutch accounting firms.[1] We did not sample Dutch accounting firms from the population, but instead collected data from directories of accountant associations that appeared at one- to five-year intervals. These directories provided information on the name, address, educational attainments, and status (partner or associate) of each accountant in the professional association. Also provided was the employment affiliation: the name of each individual's employing accounting firm, business firm, or governmental agency. Since the first Dutch accounting firm was founded in 1880, we did not face the problem of 'left-truncation' of data. The complete industry comprised 2081 firms over the 110-year period. However, a few firms founded between 1986 and 1990 were not included in the analysis, because 1990 was the last year for which data were collected. Firms founded between 1986 and 1990 could not be identified as either 'right-censored' or as having dissolved. The analyses therefore are based on almost two thousand firms – but see each chapter for some differences. We used firm intervals rather than firm years as we did not have membership information for each and every year. Membership directories were published every other year, rather than annually. During World War II, directories were not published at all, resulting in a hiatus of five years. In other cases, owing to the need to economize on exorbitant data collection expenses during the latest parts of the observation window, we even skipped some membership directories; doing so resulted in four-year, rather than two-year, intervals. Most of our chapters included in this volume cover a total of 110 years with 53 observation points and the relative percentage of observations in each interval is 24 per cent for 1 year, 60 per cent for 2 years, 6 per cent for 3 years, 8 per cent for 4 years, and 2 per cent for 5 years.

CONCLUSION

The partnership as organizational form was robust in the decades before the industrial revolution as it is now, in the time of the so-called 'knowledge economy'. Partnerships have received relatively limited attention from writers on organizations who tend to focus more on private and public corporations. With a history of well over 100 years, the accounting sector in the Netherlands has witnessed significant innovations, both overall and in the governance of its firms. The Dutch audit industry provides therefore an interesting theater for documenting the evolution of organizational forms in general and partnerships in particular.

While reviewing the history of the accounting sector and its prevailing organizational forms we have also encountered the role of human agency. Organizations comprise individuals and it behoves us to recognize that obvious fact. Obviously, we cannot understand the conduct of a partnership's members by summing their motives and propensity to atomistically pursue their self-interests. The partners in partnerships are individuals, but they are also embedded in social networks and institutionalized settings such as their current or previous firm. As we have seen in Chapter 1, they are neither over-socialized (Wrong, 1961; Granovetter, 1985) into the structure and culture of their collective enterprise and follow the internalized scripts that come with organizational affiliation and socialization or under-socialized. Wrong (1977) argued that the social order derives from the individual following widely agreed upon norms and values, thus reducing him to a *homo sociologicus* (Dahrendorf, 1966) and pleaded for a widening of perspectives that is analogous to the debates in sister social sciences – for example in economics about behavioral (for example, Thaler, 1997) versus neoclassical economics. We should thus be wary of an atomistic concept of partners and presume them to be embedded in partnerships that may constrain the pursuit of their individual intentions. The accounting sector is knowledge-intensive, as well as human asset-intensive. The members of its firms – whether owners or employees – are carriers of the intangible assets that constitute the core of their capabilities and confer a competitive advantage. Their individual actions have profound externalities discernable at the firm and sector level.

In this chapter, we have highlighted the dual nature of the audit firm's structure: governance and organization structure. Accounting firms attend to the strategic governance of competencies that permit them to earn a premium over rivals. Accounting firms are also complex organizations with horizontal and particularly vertical differentiation, most notably between owners or partners and employees or associates. The firms comprise single or multiple individuals and in fact the accounting sector data exploited in this volume's chapters derives from individuals being members of accounting associations.

The studies from the Dutch empirical setting reported here combine information concerning multiple levels of analysis, including sector, firms and individuals. The long window onto this sector allows the researcher to spot both economic and sociological developments at the firm and the sector level of analysis. The studies reported here are unique, partly because they furnish a longitudinal window on individual conduct against a backdrop of firms, their structure and performance in a competitive spatial environment. Given their geographic embeddedness, in fact, interesting insights on the locational aspects of organizations also come to light and are thoroughly discussed.

NOTE

1. Firms in our data set were owned by accountants who were licensed to provide public auditing services. The activities of these firms, however, were not confined to auditing services, as the firms also provided tax and management consulting services. Since the 1960s, the partnership governance structure has become prevalent, as has been the case in other Western countries. Through international mergers and acquisitions, the Dutch accounting industry has become increasingly concentrated and linked with peer firms across national borders. As elsewhere, single proprietorships are also conspicuous in the Netherlands. Accounting standards, which have become increasingly internationalized, likewise contribute to homogenization across borders.

PART II

The intangible asset of human-intensive organizations

3. Social capital of organizations: conceptualization, level of analysis and performance implications

INTRODUCTION

Organizations are presumed to have boundaries. They are endowed with various kinds of assets on which they make ownership claims, and which are protected with isolating mechanisms such as patents and contracts. They are liable for the products and services they produce. Also, they have members whose inclusion in the organization is usually beyond dispute. In fact, the firm as a collection of individuals is often bracketed when considering the competitive game it is playing with other firms. Yet, organizational boundaries are precarious and certainly permeable. They have exchange relationships with suppliers and clients, collude with competitors, and forge all kinds of alliances with them because they cover only part of the value added in their value chain. In their positioning across the chain they face such decisions as whether to 'make or buy' components and supplies, whether to share or even outsource R&D efforts, or to operate on a stand-alone basis. Their coherence and integrity might decline and bundles of resources often unravel into discrete parts, but these resources might also become combined – for example in divestments and acquisitions, respectively.

Organizations are embedded in a web of relational ties. In this chapter, the term 'social capital' captures this relational web. Social capital of organizations constitutes a distinctly collective property that might be mediated by individuals, yet is uniquely organizational. Social capital complements financial and human capital as assets that are more or less valuable, scarce and imperfectly tradable (Barney, 1991). Social capital is even more unique and difficult to appropriate than these other types of assets as it hinges on the continued involvement of two or more parties. Firms, as repositories of unique resources require complementary assets in order to compete successfully. Social capital is crucial in bundling intangible assets and provides the absorptive capacity to merge proprietary knowledge with that of others. Organizations need to coordinate their interdependencies in the value chain and negotiate a position in their industry. By forging external networks, the organization maintains optimal boundary conditions and remains in tune with external trends and events. At the same time, its boundary structures preserve an organizational modicum of identity and protection against erosion of its assets.

The benefits of social capital seem beyond doubt; less intuitive might be the cost of social liability. Social embeddedness endangers a firm's appropriability regime, and might also envelop the firm so tightly in a web of ties that it stifles its ability to change or impedes its innovative capability. While network relationships are often viewed as conferring various benefits, we should therefore also examine their undesirable consequences. Social capital means the ability to sustain long-term relationships and associations. The concept originates in sociology, with two writers standing out: Bourdieu (1980, 1994) and Coleman (1990). In this chapter we extend their representation of social capital by treating it as a unique *organizational* resource. We will further reflect on the nature of organizations, and ask how such human aggregates or their social organization are capable of possessing social capital. As with human capital, we need to emphasize the tension between individual and organizational levels of analysis. While it is tempting to anthropomorphize the firm as a human aggregate and impute an ability to mold its surrounding network, we need to ask how such semblance comes about, who the agent is, and what collective motives are operating. After having considered these issues, we explore the implications of organizations that have accumulated social capital. We do so by comparing two contrasting types, business groups and professional service firms, as stylized forms which can be used to illustrate the firm as rational and political actor respectively and, by implication, the sort of aggregation issues that color the ways in which we depict their social capital. Below, we also utilize these metaphors to highlight aspects of corporate social capital. We conclude by spelling out implications and future research opportunities.

CONCEPT OF ORGANIZATION AND ITS SOCIAL CAPITAL

It has not been customary to view organizations as embedded in a network of relationships, although person-based networks have been used to describe a firm's external linkages (for example, Levine, 1972). Much of the pertinent literature has focused on individuals (for example, Burt, 1997; Coleman, 1988; Granovetter, 1985; Uzzi, 1997), their place in some larger network, and the impact it has on their behavior and attitudes. Many views stand in sharp contrast with an 'over-socialized' view of man. Economists tend to couch transactions in personal, self-interest seeking terms. As parties in a market, people engage in 'arm's length' relationships and their interaction is solely conditioned by the need for exchange. Contrary to such a utilitarian tradition, norm theory in modern sociology assumes that people are overwhelmingly sensitive to the expectations of others (Wrong, 1961). Sociologists often stress the structural context within which parties meet and which might give rise to small number conditions in which actors develop personal bonds, based on trust and mutuality. Uzzi (1997) calls such links 'embedded ties'.[1] Within such bounds, utility maximization is often suspended for the sake of preserving reciprocal, even altruistic relationships. The next issue involves the extension from the individual per se to the individual as an 'office holder'. Size also matters; for example a market with single proprietorships (for example, the diamond industry) entails rather different inter-firm networking than the US banking world in which firms are tied together, for example through interlocking directorates.

Entrepreneurs, new ventures, and small firms differ markedly from large corporations in terms of the links they maintain. The links that bind them might vary from those that are heavily endowed with trust to those that fit the arm's length relationships. The large corporation tends to have arm's length relationships with external actors, but as we will see, they often invest in boundary-spanning systems in which personally-mediated links are discernible. Small firms are more likely to develop bonds of trust and mutual adjustment with external actors such as suppliers and clients, although some conditions give rise to arm's length relationships (for example, Uzzi, 1997).

We need to position these distinctions against the 'model' of the firm which is often implicit (Allison, 1971; Simon, 1957; Thompson, 1982). Organizations have often been viewed as 'rational actors' (Allison, 1971) or have otherwise been treated as unitary economic agents. As a singular agent, the firm might be embedded in a multiplex web of inter-firm relationships as manifest in contracts, joint ventures, stock cross-holdings, and so on. As units with clear legal boundaries and other isolating mechanisms firms complement each other in the value chain. The ties that bind them can be viewed as social capital for coordinating inter-firm activities. If we, however, view organizations as human aggregates – as Allison (1971) for example stipulates in his organization as 'political actor' – we might attribute social capital to the organization by virtue of the aggregate social capital of its members. The presumption of firms being endowed with social capital appears non-problematic but the implications are rather different in the two scenarios thus depicted. In this chapter we will visit the issue of the firm as rational versus political actor in greater detail.

In this chapter, for the sake of argument, we juxtapose the stylized notion of the rational actor with its political actor counterpart and examine social capital as an integral part of these models.[2] In the case of the firm as rational actor, we treat individuals as a component in what often appears to be a multi-layered network; partly mediated by individuals and partly by other linking vehicles. In the case of the firm as political actor, the link will often be personal, based on trust and tacitness.[3]

We want to stretch the concept of social capital such that it might become an extension of the individual as an office holder in an organization and consequently, become an accessory for his firm's functioning. For example, an early study by Pettigrew (1974) on the 'politics of organizational decision-making' narrates the position of an information technology specialist as a boundary-spanner between his firm and external vendors. As office holder his significance derives from the quality of internal and external embeddedness. We might then ask whether the office holder's network connections can be combined with that of others into an index of organizational social capital. Furthermore, inter-firm links might also be discernible beyond the IT specialist, for example by the long-term outsourcing of data storage and retrieval services, or the presence of a hotline with the IT consultants. Such a link is not 'simplex', but what might be called 'multiplex'. The Pettigrew example illustrates the transition from the firm as a human aggregate to the firm as a coherent, singular entity where the issue of aggregation becomes bracketed, or remains outside the purview of the observer.

LEVEL OF ANALYSIS

It is problematic to move from the individual to the organizational level of analysis when analyzing inter-firm networks. The issue of aggregation from the member to the organization is primarily an issue when we view the organization as a political actor in which the members' social capital aggregates to that of their organization. Nevertheless, people associated with the organization as rational actor carry out actions on behalf of their firm, and while the model is agnostic about their integrity, we could also focus on their roles as distinct linking mechanisms.

At face value, the individual–collective distinction seems more conceptual than real. The issue oscillates between two frames: do individuals as agents or office holders connect organizations and other human aggregates? Or do organizations and other human aggregates connect individuals? In this chapter, we are mostly concerned with the first type of framing. Nonetheless, we recognize that many inter-firm links condition the intermediation of individuals. In abstracting away from individuals as mediators of inter-firm links we shift from the view of the firm as a political actor to that of a rational actor (Allison, 1971). The level of analysis becomes moot and little need exists for acknowledging cognitive, cultural, or strategic differentiation – whether in the organizational core or at its boundaries.

To the extent that aggregation surfaces as a salient feature, we should abandon the neoclassical notion of the firm as a unitary actor with a well-defined preference ordering for which the firm's strategy is clear and unambiguous. This firm's membership has a singular identity. The challenge is to consolidate divergent identities into a coherent one such that they might even approximate the firm as a unitary integrated actor. The members are assigned to interlocked sets of roles and they develop informal sets of hierarchical and horizontal relationships with other people inside and outside the organization. A large chunk of organizational social capital exists by virtue of individuals whose relationships span organizational boundaries.

Some organizational participants contribute more to the firm's social capital than others, depending on their involvement in the focal firm and its transacting partners. Indeed, not all members are equivalent in their ability to leverage their social capital for the firm. Members vary not only in their contribution to external ties but also in their participation in the organization (for example, Cohen et al., 1972). When aggregating the social capital of members to arrive at a stock index of firms, there is also the issue of redundancy. A network link is redundant if the marginal increase in benefits from acquiring or maintaining that link equals zero. Redundant ties have been well documented at the individual level – see, for example, Granovetter's (1974) 'weak' versus 'strong' tie and Burt's (1992) presence or absence of 'structural holes'. The aggregation of the networks of organizational participants tends to have redundant contacts. The number of members maintaining contact with representatives of other organizations might produce 'stronger' ties that are particularly beneficial for the transfer of sophisticated knowledge. For the transmission of information or what might be called 'explicit knowledge', such strong ties are hardly efficient (compare Hansen, 1997). Furthermore, not all social capital of members aggregates to the social capital of the organization. The social contacts of certain organizational members may have little or no instrumental value for their organization.[4] Only overlapping membership in groups and organizations that are operationally or strategically relevant matter when aggregating individual social capital to that of the organization; the most common example is interlocking directorates (Pennings, 1980; Stokman et al., 1985).

Boundary Spanner or Multiple-group Membership

The concept of overlapping membership as a way to represent an individual's social capital should also be invoked to revisit the issue of a firm's boundaries. If members vary in their inclusion in the focal organization, their external contacts should vary in value as well. Even if organizational members have valuable external ties, they become a valuable component of the firm's social capital only if the members enjoy access to certain peers – for example those with power, information, and other resources. If inclusion is highly partial, their social capital becomes marginalized as well.

For simplicity's sake, organizational members might be stratified into a *core* group, a *regular or associate* group, and *temporary or marginal* workers. The core group consists of essential employees, that is, long-term employees and owners. Their fate is usually tied to that of the organization. The regular or associate group consists of rank-and-file employees who have been involved in the organization for some time and face good prospects of joining the core group. Many members who participate in that tournament will plateau, become sidetracked or might even be terminated. The temporary or marginal category includes temporarily hired workers and employees of subcontractors, that is, workers who fill the jobs not requiring firm-specific skills and who have little chance of moving into another category of members.[5]

It follows that the social capital associated with the core group is more important than that of the regular group. The reason is twofold. First, members in the core group are more likely to use their social contacts on behalf of the organization. Consistent with the 'garbage-can' model (Cohen et al., 1972), these members have the highest 'net energy load', as their fate is closely tied to that of the organization. Second, they are likely to maintain more valuable social contacts for the organization. They are more central to the access structure, and enjoy higher positions with more power and authority. Many of the firm-relevant social contacts are based on the job and title of individual members. A CEO becomes a board member of a peer organization, supplier or some other organization; a partner in a consulting firm befriends senior executives in the firm he works for, and so on. Compared to the employees in regular or temporary groups, members in the core group tend to have social ties with people who occupy higher, more visible and more prestigious positions in their organizations. In other words, people who have social contacts with members in the core group of a focal organization tend to have more valuable resources at their disposal for the focal organization than do the people who have primarily social ties with members in more peripheral organizations. Core members also stay longer with their organization such that their organization stands to benefit more from their social capital. Overall, we need to focus on the

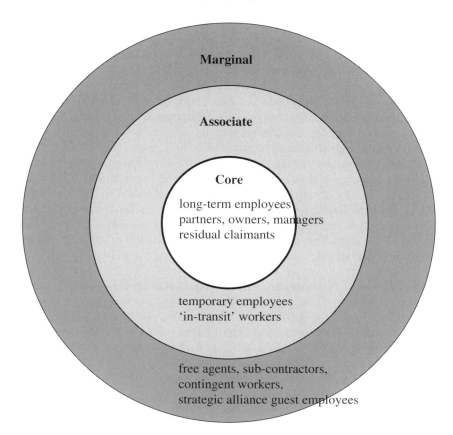

*Figure 3.1   The stratification of members in the contemporary
organization*

nature of the employment relationship to weigh an individual's ability to
link his firm with others.

Figure 3.1 provides a graphical display of organization stratification in
terms of magnitude of personal inclusion.

There are more ways than this in which to characterize the firm as a community of people who are endowed with human capital, and who are
differentiated by skill, function, types of markets, products, or technologies.
Firms have either a functional or divisional (and in many cases some hybrid)
structure whose boundaries define identities. In fact, although firms claim
to be hierarchies that economize on transaction costs (Williamson, 1975),
they in fact comprise numerous sub-cultures, with their own identities and

parochial interests. While hierarchy and lateral linkages integrate disparate units, they often face major hurdles in consolidating skills or knowledge, or more generally in bundling their contributions to the common good (Brown and Duguid, 1997; Kogut and Zander, 1994). A firm's internal networks, such as heavy duty project managers (Clark and Fujimoto, 1991), overlapping teams, and interdepartmental career paths, become vehicles for knowledge migration, but such networks are often comparatively deficient because specialization impedes knowledge transfer, especially knowledge that is difficult to package. Ironically, communities of knowledge within the firm often have easier access to like communities in other firms than they do with the sister departments within their own firm. The implication is that such external networks are often more efficacious in connecting the firm with external actors than are networks that embrace the total organization. By way of example, we might consider a firm's participation in an 'invisible college' as less problematic than its participation in a trade association (Powell, 1990; Lazega, 1999).

Multiplex Versus Personal Forms of Organizational Boundaries

At the level of inter-organizational relationships, we could make an even stronger argument about the individually anchored social capital of organizations. When the vendor of a software firm leaves, s/he might appropriate the connections with clients that s/he has built up during his tenure. One might thus argue that the social capital of organizations is tied up in the individuals they employ.

Yet, as with all intangible assets, social capital can also be treated as an intangible asset that is not exclusively buried in personal networks. Social capital is often 'depersonalized' or is couched in multiplex forms. Inter-organizational links established through individuals might begin to lead a life of their own. Or such links are reinforced by other elements such as contracts, traditions, and institutional arrangements. The members who are then a complement to a system will in fact also be governed by the norms and beliefs that are endemic to local social arrangements.

When links become multiplex, they cease to be dependent on individuals who act as brokers. By way of example, patent citations signal proximity of knowledge among organizations and can be examined as a conduit for inter-firm knowledge transfer. Cartels amount to a clique with shared norms where the members are firms rather than people. A set of firms might be tied through mutual share holdings. Affiliation among organizations, such as *keiretzu* in Japan, *chaebol* in Korea, or business groups in Sweden illustrate bundles of inter-firm connections that cannot be reduced to relations between middlemen.

Strategic alliances such as joint ventures, R&D partnerships, and minority investments embody nodes in webs of inter-firm networks in the chemical, telecommunication, micro-electronic and biotechnology industries (for example, Ahuja, 1998; Hagedoorn and Schakenraad, 1994). Severing some of these linkages might be impossible. For instance, Microsoft has extensive lock-in agreements with PC makers, and their suppliers and PC manufacturers have contracted for the pre-arranged installation of Microsoft's operating system in what used to be called 'IBM-compatible' personal computers. Biotechnology firms' entrenchment can be inferred from patent citation networks in which their intellectual property is more or less linked with that of other firms; the tightness of their links is derived from the proximity as measured by relative citation frequencies (Stuart et al., 1997).

All of this requires us to break down the ingredients of inter-firm networks into at least three categories:[6]

(1) *link*: any sort of association between two or more firms, including equity cross-holdings, patent ties, licensing agreements, R&D partnerships, equity joint venture agreements, gatekeepers, or interlocking directorates;
(2) *ties*: human mediated links, such as interlocking director or guest engineer; ties can be 'neutral', reflexive (Pennings, 1980) or even universalistic versus parochial and particularistic;
(3) *relationships*: human mediated ties that are particularistic, as for example the guest engineer who has an OEM employment status but lives on the premises of a supplier.

In short, organizational social capital bifurcates into personalized and depersonalized forms, with relationships often augmented with ties and links; while in other instances, the link might persist without the benefit of a relationship. This distinction often corresponds to a simplex versus a multiplex web of network connections. Multiplex 'links' appear to be more congruent with the rational actor metaphor of Allison, while 'relationships' feature prominently in treatments of organizations as political actors. Table 3.1 furnishes some examples. First, the organization itself can have a link with other organizations that is instrumental for its functioning. Affiliation among organizations, such as *keiretzu* in Japan or *chaebol* in Korea, is a social link of the organization itself rather than of organizational members. As a legal entity, the firm is capable of contracting or of acting as a partner in any market relationship, including the setting up of joint ventures, the acquisition of another firm, or the shedding of a business unit to other firms, and so on. Indeed, independent of

Table 3.1   Examples of social capital among organizations

Mediated by individuals (simplex)	Mediated by systems (multiplex)
Interlocking directorates (Pennings, 1980)	Business groups (Acevado et al., 1990)
Guest engineers (Dyer, 1996)	*Chaebol* (Kim, 1997)
Social register (Useem and Karabel, 1986)	*Keiretzu* (Gerlach, 1987)
Revolving door syndrome (Pennings et al., 1998)	Investment bank syndicates (Chung et al., 1995; Podolny, 1995)
Alumni (McKinsey)	Joint ventures
Double agent	R&D partnerships
Gatekeeper (Tushman, 1978)	Guanxi-si-sen (Tsui, 1997)
Emissary	Electronic clearing house (Pennings and Harianto, 1992)

its members, the organization often maintains social capital through repetitive exchanges with other organizations. The pattern of exchanges has stabilized, even if the individual members who participate in the process have been changed (Chung, 1996). Investment banks perpetuate their collective efforts when they syndicate public offerings (Chung et al., 1995). Semiconductor firms joined SEMATEC when they sought to acquire greater economies of scale.

Whether one assumes a personal or impersonal link (or a hybrid form comprising both links and relationships) between organizations, links are constituted of the ingredients of arrangements that govern the firm–environment interface. In some cases the arrangements can be viewed in their own right, but their efficacy in managing external dependencies depends critically on the quality of the relationship with internal and external decision-makers. Adams (1976) was one of the first writers to review such arrangements. He refers to so-called 'boundary transaction systems'.

Boundary Transaction Systems

Social capital fits with the notion of more or less permeable boundaries of organizations that become spanned by a 'boundary transaction system' (Adams, 1976). Figure 3.2 provides a graphic representation. As Table 3.1 indicated, such systems diverge into pairs of individual dyads such as the interlocking director or guest engineer whose role in maintaining the firm's network depends critically on a balanced overlap between the inside and the outside. Or boundary transaction systems are larger and more

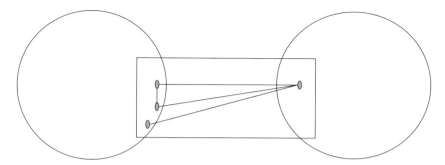

Figure 3.2 Boundary transaction system comprising four individuals and two organizations

elaborate entities – for example *kereitzus* and **R&D** partnerships. In the latter case the inter-firm link is not nearly as dependent on the presence of boundary-spanning individuals, to the extent that the significance of their mediation is comparatively minor. Personal ties often complement non-personal ones such as reciprocal ownership arrangements and **R&D** partnerships.

Furthermore, the relative salience of the system hinges on the duration of links that are maintained by individuals that make up the system. The longer the tenure, the more distinct the boundaries of the transaction system and the greater the likelihood that its members 'go native', that is, acquire an identity different from the firms they span. Consider the boards of directors or executive councils of Japanese business groups who over time might become closely knit teams. Employees originate from leading universities, where they have already formed friendship networks, and synchronically move upward through equivalent organizational ladders, such that the 'old boy network' remains intact from university years until retirement. The implication is that succession patterns further strengthen the boundary system's identity (Yoshino and Lifson, 1986). For example, Toshiba and Tokyo Power maintain close buyer–seller relationships; they both draw graduates from Tokyo University who get promoted in their respective companies, and they move in tandem; their roles might change but their mutuality stays intact. The demography of the system co-evolves with that of the respective organizations. Such evolutionary arrangements ensure network continuity throughout the firms' history.

The boundary transaction system is useful in that it points to the role of members' social capital in producing organizational social capital. Likewise, by recognizing that the system often evolves into a system that cannot be reduced to the participating members, social capital might become depersonalized. The system might become part of a business group, cartel, a joint venture, a long-term licensing agreement or an R&D partnership. Such systems are bound to become semi-free standing entities when three or more firms decide to participate. For example, SEMATEC and ESPRIT are consortia of semiconductor firms that joined forces at the behest of the US and European Union governments respectively to create what we might call a boundary transaction system.

A key difference between a simplex and multiplex boundary system involves the notion of trust. In a simplex system, trust is anchored in a dyad of trustor and trustee who maintain a form of personal trust that Simmel calls 'mutual faithfulness'. Bradach and Eccles (1989) refer to expectations that the other side will not behave opportunistically. It accords with the definition of trust by Mayer et al. (1995: 712) – a willingness of a party to be vulnerable to the actions of another party based on the expectations that the other party will perform a particular action important to the trustor, irrespective of the ability to monitor or control the other party. This definition excludes the social context of the dyad.

In multiplex systems, the social context becomes central and will in fact color the nature of the relationships between individuals who are part of that system. The context includes not only traditions, ties inherited from individuals who are no longer part of the system, contracts and financial leverage, but also forms of institutionalized trust (Luhmann, 1979; Shapiro et al., 1992; Zucker, 1986). The institutionalization evolves both temporally and spatially. Firms often have recurrent contacts with other firms, and the history of their relationship provides a platform for the current boundary system. Firms are also entrenched in larger entities, most notably business groups. The firms that make up a business group share norms about inter-firm transactions, have developed routines for contracting, and enjoy a group-derived reputation that molds the dynamics of interpersonal rela-tionships within a boundary transaction system between two member firms. And history matters here, too: the member firms have collectively gone through actions that resulted in shared practices, mutual stock own-ership, exclusive supplier–buyer relationships, or investments in transac-tion specific assets (Dyer, 1996). The historical and spatial context for two individuals who span their respective firms is therefore critically important in comprehending corporate social capital.

The fact that building up such capital requires time was neatly illustrated in the recent difficulties between Ford and its suppliers. Ford sought to redesign its Taurus model, while at the same time redesigning its boundary transaction system (Walton, 1997). For example, the firm attempted to move from multiple, arm's length ties with suppliers to single source rela-tionships. Having made few investments in social capital, its 'relational competencies' (Lorenzoni and Lipparini, 1997) for managing such supplier relationships were grossly inadequate. The boundary system included individuals such as Taurus project managers and representatives from 235 suppliers. The project's social architecture was to embrace a Japanese-style long-term cooperative relationship with suppliers. Yet, the culture of the system could be described as 'You could not trust them'.

The boundary transaction system should not be confined to individuals who initiated the system or were involved in its perpetuation. It ranges from dyads of individuals to complex social, economic, and technological arrangements. It evolves from individuals who interact frequently so that the firms become familiar with each other. Familiarity alleviates transaction costs, improves coordination across organizational boundaries, and reduces agency problems – in short the familiarity that comes with organizational networks confers benefits. Familiarity also produces group-think, cuts the firms off from important external stimuli, and renders it increasing inflexible. More specific benefits of social capital and the harmful effects of social liability are discussed next.

PERFORMANCE IMPLICATIONS OF SOCIAL CAPITAL

At the start of this chapter, social capital was mentioned as an integral part of the organization's intangible assets. The reference to assets suggests a rent-producing potential. However, social capital as such cannot produce rents, but it contributes to greater rent maximization of other resources that complement social capital.

Burt (1992) points out that social capital is owned jointly by the parties to a relationship whereas financial and human capital are the property of individuals or firms. In other words, social capital is embedded in the positions of contacts an organization reaches through its social networks (Lin et al., 1981). Further, social capital is related to rate of return in the market production function whereas financial and human capital pertain to the actual production capability. We should ask: What is the role of social capital in economic transactions? Under perfect competition, social capital cannot generate any economic rents (Burt, 1992). The market however is hardly perfect and information is not costless. The member's social capital strengthens his/her firm's ability to retain clients, perform market intelligence, and learn about new technologies. This is particularly true in our knowledge economy where many industries are characterized by abstract products or services, whose quality and other dimensions are difficult to articulate and where delivery of output is highly coupled with reputation (compare Burt, 1992). Clients resort to their social contacts to screen their suppliers because assessment criteria for quality might be hard to come by. While social capital is not part of the production function, it has profound impacts on the benefits that firms derive from their productive capabilities. Putting it differently, social capital creates the opportunities to exploit financial and human capital at a profit.

In the next two sections, we concentrate on these implications by reviewing two examples with rather different manifestations of interfirm ties: industrial firms that make up business groups such as *keiretzus* and *chaebols* and professional services firms that comprise the audit industry. We have hinted that these two examples present different manifestations of a firm's external networking. Firms that belong to a business group are typically depicted as rational actors in a conglomerate-type setting with mutual equity ownership, long-term supplier-buyer transactions, and shared directorships. The relational structure that business groups have is assumed to furnish social capital to member firms. We impute such benefits to the firm without confronting aggregation issues or delving into internal factions. Individuals are merely one of the threads that make up the fabric of networks of business groups. Thus the member firms of business groups are depicted as integrated, unitary actors who might benefit from their inclusion. The groups furnish interesting data on the benefits of social capital and costs of social liabilities among firms that come close to the stylized Allison-type rational actor.

In contrast, professional services firms belong to the sector that resembles a cottage industry, where individual professionals appear to be the most salient participants. While many professionals join a partnership and thus become co-owners of the firm, these organizations are very flat and by dint of the professionalization comprise members whose loyalty might be as strong to their firm as it is towards the profession. The social capital of the firm might in fact be the social capital of individual professionals. Even if we aggregate their social capital to that of the firm they belong to, there always remains the issue of whether it is the partner, the partner's peers as co-owners, or the firm which can make claims on the social capital that is mediated by the professional. The professional has a roster of clients to which he/she might feel more loyal than to the professional brethren who constitute the partnership. The professional's ties, and by implication the firm's links, often fit the notion of embedded ties. Arm's length transactions are incompatible with the rendering of services, although some emotional distance with the client is often deemed appropriate. Since partnerships often break up, or witness an exodus of partners, the sketch of Allison's political actor might sometimes be quite appropriate as a general descriptor. Yet, as we will see we often have to qualify this sketch.

Business Groups

Social networks have been a pervasive feature of Asian societies in general. According to Hofstede's (1980) landmark study, Asian societies stress collectivist values and cherish loyalty and commitment to family, organization, and community. At the corporate level we also discern a preponderance of networking – most visibly in business groups. Business groups include Japanese *keiretzus*, or their pre-war predecessors, called *zaibatzus*, and Korean *chaebols*. These groups contain myriad firms held together by ownership links, supplier–buyer relationships and mutual guarantees for bank loans. Other countries, most notably Sweden (for example, Hakanson and Johanson, 1993; Sundqvist, 1990; Berglov, 1994) and Argentina (for example, Acevado et al., 1990), harbor business groups, but in a local, idiosyncratic form. Therefore it is prudent to limit ourselves to a relatively homogeneous class of cases (compare Guillen, 1997). Furthermore, some other Asian countries manifest distinct forms of social capital among organizations; we could mention bamboo networks that are depicted as a *guanxi* (relation)-based cluster of Chinese firms (compare Tsui, 1997; Weidenbaum and Hughes, 1996). In these cases, the individual as family member performs a primary role in forging inter-firm links, and the family rather than the firm appears to be the most salient unit of analysis. Unlike more centrally coupled business groups in Korea and Japan, these Chinese forms of organization are octopoid and opportunistically diversified (Tam, 1990). In this section, we restrict ourselves to *keiretzus* and *chaebols*.

Chaebols Korean business groups manifest several features that set them apart from Western-style business groups (Kim, 1997). They display family ownership and management, controlled by a powerful chair. The chair's power derives from stockholdings and from the position of father or senior family member among heads of member companies. Kim (1997) even refers to unquestionable filial piety and patriarchy-based family control within modern multinational firms. A founder's descendants actively participate in the top management of the *chaebols*. When the founder dies, his descendants succeed as heirs. When a founder with multiple descendants dies, 'his' *chaebol* sometimes divides into several mini-*chaebols* as the case of Samsung indicates. The kinship and family networks continue to link the member firms of those mini-*chaebols*.

   Chaebols also exhibit high flexibility in mobilizing financial capital, technology and human resources. Unlike *keiretzus* and *zaibatzus* (although the same Chinese character is used to denote this extinct type of Japanese business group as well as *chaebol*!), which are governed through consensus-building and psychological commitment, *chaebols* are nimble in their deployment of resources and the patriarch can implement strategic decisions without consulting others. There is widespread rotation of key personnel, R&D efforts are pooled across companies, transfers of cash can be arranged through financial services firms, and the member companies can guarantee each other's borrowings from financial institutions.

Finally, the complex set of networked firms that make up a *chaebol* are exceptionally broadly diversified. Kim (1997) shows that a *chaebol* like Samsung operated in light and heavy manufacturing as well as in financial and other (for example, construction, media, hospitality, and advertising) services. Presumably, such diversification allowed the *chaebol* to offset any lack of high-tech skills by exploiting semi-skilled and unskilled labor in a way that would not be feasible to a non-networked competitor (Amsden, 1989), while at the same time producing products that are price-competitive rather than quality-competitive in the global markets. Compared to *keiretzus*, *chaebols* are shaped on the basis of the founding family. Financial institutions are of less importance in forming relationships within the *chaebol*'s member firms, because *chaebols* are blocked from owning more than 8 per cent of shares in commercial banks.

Keiretzus   *Chaebols* should thus not be confused with *keiretzus* or even with their earlier manifestation as *zaibatzus*, although the degree of contrast is a matter of controversy. After the Second World War, *zaibatsus* were dismantled, only to reappear in a different form, as *keiretzus*. As a result of the transformation, the founding families of the *zaibatsus* lost their shares and power and thus were no longer a source of connections. The insurance companies are at the *keiretzus*' apex, and from them cascade a transitive pattern of equity cross-holdings – the implication being that the insurance firms and their executives are the ultimate center of power and influence (Nishiyama, 1982). *Keiretzus*' governance is much more decentralized with decision-making among firms by consensus rather than through fiat by the *keiretzus*' insurance firm's executives. The *zaibatsus* provided a template which was mimicked by Korean entrepreneurs and in any event evolved into a prominent form during Korea's industrial revolution. *Zaibatzus* and *chaebols* share characteristics such as family ownership, management by patriarch, and unrelated diversification. However, unlike the *chaebol*, the *zaibatzu* also controlled commercial banks, giving them access to capital markets.

Keiretzus are laterally federated with transitive stock ownership arrangements that induce minimal interference in between-firm interactions, rather than resembling a *chaebol*-like holding with a vertically arranged governance structure.[7] Gerlach (1987: 128) refers to them as 'business alliances', which he defines as the 'organization of firms into coherent groupings which link them together in significant, complex long-term ownership and trading relationships'. They are distinct in the manner in which they have established coordinating mechanisms to govern their relationships. These include high-level councils of executives, the shaping of exchange networks, and external presentation as a coherent social unit, for example through advertising and product development activities. Prominent, but largely invisible in the structuring of network links is the role of financial institutions, which unlike the *chaebol* are an important component of the Japanese style alliance. The member firms are heavily indebted to the *keiretzu*'s main life insurance company and bank. The cross-equity holdings constitute an important link over and beyond the relationships that could be uncovered if one were to have access to their inner circles. Unfortunately, no research exists on the power structure within such circles, and the sort of collective decision-making processes that ensue. Thus we are also deprived from reaching strong conclusions regarding the stock of social capital among *keiretzu* firms. These links are not merely leverage tools, but in fact might acquire a significant symbolic meaning on their own and complement other media of networking such as exclusive R&D projects. The *keiretzu* as a somewhat hierarchical network is therefore multiplex – debt holdings, cross-equity holdings, supplier–buyer links, and personnel bonds are part and parcel of the connections that bind the firms into a tight and relatively unified alliance.

Social capital of business groups Firms that are part of *chaebols* and *keiretzus* are presumed to benefit from the social capital that ensues from their membership in these alliances (for example, Kim, 1997; Lawrence, 1991). Social capital is manifest in two ways: first business groups provide member firms with access to resources from other firms. As a quasi-holding or federation of businesses, they can furnish superior access to financial capital through a member financial services firm and cross-guarantee each other's bank loans. Similarly, business group-specific suppliers and their original equipment manufacturers (OEMs) belonging to the same group display shorter lead times in new product development because they circumvent transaction costs, for example by making significant asset-specific investments that in the absence of a business group context would incur significant hold-up problems (for example, Dyer, 1996; Gerlach, 1992). The inclusion in the *keiretzu* reduces the outsourcing to one or at most two suppliers, and the relationship is typically based on trust and mutuality. By way of contrast, Toyota relies often on a single, *keiretzu*-anchored supplier, while US auto manufacturers such as GM usually rely on as many as six suppliers, with whom they interact opportunistically and at arm's length (Dyer, 1996; Noteboom, 1999). The suspension of the hold-up problem also results in joint R&D and in the geographic clustering of OEM and their suppliers, thus economizing on value chain coordination costs, transportation distance, and inter-firm transfer of tacit knowledge (for example, Hansen, 1997).

The social capital of business groups, however, is not confined to intra-group relationships. Since their boundaries are also salient at the group level, they can enjoy scale advantages not unlike those accorded fully vertically-integrated firms. Such assertions question the saliency or distinctiveness of boundaries, and in particular the issues associated with vertical integration, governance, and transaction costs (Williamson, 1996; Powell, 1990). Even though inter-firm links are not exclusively mediated by individuals – as we have argued they are multiplex, to say the least – the links that bind them might be so strong that the focal attention often shifts to that level of analysis when discussing social capital. They maintain levels of flexibility in moving around human resources and other assets, and because of superior access to cheap and unskilled labor are able to claim cost leadership positions in the their world of multi-point competition (Kim, 1997: 180–95). Yet, on the next higher level of analysis, these groups commanded clear benefits that surpassed inter-firm arrangements, as reviewed by Powell (1990).

Empirical Evidence

For example, in Korea there is the often documented 'cozy' *chaebol–*government interface. *Chaebols* as groups are often endowed with a good deal of social capital because of the support they have extracted from the South Korean government. Compared to non-*chaebol* firms, *chaebols* have had better access to state-controlled resources, and have thus been able to exploit governmental powers for their own benefit (Kim, 1997). The *chaebol*-dominated segment of the economy grew much faster than the economy as a whole.

Chaebols have received a great deal of governmental support for two reasons. First, the sheer size of *chaebols* has made them very important for the development-oriented Korean government. For instance, the value added by the 30 largest *chaebols* has been around 15 per cent of GNP and their sales volume has been around 80 per cent of GNP (Cho et al., 1998). Because *chaebols* have been used as a tool for the government's industrialization policy, the Korean government has provided many favors to them, including soft loans, import prohibition, tax breaks and the like. Second, relationships between elite university graduates has strengthened the relationship between the Korean government and *chaebols*. People who graduated from elite universities have occupied major positions in the Korean government, banks, and parliament. As a result, *chaebols* appointed elite university graduates as CEOs to lubricate their relationship with external entities. For instance, 62 per cent of CEOs of the seven largest Korean *chaebols* in 1985 graduated from Seoul National University (Steers et al., 1989).

There is also some provisional evidence that member firms within a *chaebol* or *keiretzu* might encounter the adverse effects of 'over-embedddedness'. In Korea we have the case of the Kukje *chaebol* and recent bankrupties of major *chaebols*, while in Japan the differential learning of *keiretzu* versus non-*keiretzu* suppliers provide testimony to the harmful effects of social embeddedness. The Kukje case emerged in February 1985 and evolved from an ordinary bankruptcy into a scandal when the Chun government disbanded the *chaebol* due to 'reckless management, and exceeding high debt rates'. It is most relevant for our argument because of 'nepotic management by the sons of the founder' (Kim, 1989). The bankruptcy case is somewhat ambiguous and opinions varied as to whether it was over-embeddedness among member firms or deficient external social capital that accounted for the disbanding of Kukje. Yang, the *chaebol* president, claimed favoritism on the part of the Chun government. In any event, further research should identify whether it was social capital at the group level or at the group–state level that explains the demise of Kukje.

Due to their risk-sharing role, Korean *chaebols* enjoy very high survival rates and thus only a few *chaebols* experienced bankruptcy. During the period between January 1997 and January 1998, however, nine of the 30 largest *chaebols* experienced insolvency. The mutual guaranteeing of bank loans made whole member firms rather than some parts of them insolvent. In some cases, the failure of one member firm became the reason for the bankruptcy of the *chaebol*. Over-embeddedness to other member firms rendered profitable and financially sound member firms bankrupt, thus revealing the 'dark side of social capital'.

Keiretzus in Japan also function as a tool for risk-sharing among member firms (Nakatani, 1984) and thus they also enjoyed a low bankruptcy rate (Suzuki and Wright, 1985). However, criticism has surfaced regarding their traditionally claimed advantages. Gerlach (1992) sees the potential unraveling of *keiretzus* now that their benefits have appeared to wane. Nobeoka and Dyer (1998) have recently completed a survey of OEM–automotive supplier relationships and produced evidence indicating that suppliers that diversify away from a single *keiretzu*-based OEM are more profitable compared with firms who are locked in a close single-source relationship. They interpret this finding as being the result of either superior bargaining power or a broader exposure to technological know-how; such firms diminish their dependence on a single OEM or they witness learning benefits in that their know-how is likely to be more generic and less firm-specific.

Similarly, Lincoln et al. (1997) provide evidence from Toyota the auto manufacturer and Toyota the *keiretsu* member which diversified away from *keiretsu*-based automotive suppliers. These authors report that intra-*keiretsu* knowledge was not only limited, but that Toyota did not even attempt to elevate its 'internal' suppliers to the standard that would meet its needs. The implication is that, in spite of trust and inbred capabilities, the firm begins to question the benefits of traditional arrangements. Such precedents might lead the *keiretsu* along a path of further unraveling its stale social capital and the substitution of a fresh one.

Summarizing, the business group's endowment of social capital should be differentiated into that social capital that is discernible at the group level versus that which resides at the interface between the business group and external actors. The beneficiary of social capital is the firm or group of firms who are portrayed as unitary actors operating in their economic-political arena. The evidence so far has shown social capital to be beneficial, but more recent evidence shows also that over-embeddedness might be harmful.

Audit Firms

The accounting sector presents another setting in which the costs and benefits of social embeddedness are evident. Unlike markets with industrial firms, as is the case with industries comprising business groups, the accounting sector produces largely intangible and abstract services. The measurement of product quality is elusive, the production flow is exposed to the client who is often an active co-producer of the services rendered. The firm has some degree of hierarchy but is usually fairly flat. In fact most firms are stratified into partners (that is, owners) and employees, some of whom expect to join the partnership. Their close exposure to the market place and their intense involvement with clients makes social capital a central feature of operations and a key driver of organizational performance. This sector resembles numerous cottage industries where personally mediated ties predominate, not unlike the settings of garment district members (Dore, 1983; Uzzi, 1997) or investment bankers (Burt, 1997).

Ironically, social capital can be viewed as a substitute for objective criteria of quality, reliability and consistency. In the absence of objective, verifiable and measurable product attributes, clients might rely on their networks to select auditors or to remain loyal to them even after the honeymoon period has passed (compare Polodny and Castelluci, 1999). The endowment of social capital is therefore a critical resource in such sectors. Absent social capital, the firm might not extract much rent from its human capital. Furthermore, social capital allows the firms to leverage their human capital thus extracting more quasi rent from that asset. Social capital is not only valuable as rent-producing potential, but is also both scarce and difficult to appropriate. These aspects suggest social capital as a resource not unlike brand equity, reputation and goodwill, and should be further explored here.

As we indicated at the start of this chapter, social capital fits Barney's (1991) criteria of the resource-based view of the firm. Resources that provide a competitive advantage should be valuable, rare, hard to imitate, and imperfectly substitutable. Applying these conditions to accounting firms and other professional service sectors, it appears therefore obvious that the social capital of an audit firm forms a major source of competitive advantage in this 'knowledge' sector. Social capital of audit firms has a rent-producing potential in that it is valuable and scarce (product market imperfectness) as well as imperfectly tradable (factor market imperfectness). Let us review these aspects of social capital in closer detail.

Value   As far as the value argument is concerned, a substantial number of studies in sociology have shown that social ties transfer influence and information (for example, Burt, 1992, 1997; Coleman et al., 1966). At the individual level, the benefit of having supportive relationships has been well established. These contribute to getting a job (Granovetter, 1974), high compensation (Boxman et al., 1991), and promotion (Burt, 1992). We argue that this argument pertains to the (audit) firm level as well. Burt and Ronchi (1990) and Burt (1992) applied the notion of social capital to organizations. Burt (1992: 9) pointed out that 'the social capital of people aggregates into the social capital of organizations'. Social capital amassed in the organization's members is among the firm's most valuable productive assets (Burt and Ronchi, 1990). Unlike the setting of business groups, in this sector we can define an organization's social capital as the aggregate of the firm members' social capital. An individual member's social capital is captured by his connectedness with client sectors.

Why would audit firms with social capital enjoy competitive advantages and higher survival chances? That is, what is the role of social capital in the economic transaction of providing audit services? Under perfect competition, social capital cannot generate any economic rent (Burt, 1992). However, the market for auditing services is hardly perfect, and information about audit services is not costless. The owner's social capital strengthens his firm's ability to retain and attract clients. This is even truer in the audit industry, where information with respect to qualities of professionals is hardly perfect (compare Burt, 1992; Polodny and Castelluci, 1999). Clients resort to their social contacts to screen their service providers, because assessment criteria for auditing quality are hard to come by. Crucial contacts include those that involve the client sectors that an audit firm serves. There are three reasons why network ties with client sectors may well facilitate the building and retention of clientèle.

First, people tend to rely on their current social relations to alleviate transaction cost (Ben-Porath, 1980). A stranger who does not anticipate an enduring exchange relationship has an incentive to behave opportunistically. To curb this malfeasance, ill-acquainted exchange partners typically rely on elaborate, explicit, and comprehensive contracts. These contracts, however, are difficult to write and hard to enforce (Williamson, 1975). Mutual trust between the actors, developed through repetitive exchanges, obviates the need for writing explicit contracts. If the creation of trustworthy social relations were costless, however, the existing network ties would not confer benefits to those who nurtured them. In reality, individuals and organizations have to invest substantial time and energy in forging durable relations with others (Burt, 1992). Variations in networking among firms should then contribute to differences in the firms' ability to attract clients. Second, trustworthy relations produce information benefits for the linked actors (Burt, 1992). Information is not spread evenly across all actors. Rather, its access is contingent upon social contacts (Coleman et al., 1966; Granovetter, 1985). An actor cannot have access to all relevant information, nor can s/he process and screen all important information singlehandedly. Being embedded in a network of relations allows a particular actor to economize on information retrieval. Second-hand information, at least serves to signal something to be looked into more carefully (Burt, 1992). Personal contacts also make it possible for the involved actors to acquire information earlier than others. Third, trustworthy relations enhance the possibility for an actor to refer his contact person (for example, an auditor, physician or management consultant) to a third party ('tertius'). Burt (1992: 14) puts the benefit this way: 'You can only be in a limited number of places within a limited amount of time. Personal contacts get your name mentioned at the right time in the right place so that opportunities are presented to you.' The counterpart in a dyadic relation can play a role as a liaison to link the social actor to third parties.

Scarcity   The argument as to the scarcity issue is, again, specific to the CPA profession. The CPA profession is there to attest financial outlets of organizations. In effect, this was the very reason for the origination of the profession. In a way, this is comparable to other public professions. For example, police officers are trained to perform their public and legally protected role of preventing and bringing action against violations of the civil order. In a similar vein, CPAs are expected to prevent and bring action against violations of the 'financial order'. Therefore, CPAs are trained to perform their public attesting role – this is the core of any CPA education program. The very nature of the profession, therefore, implies that the majority of CPAs are employed in public practice, working within audit firms rather than client organizations. Only a minority are attached to internal control jobs within client organizations. Hence, social ties that come with current (or previous) partners or associates with previous (or current) employment outside the audit industry – that is, through jobs in governmental bodies or private enterprises – are not abundant. For example, in 1920 roughly 80 per cent of Dutch CPAs worked in public practice. In the period from the 1960s to the 1980s, this percentage dropped to slightly above 50 per cent. Hence, there is much room for audit firm heterogeneity in this respect, both in time as well as over time.

Nontradability   Apart from product market imperfection (resource value and scarcity), nontradability is needed to guarantee the sustainability of rent appropriation. Social capital is tradable, however, if imperfectly. Within audit firms, an individual CPA handles a set of client accounts, which means that from the perspective of the client there is a double tie to the audit service supplier – to both the audit firm and the individual auditor. Client loyalty to the audit firm is often fairly high. This is particularly true for large companies, which rarely switch from one audit firm to the other (Langendijk, 1990), although among small and medium-sized client firms audit firm switching may well be more common. Additionally, however, a client's financial reports are attested by an individual CPA, which introduces a tie to the individual auditor. In many cases, the auditor's position involves confidentiality and trust. In a way, the auditor develops into a mediator who plays an advisory role in a wide array of financial and even non-financial issues. So, social ties are partly linked to the audit firm, and partly to the individual auditor. This implies that by moving to another firm, an auditor only depreciates part of this social network, because client sector ties are both an integral part of the firm and linked to the trust relationship with the individual CPA. Of course, here the partner–associate distinction is relevant from the very observation that ownership is associated with limited mobility.

Finally, we should mention that during the last half century partnership contracts have further diminished the portability of social capital. In the US, Europe and elsewhere, partnership agreements typically contain a clause that blocks partners from taking clients with them in the event they leave the firm. Needless to say, such contractual constraints bolster the nontradability assumption of a firm's social capital. Such clauses have become standard since the Second World War and diminish the mobility of a partner's roster of clients.

In sum, a firm whose partners are tied with potential clients is better positioned to build clientèle since a potential client can (1) actually become the firm's client, (2) provide valuable information about potential markets, and (3) refer the firm to other potential clients. These aspects should strengthen a professional service firm's survival chances.

What Further Implications Regarding Social Capital?

This chapter illustrates the benefits and drawbacks of social capital, either mediated by individuals or formed through an array of linking vehicles such as cross-stockholdings and long-term buyer–supplier relationships. We have suggested that the model of the firm conditions the conceptualization and operationalization of social capital and the consequences associated with it. Firms are conceived of as unitary actors which interact with other actors (for example, peer firms in business groups), or they can be conceived as a community of practices and aggregates of individuals with their distinct objectives and unique agendas (for example, professional services firms). Allison's (1971) labels of rational and political actor correspond with these stylized forms of organization. In the former case, social capital can be operationalized through the multiplex arrangements that bind a firm to other actors. In the latter case, we focus on individuals and their ties, which aggregate to organizational social capital. We then set out to review the benefits of social capital as a distinct organizational (intangible) asset.

Mediated by individuals, social capital nonetheless can be viewed as an organizational property. The individuals might be stationary (as illustrated by the linking pin (Likert, 1961) or double agent) or they might migrate between firms (as illustrated by the revolving door syndrome). The relative inclusion of the individual defines the individual's functionality for information and knowledge transmission: the individual needs to be available for external linking, yet also requires sufficient proximity to internal members and groups who can convert the flow of knowledge and other resources into some competitive advantage.

Individuals can also mediate social capital in the case of business groups. In fact, some of the pertinent literature has focused on individuals as transmitters of knowledge between firms that they span – for example, so-called guest engineers who are employed by the OEM or its supplier and are assigned to work in the partner's site, or civil servants who have been recruited by a *chaebol* firm and join their ranks. For example, in the Kukje bankruptcy, it was suggested that the *chaebol* management shunned participation in semi-public sectors such as the Ilhae Foundation, thus depriving themselves of individually-mediated social capital. The Pusan-based *chaebol* neglected to maintain part of its boundary transaction system. What sets business groups apart from partnerships, among others, is that business group links are typically multiplex, comprising both personal and impersonal means for maintaining durable links.

In spite of such differences, this chapter has indicated that network embeddedness can have both positive and negative consequences. The links that bind provide access to competitively critical resources, but they can also be so binding that they are stultifying and potentially harmful. The case of Kukje illustrates the deleterious effects of embeddedness that becomes fractured as a result of governmental interventions. The inclination of Toyota to reduce its embeddedness within its *keiretzu* signals a desire to increase the flow of novel information that current links cannot furnish; its conventional supplier links might be too limited in contributing potentially innovative ideas. The negative first-order effect and positive second-order effect of social capital on performance in the apparel industry might be the most robust finding to date regarding the paradox of embeddedness (Uzzi, 1997).

Uzzi (1997) makes the important observation that embeddedness is a two-edged sword. Embeddedness ranges from 'under-embedded', via 'integrated' to 'over-embedded networks'. As was shown, this distinction hinges largely on whether links are 'arm's length' (that is, contacts based on selfish, profit-seeking behavior) or 'embedded' (that is, contacts based on trust and mutual intimacy). A firm's network that comprises largely arm's length links does not confer much advantage in knowledge transfer, coordination, or strategic alignment. Conversely, a firm that is strongly entrenched in embedded networks might become so insular that it suspends exposure to markets and technologies which reside outside its immediate environment.

It appears that these distinctions do not readily map on the two contrasting cases we presented in this chapter. The partnerships in a professional services sector fit the conceptual distinctions between arm's length and embeddedness, together with their functionality such as the trust, tacitness of knowledge being transferred, and mutual adjustment (Thompson, 1967) as the coordination mode. At face value, partnerships are internally personalized and anchored in trust, and so we would expect some of the relationships to be among professionals and their clients. Uzzi's (1997) case involves similar *Gemeinschaft*-like firms, that is, small entrepreneurial firms, mom and pop, a trade making up a cottage industry – in short, organizations in which face-to-face relationships predominate and which often become extended externally. The apparel world resembles the Chinese 'bamboo network' (Tsui, 1997) and Dore's (1983) description of the Japanese textile industry, which he labels as 'cottage industry' and in which goodwill becomes the central feature in describing the prevailing trust and mutuality. The network ties are largely mediated by individuals.

How do we map these descriptions on to the social capital of firms in business groups which tend to be multiplex? Are such links more *Gesellschaft*-like in their appearance and functionality? What sort of processes can we envision in a boundary transaction system in which personal ties complement contracts, equity cross-holdings, and traditions that outlive their instigators? We should ask such questions particularly when the individuals in the boundary transaction system do not 'go native', and continue to link up with people and groups in the firms they span, together with other elements that define their inter-firm context. The issue is germane to our earlier review of the firm as a layered entity in which the boundary-spanning system resides largely in the more peripheral bands. Such networks abound with actors possessing 'structural autonomy' (Burt, 1992) and creating opportunities for opportunism, information asymmetry, and knowledge hoarding – opportunities which Uzzi considers antithetical to embedded ties.

The implication of these observations is to recognize the two faces of organizations and to develop divergent frameworks for capturing the performance implications of network embeddedness. Without forcing us onto a meso-level of research, by artificially integrating face-to-face and small group dynamics with large scale firm-interface arrangements, we might develop a middle range theory of social capital that fits the specific questions we might ask. Whether organizations have at least two faces, or whether we invoke two cognitive models of organizations might be an issue left to philosophers and epistomologists. Empirically, we might envision a continuum in which organizations range from highly cohesive, well bounded aggregates that are tightly coupled and present few if any intra-firm hurdles for coordination, knowledge sharing, and strategic positioning. We can also envision organizations that are loosely coupled, with permeable boundaries and few isolating mechanisms, barely holding them together and maneuvering on the brink of dissolution. In either case, the firm is part of a larger context. How they position themselves onto this continuum, and what image we impose on them remains a never-ending challenge. The research on social capital will shed further light on how they negotiate their embeddedness, and what sort of advantages and shortfall they derive from that capital.

NOTES

1. Note that embedded ties could have two (if not three) rather divergent meanings: (1) ties that are reinforced by mutual feelings of attachment, reciprocity, and trust; and (2) ties that are a link within a larger set of links and nodes. Since Uzzi's (1997) work is confined to dyads, the first meaning applies. When the members of a dyad become affected by third

parties who envelop their tie, as in Burt's (1992) work on structural holes, the second meaning applies. In both cases, the concern is with a focal person. If one moves to an even higher level of analysis, as for example the internet, transactions among textile traders in fifteenth-century Florence and Flanders, or community power structures, then the network takes primacy over the ties between individuals who are embedded in those networks. A person's or firm's 'centrality' conveys relative access to other actors in the network such that a focal actor's social capital hinges partly on the direct and indirect ties that the tied partners possess (for example, Levine, 1972).

Empirically the effect of centrality on firm behavior or performance has not been studied adequately.

2. Note that the rational model of the firm does not presume anything about its embeddedness here. In either the rational or political scenario, we do not assume organizations to behave as if they are atomized from the impact of their relations with other organizations, or from the past history of these relations. If we were to extend methodological individualism to the embeddedness of firms, we would not be able to furnish an adequate account of how firms' actions combine up to the level of the value chain, markets or institutions. We only make the analytical distinction based on the relative saliency of aggregation when examining social capital as a firm-specific asset.

    Hence, our reluctance to include Allison's (1976) second model, the 'organizational actor model' in our review. This extrapolates to over-socialized individuals reduced to mentally programmed automata who mechanically replicate the routines that the organizational socialization process has imprinted onto them. As performers of a role they would have no discretion to embellish their positions or protect personal interests, nor could they be construed as the personal authors of their social network.

3. Some examples might illustrate the issues at hand. Firms are tied to each other through trade associations, business groups, consortia, cartels, joint ventures, and directors who sit not only on their board but on the boards of other organizations as well. They are locked into licensing agreements and long term supplier–buyer arrangements, and might have made significant investments in specific inter-firm relationships. The presence of such links and their benefits seem obvious when that capital is treated as firm-level or individual-level phenomena.

    For example, Boeing's 747 aircraft requires the input from numerous contractors and sub-contractors – only certain chunks of the cockpit and wings are developed and produced by Boeing. Such inter-firm transactions result in long-term links that become independent of the members who forged them originally. Many firms occupy positions in the value chain with interdependencies so dense that one occasionally might consider the value chain to be a more salient unit of action than the firms that exist within the value chain. A simple illustration from the computer industry might further illustrate this observation.

    During the main-frame computer era, it was common for firms like IBM and Hitachi to control all the steps in the value chain, from silicon, computer platform, system software, application to distribution and service. The firm was the value chain, and competition between corporations matched competition between value chains. In the late 1990s, we observe a fragmented horizontal competition between firms, but vertically dense complementarities have surfaced. Microsoft competes with Apple and Unix, but is symbiotically linked with upstream PC manufacturers and their suppliers, such as Intel. Downstream, the firms relate to distribution and service firms such as computer stores and mail order firms. Microsoft has been a shrewd exploiter of network externalities: the various technologies require complementary products, lead to the formation of virtuous cycles such as software developers writing more Microsoft Windows applications, and when these become available, more customers adopting Microsoft Windows. Increasingly all firms in the value chain become 'locked-in' (or locked-out!) resulting in a complex string of links that are straddled around a dominant computer design (for example, Yoffie, 1996). In such a value chain, links are often depersonalized and it is the organizations that become the salient unit of the network. The ties in such networks are critical for the firms involved as their products and technologies become heavily intertwined with those of others.

Much of the social capital literature has an individual slant (for example, Burt, 1997) and firm attributes have often been examined as an individual manifestation. Burt's (1997) study examines investment banks but really focuses on its traders and the 'structural holes' that benefit the size of their performance-based bonuses. One might also focus on their banks' tombstones and the social capital that could be inferred from them. Coleman's (1988) classic example involves the tight social circle of diamond traders in New York whose smooth and paperless transactions hinge on the social ties that they maintain with other traders. The trust that is sustained within such a network results in a substantial reduction of transaction costs. Likewise Coleman (1988) shows that children whose parents know other parents and teachers are better embedded in their school community and show lower dropping-out rates. Finally, Uzzi (1997) recounts the linkages among individuals who make up the New York apparel industry. In such instances, the issue of aggregation and the presumption of the firm as a unitary actor is rather moot: the entrepreneur is the firm. In these and many other contributions, social capital is a resource that belongs to the networking or interacting individuals and that might affect the venture with which the embedded individual is associated.

4. By the same token, an individual who is neutral to the bridging between two firms cannot easily be incorporated in the organization's social capital. Referee, arbitrator, or mediator roles are sharply different from those we associate with ambassador, spy, or guest engineer. The former's neutrality might depreciate or sanitize whatever information or knowledge the 'middle-man' furnishes to the linked organizations. His neutrality also precludes intimacy and creates social distance. We assume that organizations have discrete bundles of knowledge and information whose rents will be augmented by the development of 'proprietary' social capital.

5. Sherer (1995) identifies three major types of employment relationship. The first is the employment relation coupled with ownership. It includes employees who share the risk of organization via various incentive systems which link their earnings to the performance of the organization. Employees in that relation constitute the *core* group in our analysis. The second is the traditionally described employment relation in which employees receive a fixed amount of earnings, provide a fixed length of time, and perform work based on the direction from the supervisor or job description. Employees in these types are designated *regular* in the present discussion. The third embodies relationships that involve temporary employment or contracting out. Employees in this type form the *temporary or marginal* group. Note that with the rise of temporary employment agencies, outsourcing and sub-contracting, this latter group has acquired huge proportions. Analogous distinctions have been made by Jensen and Meckling (1976) and Milgrom and Roberts (1992).

6. The classification was suggested by Jon Brookfield.

7. The term *transitive* cross-equity holding refers to a string of *keiretsu* firms between which ownership is mutual yet unequal. Nishiyama (1982) reports the pattern of large block holdings in the Sumitomo Business Group, with Sumimoto (S.) Life Insurance owning a larger percentage of shares in S. Bank, S. Metal, S. Chemical, S. Electric, and so on than vice versa; it augments its power over these firms because these firms in turn own shares in each other, such that cumulatively, S. Life Insurance scores highest on the 'comprehensive power index'.

4. Human capital, social capital and firm dissolution

INTRODUCTION

Many authors, expressing the view that the modern world is becoming a 'knowledge society', have discussed the importance of organization-level human and social capital for organizational performance and survival (for example, Kogut and Zander, 1996; Pfeffer, 1994; Uzzi, 1996). However, only a few studies have examined this relationship empirically, looking at the effect of founders' human and social capital on organizational performance, and particularly, organizational survival (for example, Bates, 1990; Brüderl et al., 1992; Uzzi, 1996). Similarly, studies of the role of CEO characteristics have revealed that CEOs' human capital features have an impact on organizational behavior and performance (for example, Boone et al., 1996). As was expected, in those studies higher founder or CEO human capital was shown to enhance organizational performance. But although founders' and CEOs' human and social capital are important to organizational success, other organization members' human and social capital also play a critical role in organizational performance.

This chapter attempts to deepen understanding of the determinants of organizational dissolution by introducing firm-level human and social capital in a hazard rate model of firm dissolution. We argue that organizational human and social capital decrease the likelihood of firm dissolution and that the specificity and non-appropriability of those forms of capital affect their contribution to firm dissolution. Of course, the message that people matter is hardly new (for example, Pfeffer, 1994). However, systematic theorizing and testing at the organizational level is rare, as most studies have restricted their analyses to single CEO or management team features. The key contribution of this work is the proposal and testing of firm-level hypotheses on the likely impacts on organizational dissolution of human and social capital in general and of their specificity and non-appropriability in particular. For this purpose, we offer an in-depth analysis of a population of Dutch accounting firms in the period 1880–1990. We conducted this inquiry into the role of human and social capital while controlling for firm, industry, and population-level conditions (compare Hannan and Freeman,

1989; Schmalensee, 1985) – most notably, industry density and firm age, as these variables have acquired undue prominence in the explanation of firm dissolution.

THEORY AND HYPOTHESES

We argue that the firm-level aggregates of human and social capital may well explain organizational dissolution, particularly in the context of professional service markets such as the accounting industry. The success of professional service organizations like accounting firms hinges on their ability to deliver high-quality services (production capability) and to attract and retain clients (selling capability).

To produce and deliver high-quality services, professionals should have adequate knowledge and skills – the human capital carried by certified accountants (Maijoor and Van Witteloostuijn, 1996). The human capital of a firm is defined as the knowledge and skills of its professionals that can be used to produce professional services. Human capital theory distinguishes industry-specific from firm-specific human capital (Becker, 1964). Industry-specific human capital in this study is knowledge about complicated auditing routines (for example, statistical sampling, risk analysis, and analytical review) and financial accounting (for example, measurement methods, regulations, and standards) that cannot be completely transferred to other industries and can be developed through professional education and industry experience. Firm-specific human capital is knowledge about unique routines and procedures that have limited value outside the firm in which the capital base has been developed. In effect, all leading accounting firms have extensive and obligatory internal education and training programs. As professionals' time with a given firm grows, they develop more firm-specific human capital through within-firm training programs and on-the-job experience.

A professional firm's ability to attract and retain clients depends not only on its competence to produce high-quality services, but also on its connections to potential clients (Maister, 1993; Smigel, 1969), because social relationships mediate economic transactions (Granovetter, 1985). This observation points to the role of social capital, which we define in terms of supporting relationships with other economic actors, most notably, potential clients. Such relationships can be formed in many different ways: mutual schooling, family and other personal connections (*guanxi*), overlapping memberships, inter-firm mobility, joint ventures or other collaborative arrangements, and more. In this study, we focused on connections to potential clients that grew out of certified public accountants' (CPAs) interfirm mobility – that is, professionals' migration from a potential client firm to an accounting firm, and vice versa.

Below, we pursue two arguments. The first argument relates to the absolute value of firm-level human and social capital. We explain why our indexes of human and social capital stock may have a negative impact on organizational dissolution. The second argument goes into the relative importance of the two types of capital. Is there any reason to expect that different types of human and social capital will vary in their effects on organizational dissolution? For example, forms of human and social capital vary in the degree to which they are idiosyncratic to firms, with the proviso that the more idiosyncratic a given form is, the greater its contribution to firm survival. Similarly, intangible capital tied to partners is more 'sticky' than that associated with employees. Here, we apply the concepts of firm specificity and of ownership or property rights to the uniqueness or distinctness and the nontradability of that intangible capital, respectively.

The Absolute Value of Firm-level Human and Social Capital

At least two arguments support the absolute contribution of human capital investment to firm survival. First, professionals endowed with a high level of human capital are more likely to deliver consistent and high-quality services (Becker, 1964; Mincer, 1974), and their firms are therefore better able to retain clients or attract new ones. Industry-specific and firm-specific human capital help professionals produce high-quality professional services. Second, potential clients may use a professional's human capital credentials as a screening device for choosing their service providers (for example, Arrow, 1973). Professional degrees and industry experience, two indicators of industry-specific human capital, function as screening and filtering devices, because (1) people with high initial ability have good access to professional education (Arrow, 1973) and (2) less gifted people are more likely to be selected out during their early careers. In the absence of information about the qualities of service providers, educational attainment and industry experience act as surrogate indicators of ability and competence.

Other things being equal, firms whose professionals reflect a high level of human capital are less likely than other firms to dissolve, because they can retain and attract more clients. However, we have to consider the effect of aging in formulating hypothetical effects of human capital developed through either industry or firm experience. These two types of capital are basically measured by industry tenure and firm tenure, respectively. When they become old, accountants will quit their firms, die, or dissolve their firms, so increasingly higher levels of industry-specific human capital and of firm-specific human capital will trigger a greater propensity toward firm dissolution. This formulation produces a two-pronged hypothesis:

Hypothesis 4.1a   Organizational dissolution is negatively affected by firm-level industry-specific human capital developed through professional education.

Hypothesis 4.1b   Organizational dissolution has a U-shaped relationship with industry-specific human capital developed through industry experience and firm-specific human capital.

Firm-level social capital can also decrease a firm's likelihood of dissolution just as it strengthens the firm's ability to retain and attract clients. We defined an organization's social capital as the aggregate of firm members' connectedness with potential clients. Such ties are among a firm's most valuable capital (Burt, 1992), because, other things being equal, potential clients will choose a firm as a service provider on the basis of previous interpersonal relationships with the firm's professionals. The benefits of having organization members endowed with valuable social relationships have been illustrated in previous studies. For example, an owner's strong ties with powerful suppliers or buyers enhances his or her company's survival chance (Uzzi, 1996). Social capital plays a more important role in economic transactions when information with respect to qualities of professionals is imperfect, as is the case in professional service industries (compare Burt, 1992; Pennings and Lee, 1999). Crucial relationships in professional service industries include those that involve the potential clients that the firm serves. This argument provides the following hypothesis:

Hypothesis 4.2   Organizational dissolution is negatively associated with firm-level social capital.

The Relative Values of Firm-level Human and Social Capital

The relative contributions of firm-level human and social capital to firm survival depend upon both the capital's firm-specificity and ownership claims. The more specific the capital to the firm, the higher its contribution to firm survival. As professionals develop more capital specific to a firm, they are less likely to leave or dissolve it since they cannot take advantage of that capital elsewhere. Firm-specific human capital has limited value outside the firm in which the capital base was developed (for example, Wernerfelt, 1984). Industry-specific human capital has less firm specificity, since any professional can move from firm to firm throughout a market without diminishing the value of his or her industry-specific human capital. Finally, social capital has an intermediate degree of firm specificity. Within professional service firms, an individual professional handles a set of client accounts. Thus, from the perspective of the client, there is a double tie to the service supplier – to both the firm and the individual. In many cases, the professional's position involves confidentiality and trust. In a way, the professional develops into a mediator who plays an advisory role in a wide array of issues. By moving to another firm, a professional only loses part of this social capital, so the old firm loses 'rent-producing' potential with each such move. The specificity argument provides the following hypothesis:

Hypothesis 4.3 Firm-specific human capital and social capital have stronger negative associations with firm dissolution than industry-specific human capital.

Ownership also determines the relative value of human capital. Many professional service firms have adopted a partnership arrangement. In professional service firms, the owners' (the partners') human capital is more pertinent to the firms' profit potential than that of the employees (the associates). Three reasons justify this statement. First, partners, as residual claimants, have a greater incentive to use their human capital for firm growth and performance than do associates, who are fixed claimants. Second, organizations cannot fully appropriate the rents from associates' training and experience because an associate whose compensation falls short of his or her marginal product is likely to move to more remunerative employment. Third, ownership ties a professional to property, thus decreasing incentives to leave a firm. Partners invest in their property both financially and non-financially and thus have 'exit barriers' that are higher than those of associates, who are still participating in a tournament and striving for ownership status. This argument suggests the following hypothesis:

Hypothesis 4.4 Partners' human and social capital has a stronger negative association with firm dissolution than associates' human and social capital.

The beneficial role of human and social capital can also be examined when the integrity of the role is jolted during disruptive events like schisms and acquisitions. The firms emerging from a schism are more likely than *de novo* firms to be dissolved because of a lack of complementary knowledge and skills among professionals. A break-up leads to a severe partitioning of joint experiences, loss of the home-grown complementarity of skills among professionals, and the disappearance of valuable social capital. During a schism, a firm's intangible capital becomes disassembled, and the event can be viewed as producing two nearly new firms. Those firms would have to develop new methods of dividing labor and cooperation and reconfigure bundles of complementary skills among professionals. The putative benefits of 'congenital learning' (for example, Ingram and Baum, 1997) emanating from the inherited partners of the old firm are more than offset by the unraveling of those bundles of capital, most notably firm-specific human capital.

In the case of an acquisition, the disruption is also profound, especially when the firms involved are similar in size. The integrity of proprietary capital is at risk when the human and social capital of one firm mingles with that of another. Organization members from the acquired firm will forget previously acquired firm-specific human capital as they learn new routines and procedures, and a new way of cooperation. In other words, they have to acquire human capital that is specific to the acquirer. A new organization created by an acquisition should put many resources into amalgamating the skill-sets of the two firms. The extent of disruption depends on the relative sizes of the firms. When a large firm acquires a small one, only a few professionals will learn a new way of doing things. When the two firms are similar in size and decide to stick to the routines that one firm previously used, about half the professionals will learn a new way of doing things. In the professional service industry, the resulting firm usually adopts a new name to signal a departure from the past. Additionally, name change without acquisition does not change the human and social capital of a firm. So we expect that firms that emerge out of such an acquisition are more likely to dissolve than either firms that experience acquisitions without name changes or those that change their names without acquisitions. Therefore, we propose collateral hypotheses:

Hypothesis 4.5a   Newly-created firms emerging out of splits will show higher dissolution levels than *de novo* foundings.

Hypothesis 4.5b   Firms emerging out of acquisitions involving name changes will show higher dissolution levels than firms created by acquisitions with no name changes and firms that experienced name changes without acquisitions.

METHODS

Data and Measures

Figure 4.1 graphically shows the Dutch accounting industry's evolving density, with sole proprietorships (firms with one owner) broken out. The

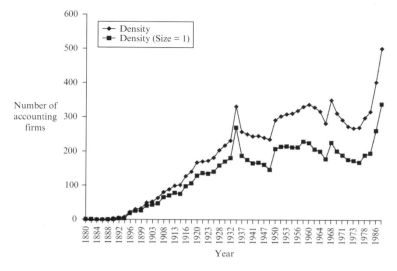

Figure 4.1   Historical variations in density for the population of Dutch accounting firms

graph indicates a positively accelerating density, with the total number of firms dramatically increasing during the last decade. The total number of firms and the number of sole proprietorships declined after 1966, but climbed from 1974 onward.

Organizational foundings, dissolutions, and other events were measured by examining the changes in accountants' organizational affiliations. To identify organizational founding and dissolution, we traced various organizational changes such as acquisitions, splits, and name changes. When two or more firms joined together, the event was coded as an acquisition. We differentiated between two types: acquisition without name change and acquisition with name change. When a resulting firm adopted one of the pre-existing names, the event was coded as an acquisition without name change. The firm that maintained its name was coded as an acquirer, whereas the other or others were treated as acquired firms. When two or more firms joined and adopted a new name, the event was coded as an acquisition with name change. The largest of the firms involved in an acquisition was classified as a going concern, and its smaller counterparts, as acquired firms. When the sizes of the involved firms were equal, the newly named firm was labeled as the continuation of the firm whose name came first in the alphabet. There were 158 cases of acquisition with name change and 258 cases of acquisition without name change.

Name changes were coded when the name of a firm differed from its previous name but at least two-thirds of its partners had continued their affiliation with the firm. The name changes did not include mutations due to acquisition, or cosmetic name changes, such as modifications in the order of partners' names. There were 231 incidences of name change. A split was coded when at least two partners left and formed a new firm. We counted 103 organizational splits, from which 103 foundings resulted. A founding was coded when a new name appeared in the directories for the first time and neither an acquisition nor a name change accounted for the new entry. For the test of Hypothesis 4.5a, we created a dummy variable, *founding type*. It was set to 1 if a particular firm was founded by a split and to 0 otherwise. Firms that emerge out of a split face unusual challenges since they have to restart the process of accumulating firm-specific human capital. These events amount to an unraveling of intangible capital and could be injurious to the firms. In terms of measurement, the owners of a firm emerging from a split are resetting the collective firm-specific tenure clock. Dissolution was coded when the name of a firm permanently disappeared from the directories without the incidence of an acquisition or name change.

Human capital as broadly defined here was, among other things, a firm's ability to produce a high-quality service, an ability basically held by individual accountants. It was captured by six variables. *Partners' industry-specific human capital* was measured by two indicators. The first was the proportion of partners possessing masters' or higher degrees. Even though formal education is considered to develop general human capital, graduate education in accounting develops industry-specific human capital because most CPAs have degrees in accounting and finance. In the Netherlands, masters' and PhD degrees confer titles that can be appended to individuals' names and diplomas that can be conspicuously displayed. The second proxy for partners' industry-specific human capital was average years of industry experience.[1] We decomposed each accountant's career into an industry and firm component, subtracting his or her tenure at a current firm from industry tenure, since industry tenure automatically increases as firm tenure increases. Before aggregating to the firm level, we took each partner's industry-specific human capital as proxied by the natural logarithm of tenure in the accounting industry, net of tenure with the current accounting firm. We measured a firm's *associates' industry-specific human capital* using the same procedure. However, associates typically do not accumulate industry tenure net of firm tenure as they enter firms as novices. The implication is that after subtracting an associate's duration with a firm from his or her career in the industry, the associate's industry tenure would drop to zero.

We measured a firm's *partners' firm-specific human capital* as the average of the natural logarithms of their tenures (in years) at the firm. Associates' firm-specific human capital was similarly measured. To avoid logarithms of zero, or negative infinity, we added one year to both the industry tenure and the firm tenure of all accountants. By taking the natural logarithm, we assumed that the speed of specific knowledge accumulation decreased over an accountant's tenure.

A firm's social capital was measured by eight variables. *Partners from client environments* was the proportion of partners who had worked in other industries or in government agencies before joining the accounting firm and were thus likely to have many valuable ties with potential clients. Similarly, *associates from client environments* was the proportion of associates who had worked in client environments. Also, when partners in accounting firms leave and find employment in client environments, they have strong incentives to take advantage of their social capital and are likely to choose the firms they worked for to provide professional services to their new firms (Maister, 1993). To reflect this effect, we constructed a *partners to client environments* variable, which measures the proportion of partners who had left a firm within the previous ten years to work for other industries or government agencies. Applying the same procedure, we measured *associates to client environments*. A ten-year span was adopted for two reasons. First, as departed members develop new social relationships, the strength of their relationships to their former firms may decay. Second, the departed partners are ultimately bound to retire from the business world and will thus no longer provide economic opportunities to their old firms.[2]

Aggregating organization members' social capital into a firm's capital index raises the possibility of redundancy. If a firm employs individuals with similar backgrounds, these employees' networks tend to be redundant with respect to their client acquisition capabilities (compare Burt, 1992). To reflect this possibility, we constructed four heterogeneity variables. Accountants can join the accounting industry from three sources: universities, other industries, or government agencies. We used Blau's (1977) measure of heterogeneity to assess the number of partners in each of the three categories. Formally, *heterogeneity in partners' origins* was calculated as

$$1 - \sum_{j=1}^{3} P_j^2,$$

where P_j is the proportion of partners in the *j*th category. The second variable is *heterogeneity in departed partners' destinations*. Partners can also move to universities, other industries, or government agencies, and we used Blau's measure of heterogeneity to quantify this variable as well. Applying the same procedure, we also constructed *heterogeneity in associates' origins* and *heterogeneity in departed associates' destinations*.

We standardized all human and social capital variables for each observation period so that each variable had a mean of zero and a standard deviation of one for each observation period. If we had been dealing with one observation period, we would not have needed this standardization, because the statistical significance of independent variables did not change. When longitudinal data are pooled, however, such standardization is needed to reflect the scarcity of resources, since human capital's contribution to a firm's competitiveness depends on the amount of capital held, relative to the amount held by competing firms.

Control Variables

We needed to control for a wide range of variables to rule out a number of rival hypotheses. For example, human and social capital are likely to be highly correlated with firm age and size. A study of professional partnerships should control for the *leverage ratio*, as indicated by the number of associates per partner (for example, Lee and Pennings, 1998). We standardized the leverage ratio for each observation period. Studies on leverage ratios in professional service firms have shown that highly leveraged firms enjoy higher profit per partner (*American Lawyer*, 1995) and command higher billing rates (Sherer, 1995). The liability of newness (Stinchcombe, 1965) argument led us to control for *firm age*, which we measured as the years that had elapsed since a firm's founding, expressed as a logarithm.

Since single proprietors cannot benefit from member heterogeneity, we controlled for *single proprietorships*, with 1 denoting firms with one owner and 0, multi-owner firms (partnerships). Furthermore, a dummy variable indicated whether a firm had had any *partners leaving the firm* in the previous decade (1 = yes, 0 = no). *Firm size*, measured as the number of accountants associated with a firm, was also included. To incorporate Winter's (1990) claim that large firms generate more competition than small firms, we constructed *population mass*, which was measured by the number of accountants who were affiliated with all other accounting firms in each observation period.

Histories of the Dutch accounting industry (for example, Zeff et al., 1992) described important historical events that may have affected firm dissolution in specific years. We constructed variables to control for World War II, Indonesia's independence in 1949, and significant changes in regulations that governed the accounting profession and its clients. *World War II* was captured in a dummy variable for the length of the observation interval since there is only one five-year observation interval. Indonesia's independence was specified as having a persistent effect since this event implied a permanent shrinkage of the market (1 if year > 1949, 0 otherwise). Government regulation during 1914–18 dealing with *World War I* conditions was specified as having its effect from 1914 to 1920 (1 if year ≥ 1914 and ≤ 1920, 0 otherwise). The government *regulation of 1929* triggered by the Great Depression was presumed to have its impact during 1929 and 1931 (1 if year ≥ 1929 and ≤ 1931, 0 otherwise).

Another institutional event was the emergence of a *single association* that represented the collective interests of all Dutch accounting firms, NIvRA, which was established in 1966 (1 > 1966, 0 otherwise). The industry also experienced two significant regulatory changes (Zeff et al., 1992). First, the Act on Annual Financial Statements of Enterprises, requiring annual audits, took effect in 1971. Second, from 1984 onward, definitive guidelines for auditing were promulgated and enforced by NIvRA, in collaboration with the Dutch Ministry of Justice (Zeff et al., 1992). By increasing the complexity of accounting procedures and specifying which companies should be externally audited, both regulations significantly heightened the demand for audit services. These regulations were still effective in 1990. Two variables were specified: *regulation of 1971* (1 if year > 1971) and *regulation of 1984* (1 if year > 1984).

Because this study might also evoke an association with the population ecology program of research, controlling for key ecological variables was appropriate and essential to forestall the argument that a firm's human and social capital do not matter once industry characteristics have been controlled for.

The number of firms in existence at a particular time reflects *contemporaneous density*. Population ecologists (for example, Hannan and Freeman, 1989) have argued that density's effect on dissolution is curvilinear, with a negative first-order effect and a positive second-order effect. We also controlled for *density at founding*, the number of firms at the time of a focal firm's creation. Owing to intense competition from crowding, new entrants at a time of high density encounter difficulty in exploiting resource-rich niches and in developing replicable skills (Hannan and Freeman, 1989).

We measured *numbers of foundings and dissolutions during the previous observation period* by dividing the number of firms founded or dissolved during a time period by the interval length. In counting the number of dissolutions, we did not include firms that were acquired. The rationale for including this last pair of controls was predicated on the assumption that prior foundings and dissolutions respectively signal the degree of new business opportunities and the availability of abandoned resources.

The possibility of dissolution during a focal time t and time $t + d$ may be positively related to the length of d, where d is the number of unobserved years. Because d ranged from one to five years, we introduced four additional dummies to represent the length of the previous observation interval because the observed annual average number of foundings and dissolutions during the interval would depend on its length. For both current and previous intervals, we used a two-year interval as the omitted category.

Model and Estimation

The empirical analysis of this study deals with time-varying conditions that may explain organizational dissolution. Organizations that were alive in 1990 were treated as right-censored. The same was true for firms that were acquired by other firms, as the process that leads to acquisition may differ from the conditions that lead to failure (Hannan and Freeman, 1989). Since our data set involved time aggregation and right-censoring, the estimates from continuous event history analysis would at best have been biased (Petersen and Koput, 1992). Following Allison's (1982) recommendation, we employed discrete event history analysis. A discrete time hazard rate is defined by

$$P_{it} = PR(T_i = t | T_i \geq t, X_{it}),$$

where T is the discrete random variable giving the uncensored date of failure and P_{it} is the conditional probability that firm i will die at time t, given that it has not already died. Specifically, we used the complementary 'log-log function', as it provides consistent estimates of the continuous time, proportional hazards parameters, regardless of the interval length or the size of the failure rate (Allison, 1982; Petersen and Koput, 1992). Our research setting satisfied two conditions for adequately applying the complementary log-log function (Petersen and Koput, 1992). First, censoring always occurred at the end of the interval. Second, there was only one state in which dissolution could occur – that is, failure. The model is expressed as

$$P_{it} = 1 - \exp[- \exp(\alpha_t + X_{it}\beta)], \text{ or}$$

$$\log[- \log(1 - P_{it})] = \alpha_t + X_{it}\beta,$$

where α_t is a function of time, X_{it} is a row vector of firm i's state variable at time t, and β is a column vector of coefficients. All independent variables, except for the dummies representing the length of current observation intervals, were lagged by one observation period. In other words, environmental, population, and firm i's state variables at time t were used to explain mortality rates during the period from t to $t + d$, where d is the length of the observation interval measured in years. A procedure with the complementary log-log function in SAS (Allison, 1995) was used to estimate the model. The model is particularly appropriate when the intervals within an observation window are not uniform.

We estimated separate equations for the firms that were single proprietorships during their entire life spans. Single proprietorships that evolved into partnerships were therefore excluded. Three reasons forced us to conduct this subgroup analysis. First, single proprietorships had no leverage and could not diversify their social capital. Second, single proprietorships that did not change their membership provided the opportunity to disentangle the effects of industry-specific and firm-specific human capital, a task that is difficult, if not impossible, to achieve for a sample of firms in which partners change their affiliations. Third, the presence of a large number of single proprietorships in this population justified the analysis.

RESULTS

The analysis was based on 1851 firms (representing 8696 firm intervals) that had been founded by 1986; of these firms, 1164 were dissolved, 416 were acquired (158 with name change and 258 without name change), and 271 were still in existence in 1990. There were 1037 single proprietorships (3398 firm intervals) that did not change their membership during their life spans.

Table 4.1 furnishes the means, standard deviations, and product-moment correlations between the variables that were used in this study.

Table 4.2 presents the results from the regression analysis of firm dissolution with the complementary log-log specification. Model 1 presents the baseline, with controls and variables related to Hypothesis 4.5. In model 2, we added the variables measuring the human and social capital of partners to test overall additive effects. The significant chi-square test ($X^2 = 118.0$, $df = 9$, $p = .0001$) revealed that the addition of partners' human capital significantly improved the goodness of fit. Model 3 added the associates' human and social capital. We did not include associates' industry-specific human capital developed through industry experience in model 3 since most employees joined the firms without industry experience. When model 2 is compared with model 3, the increment in the likelihood is quite small ($X^2 = 14.0$, $df = 7$, n.s.). However, the addition of associates' firm-specific human capital to model 2 (results not presented here) improved the goodness of fit significantly ($X^2 = 13.0$, $df = 2$, $p = .01$). We used model 3 in interpreting the effects of independent variables on firm dissolution.

Hypotheses 4.1a and 4.1b state that organizational dissolution will be negatively related with industry-specific capital developed through professional

Table 4.1 *Means, standard deviations and correlations*[a]

Variable	Mean	s.d.	1	2	3	4	5	6	7	8	9	10	11	12	13	14
1. Dissolution	0.13	0.34														
2. Current interval: one-year dummy	0.27	0.45	−.10													
3. Current interval: three-year dummy	0.05	0.22	.18	−.13												
4. Current interval: four-year dummy	0.14	0.35	.10	−.28	−.10											
5. Current interval: five-year dummy[b]	0.02	0.15	.05	−.09	−.03	−.06										
6. Previous interval: one-year dummy	0.27	0.44	−.05	.26	−.13	−.05	−.09									
7. Previous interval: three-year dummy	0.05	0.21	−.03	−.12	−.04	−.09	−.03	−.12								
8. Previous interval: four-year dummy	0.12	0.32	.08	−.21	−.09	.84	−.06	−.24	−.08							
9. Previous interval: five-year dummy[b]	0.02	0.16	−.02	.23	−.03	−.07	−.02	−.09	−.03	−.06						
10. World War I	0.04	0.19	.02	−.09	−.03	−.06	−.02	.00	−.03	−.06	−.02					
11. Regulation of 1929	0.02	0.13	−.01	−.08	−.03	−.06	−.02	−.08	−.03	−.05	−.02	−.02				
12. Regulation of 1971	0.19	0.40	.04	.02	−.12	.79	−.08	.21	−.11	.68	−.08	−.08	−.07			
13. Regulation of 1984	0.04	0.20	.09	−.14	−.05	.52	−.03	−.14	−.05	.59	−.03	−.03	−.03	.42		
14. Indonesia's independence	0.62	0.40	.02	.18	−.05	−.11	−.03	.06	−.05	−.09	−.03	−.03	−.03	−.13	−.05	
15. Single association	0.29	0.46	.01	.23	−.16	.59	−.10	.21	−.15	.51	−.11	−.10	−.10	.75	.32	−.17
16. Single proprietor	0.69	0.46	.12	−.01	.05	−.02	.00	−.01	.01	−.02	.00	−.01	.02	−.03	.00	.00
17. Partners leaving firm	0.82	0.38	−.09	−.01	−.03	.01	−.01	.02	−.01	.00	.00	−.03	.01	.01	−.02	.03
18. Founding type	0.03	0.17	−.02	−.01	−.02	.05	.00	.00	.00	.04	.01	.01	−.01	.04	.01	.00

94

No. Variable	Mean	S.D.	19	20	21	22	23	24	25	26	27	28	29	30	31	32	33	34
19. Split	0.03	0.09																
20. Acquisition with name change	0.29	0.64	-.02															
21. Acquisition without name change	0.20	1.02	.04	-.06														
22. Name change	0.11	0.36	.00	-.05	-.03													
23. Population mass[c]	6.52	0.95	.05	-.01	-.23	.53												
24. Firm size	3.44	15.12	.01	-.05	-.03	.09	-.10											
25. Firm age[c]	1.81	1.16	-.01	-.12	-.09	-.03	-.01	.04										
26. Leverage ratio	0.13	0.43	.00	-.07	.01	-.01	.00	.03	.00									
27. Contemporaneous density	251.40	82.72	-.13	.02	-.03	.27	-.09	-.17	-.19	.31								
28. Density at founding	234.25	79.54	.07	.06	-.12	.27	-.08	.06	-.19	.24	-.08							
29. Number of foundings in a prior year	24.47	24.99	.04	-.04	-.11	-.08	-.09	.35	.00	-.06	-.11	-.27						
30. Number of dissolutions in a prior year	19.66	12.59	.33	-.08	-.27	-.01	-.08	.19	.10	-.07	-.13	-.20	-.16					
31. Partners' industry-specific human capital: graduate education	0.20	0.37	.00	-.03	-.01	.00	.03	.01	.00	.00	.02	.00	.00	.00				
32. Partners' industry-specific human capital: industry tenure	0.76	1.10	.01	.01	-.03	.03	-.03	.01	-.02	.02	-.02	.00	-.01	.04	.01			
33. Partners' firm-specific human capital	1.57	1.02	-.02	-.08	-.02	.02	.01	-.01	-.01	.02	.00	.01	.00	.02	.35	.01		
34. Partners from client environments	0.16	0.34	.00	-.02	.01	-.01	-.01	.00	-.01	-.01	.00	.01	-.01	-.01	.10	.03	.00	
35. Partners to client environments	0.05	0.10	.20	-.08	.00	-.14	-.04	-.05	.01	-.12	-.04	-.05	-.13	.31	.24	-.15	-.06	.64

Table 4.1 (continued)

Variable	Mean	s.d.	1	2	3	4	5	6	7	8	9	10	11	12	13	14
36. Heterogeneity in partners' origins	0.04	0.13	-.06	.01	.01	-.01	.02	.00	.02	.00	.01	.02	.01	-.01	-.01	.00
37. Heterogeneity in departed partners' destinations	0.09	0.28	-.06	-.01	.00	-.01	.01	.00	.00	-.01	.01	.00	.01	.00	-.01	.00
38. Associates' industry-specific human capital: graduate education	0.07	0.35	-.05	.01	.01	-.01	-.01	.01	.01	-.01	.02	.00	.00	.00	-.01	.01
39. Associates' firm-specific human capital	0.10	0.45	-.04	-.01	.01	.00	.00	-.01	.02	.01	.01	.01	.01	.00	.00	.00
40. Associates from client environments	0.01	0.09	.01	.00	.17	-.07	.00	-.02	.12	-.05	.01	.16	.09	-.11	-.01	.04
41. Associates to client environments	0.02	0.12	-.03	.01	.00	-.02	.02	.00	.00	-.01	.03	.00	.00	-.02	-.01	.03
42. Heterogeneity in associates' origins	0.01	0.05	-.05	.00	.01	-.02	.00	.01	.00	-.02	.00	.00	.01	-.03	-.01	.02
43. Heterogeneity in departed associates' destinations	0.08	0.26	-.06	.03	-.05	-.04	-.02	.04	-.04	-.03	.02	-.03	-.03	-.05	-.03	.14

Table 4.1 (continued)

Variable	Mean	s.d.	15	16	17	18	19	20	21	22	23	24	25	26	27	28
1. Dissolution	0.13	0.34														
2. Current interval: one-year dummy	0.27	0.45														
3. Current interval: three-year dummy	0.05	0.22														
4. Current interval: four-year dummy	0.14	0.35														
5. Current interval: five-year dummy[b]	0.02	0.15														
6. Previous interval: one-year dummy	0.27	0.44														
7. Previous interval: three-year dummy	0.05	0.21														
8. Previous interval: four-year dummy	0.12	0.32														
9. Previous interval: five-year dummy[b]	0.02	0.16														
10. World War I	0.04	0.19														
11. Regulation of 1929	0.02	0.13														
12. Regulation of 1971	0.19	0.40														
13. Regulation of 1984	0.04	0.20														
14. Indonesia's independence	0.62	0.48														
15. Single association	0.29	0.45														
16. Single proprietor	0.69	0.46	−.04													
17. Partners leaving firm	0.82	0.38	−.01	−.44												

97

Table 4.1 (continued)

Variable	Mean	s.d.	15	16	17	18	19	20	21	22	23	24	25	26	27	28
18. Founding type	0.03	0.17	.03	−.27	.27											
19. Split	0.03	0.29	.03	−.15	.25	.20										
20. Acquisition with name change	0.09	0.64	.13	−.21	.26	.05	.31									
21. Acquisition without name change	0.20	1.02	.04	−.20	.39	.20	.41	.36								
22. Name change	0.11	0.36	.02	−.32	.35	−.03	.19	.16	.15							
23. Population mass[c]	6.52	0.95	.73	−.05	.03	.02	.02	.10	.05	.03						
24. Firm size	3.44	15.12	.10	−.24	.28	.23	.47	.56	.59	.16	.08					
25. Firm age[c]	1.81	1.16	.00	−.31	.45	.09	.18	.19	.30	.31	.09	.18				
26. Leverage ratio	0.13	0.43	−.01	−.47	.23	.14	.11	.16	.22	.18	−.02	.28	.16			
27. Contemporaneous density	251.40	82.72	.34	.02	.03	.00	.00	.03	.04	.02	.81	.05	.04	−.02		
28. Density at founding	234.25	79.54	.47	.17	−.30	−.12	−.18	−.06	−.21	−.15	.73	−.08	−.36	−.13	.68	
29. Number of foundings in a prior year	24.47	24.99	.04	.00	.00	.01	−.01	.00	.01	−.01	.07	.00	−.05	.00	.14	.10
30. Number of dissolutions in a prior year	19.66	12.59	.45	−.03	.00	.00	−.02	.07	.03	.03	.47	.04	.01	−.01	.29	.39
31. Partners' industry-specific human capital: graduate education	0.20	0.37	−.01	−.01	−.01	−.03	.00	.01	−.02	.02	.01	−.02	−.03	.00	.01	.03
32. Partners' industry-specific human capital: industry tenure	0.76	1.10	.05	−.17	.10	.15	.02	.08	.06	.02	.05	.08	−.06	.06	.02	.01

98

	Mean	SD														
33. Partners' firm-specific human capital	1.57	1.02	.01	−.05	.12	−.04	.06	.01	.08	.13	.04	.03	.81	.07	.03	−.22
34. Partners from client environments	0.16	0.34	.00	−.03	.02	−.01	.00	.00	.02	.03	.00	.01	.03	−.03	.00	.00
35. Partners to client environments	0.05	0.10	−.19	.02	.03	−.01	−.01	−.03	−.02	−.04	−.23	−.03	−.12	.00	−.17	−.15
36. Heterogeneity in partners' origins	0.04	0.13	−.02	−.45	.30	.26	.12	.13	.19	.16	−.04	.17	.15	.14	−.04	−.17
37. Heterogeneity in departed partners' destinations	0.09	0.28	.00	−.31	.75	.22	.26	.22	.33	.27	−.01	.22	.35	.16	−.01	−.28
38. Associates' industry-specific human capital: graduate education	0.07	0.35	−.01	−.33	.26	.19	.16	.18	.25	.14	−.02	.21	.17	.35	−.02	−.15
39. Associates' firm-specific human capital	0.10	0.45	−.01	−.33	.21	.15	.12	.12	.17	.08	−.02	.17	.12	.44	−.02	−.12
40. Associates from client environments	0.01	0.09	−.15	−.14	.07	.06	.12	.01	.09	.03	−.37	.04	−.01	.23	−.35	−.36
41. Associates to client environments	0.02	0.12	−.04	−.20	.26	.10	.12	.25	.32	.09	−.03	.27	.16	.26	−.01	−.11
42. Heterogeneity in associates' origins	0.01	0.05	−.03	−.22	.23	.17	.10	.18	.33	.08	−.03	.26	.13	.36	−.02	−.11
43. Heterogeneity in departed associates' destinations	0.08	0.26	−.07	−.34	.43	.22	.15	.18	.36	.21	.01	.23	.28	.26	.06	−.19

Table 4.1 (continued)

Variable	Mean	s.d.	29	30	31	32	33	34	35	36	37	38	39	40	41	42
1. Dissolution	0.13	0.34														
2. Current interval: one-year dummy	0.27	0.45														
3. Current interval: three year dummy	0.05	0.22														
4. Current interval: four-year dummy	0.14	0.35														
5. Current interval: five-year dummy[b]	0.02	0.15														
6. Previous interval: one-year dummy	0.27	0.44														
7. Previous interval: three-year dummy	0.05	0.21														
8. Previous interval: four-year dummy	0.12	0.32														
9. Previous interval: five-year dummy[b]	0.02	0.16														
10. World War I	0.04	0.19														
11. Regulation of 1929	0.02	0.13														
12. Regulation of 1971	0.19	0.40														
13. Regulation of 1984	0.04	0.20														
14. Indonesia's independence	0.62	0.48														
15. Single association	0.29	0.46														
16. Single proprietor	0.69	0.46														
17. Partners leaving firm	0.82	0.38														
18. Founding type	0.08	0.17														
19. Split	0.03	0.29														

	Mean	S.D.							
20. Acquisition with name change	0.09	0.64							
21. Acquisition without namechange	0.20	1.02							
22. Name change	0.11	0.36							
23. Population mass^c	6.52	0.95							
24. Firm size	3.44	15.12							
25. Firm age^c	1.81	1.16							
26. Leverage ratio	0.13	0.43							
27. Contemporaneous density	251.40	82.72							
28. Density at founding	234.25	79.54							
29. Number of foundings in a prior year	24.47	24.99							
30. Number of dissolutions in a prior year	19.66	12.59	.18						
31. Partners' industry-specific human capital: graduate education	0.20	0.37	.00	.00					
32. Partners' industry-specific human capital: industry tenure	0.76	1.10	.01	.03	.01				
33. Partners' firm-specific human capital	1.57	1.02	−.02	−.01	−.04	−.15			
34. Partners from client environments	0.16	0.34	.00	.00	.01	−.05	.02		
35. Partners to client environments	0.05	0.10	−.07	.19	−.01	−.01	−.04	.00	
36. Heterogeneity in partners' origins	0.04	0.13	−.01	−.03	.00	.17	−.01	−.23	.01

Table 4.1 (continued)

Variable	Mean	s.d.	29	30	31	32	33	34	35	36	37	38	39	40	41	42
37. Heterogeneity in departed partners' destinations	0.09	0.28	-.01	.00	-.01	.07	.11	.01	.01	.23						
38. Associates' industry-specific human capital: graduate education	0.07	0.35	.00	.00	.03	.03	.03	.02	.01	.12	.18					
39. Associates' firm-specific human capital	0.10	0.45	.00	-.01	.02	.08	.02	.01	.00	.14	.10	.31				
40. Associates from client environments	0.01	0.09	-.02	-.18	.03	-.01	.00	.01	.14	.09	.08	.08	.28			
41. Associates to client environments	0.02	0.12	.01	-.02	.03	.02	.05	-.02	.01	.09	.17	.16	.12	.05		
42. Heterogeneity in associates' origins	0.01	0.05	.01	-.01	-.02	.03	.03	.00	.01	.18	.19	.18	.25	.38	.18	
43. Heterogeneity in departed associates' destinations	0.08	0.26	.07	.02	.00	.07	.07	.02	.09	.16	.31	.36	.20	.07	.14	.27

Notes:
a. Correlations ≥ .03 are significant at .01: r's ≥ .02 are significant at .05. Correlations are based on standardized variables. Means and standard deviations are based on the values before standardization. Data are for 1851 firms and 8696 firm years.
b. Variable identifies World War II.
c. Variable is a logarithm.

Table 4.2   Results of complementary log-log regression analysis of firm dissolution[a]

Variables	Model 1		Model 2		Model 3	
	b	s.e.	*b*	s.e.	*b*	s.e.
Intercept	−2.84**	1.01	−0.45	0.93	−0.56	0.94
Current interval: one-year dummy	−0.39**	0.14	−0.01	0.15	−0.02	0.15
Current interval: three-year dummy	0.92**	0.17	1.00**	0.17	0.94**	0.17
Current interval: four-year dummy	1.21**	0.26	1.66**	0.26	1.14**	0.26
Current interval: five-year dummy[b]	1.48**	0.22	1.94**	0.22	1.21**	0.22
Previous interval: one-year dummy	0.10	0.14	−0.41**	0.16	−0.41**	0.16
Previous interval: three-year dummy	−0.48*	0.28	−0.54	0.33	−0.54	0.33
Previous interval: four-year dummy	−0.48*	0.24	−0.15	0.25	−0.17	0.25
Previous interval: five-year dummy[b]	−0.98**	0.37	−0.37	0.37	−0.38	0.37
World War I	0.53**	0.27	0.67*	0.27	0.65*	0.27
Regulation of 1929	0.15	0.36	1.90**	0.43	1.95**	0.43
Regulation of 1971	−0.69**	0.29	−0.43	0.31	−0.43	0.31
Regulation of 1984	−0.95**	0.28	1.11**	0.30	1.16**	0.30
Indonesia's independence	1.87**	0.20	1.72**	0.22	1.71**	0.22
Single association	−0.70**	0.23	−0.08	0.23	−0.06	0.23
Single proprietor	0.48**	0.13	0.29*	0.14	0.36*	0.15
Partners leaving firm	−0.05	0.16	0.04	0.23	−0.05	0.24
Founding type	0.59*	0.27	0.60*	0.27	0.60*	0.27
Split	0.24	0.24	0.25	0.24	0.19	0.24
Acquisition with name change	0.35**	0.09	0.35**	0.09	0.36**	0.10
Acquisition without name change	0.05	0.12	0.04	0.12	−0.02	0.13
Name change	−0.06	0.15	0.02	0.15	0.03	0.15
Population mass[c]	1.12**	0.27	−0.63*	0.27	−0.62*	0.27
Firm size	−0.09**	0.03	−0.08**	0.03	−0.08**	0.03
Firm age[c]	−0.08*	0.04	−0.03	0.11	−0.03	0.11
Leverage ratio	−0.08*	0.04	−0.22**	0.07	−0.21*	0.09
Contemporaneous density/100	−3.78**	0.58	0.61	0.57	0.65	0.57
(Contemporaneous density/100) squared	0.68**	0.10	−0.20*	0.10	0.21*	0.10
Density at founding/100	0.49**	0.11	0.62**	0.11	0.62**	0.11
Number of foundings in a prior year/100	−0.16	0.23	0.10	0.25	0.08	0.25
Number of failures in a prior year/100	−0.37	0.70	1.48*	0.86	1.52*	0.86
Partners' industry-specific human capital: graduate education			−0.138**	0.04	−0.14**	0.04
Partners' industry-specific human capital: industry tenure			−0.11*	0.05	−0.11*	0.06
Partners' industry-specific human capital: industry tenure squared			0.15**	0.03	0.15**	0.03
Partners' firm-specific human capital			−0.24*	0.11	−0.24**	0.11

Table 4.2   (continued)

Variables	Model 1		Model 2		Model 3	
	b	s.e.	*b*	s.e.	*b*	s.e.
Partners' firm-specific human capital squared			0.23**	0.03	0.23**	0.03
Partners from client environment			−0.09**	0.03	−0.09**	0.03
Partners to client environment			−0.01**	0.00	−0.01**	0.00
Heterogeneity in partners' origins			−0.06	0.06	−0.05	0.06
Heterogeneity in departed partners' destinations			0.02	0.08	0.03	0.08
Associates' industry-specific human capital: graduate school education					−0.05	0.08
Associates' firm-specific human capital					−0.39*	0.16
Associates' firm-specific human capital squared					0.35**	0.13
Associates from client environment					0.06	0.17
Associates to client environment					0.07	0.05
Heterogeneity in associates' origin					−0.21	0.16
Heterogeneity in departed associates' destination					0.03	0.03
*Log-likelihood (*df*)*	−2.119 (30)		−2.060 (39)		−2.053 (46)	
*Chi-square compared with previous model (*df*)*			118** (9)		14* (7)	

Notes:
a. Data are for 1851 firms, 8696 firm intervals, and 1164 firm failures.
b. Variables identifies World War II.
c. Variable is a logarithm.
* $p < .10$; ** $p < .05$; *** $p < 0.01$.
All two-tailed tests.

education and will have a U-shaped relationship with industry-specific capital developed through industry experience and firm-specific experience. Supporting the hypotheses, all the human capital variables except for associates' industry-specific human capital developed through professional education had significant and predicted effects on firm dissolution. The results strongly support Hypotheses 4.la and 4.1b. Hypothesis 4.2 predicts that all eight indicators of social capital will have significantly negative effects on firm dissolution. Results show that only two variables – partners from client environments and partners to client environments – significantly decreased firm dissolutions. Neither of the two heterogeneity measures of social capital produced statistically significant coefficients. Consequently, Hypothesis 4.2 was only partially supported.

Hypothesis 4.3 states that firm-specific human capital and social capital will have stronger effects on firm dissolution than industry-specific human capital. To test the hypothesis, we conducted a series of chi-square tests by using model 3 as a full model. When two variables measured by the same metric have the same effects on firm dissolution, the full model should have the same log-likelihood as a reduced model that uses the summation of two variables instead of using the two variables separately. If the effects of two variables are significantly different, a chi-square value contrast of the two models should be significant at one degree of freedom. We could use this procedure since all human and social capital variables were standardized. To control the effect of ownership status, we compared the coefficients of the partners' and associates' human and social capital separately. Results of the chi-square tests indicated that the coefficient of the partners' firm-specific human capital was significantly higher than the coefficients of two indicators of the partners' industry-specific human capital ($X^2 = 20.6$, $df = 2$, $p = .01$ for firm-specific human capital versus industry-specific human capital proxied by industry tenure, and $X^2 = 6.9$, $df = 1$, $p = .01$ for firm-specific human capital versus industry-specific human capital proxied by professional education). A similar inference could be drawn for associates ($X^2 = 8.3$, $df = 1$, $p = .01$). However, the coefficients of the social capital variables were not significantly larger than the coefficients of the industry-specific human capital variables for both partners and associates. Thus, Hypothesis 4.3 was only partially supported.

Hypothesis 4.4 states that partners' human and social capital will have a stronger effect on firm dissolution than associates' human and social capital. To test the hypothesis, we again conducted chi-square tests. Results indicated that industry-specific human capital developed through the professional education of partners had a significantly stronger effect on firm dissolution than the comparable variable measured for associates ($X^2 = 7.3$, $df = 1$, $p = .01$). Partners from client environments and partners to client environments had significantly stronger influences than associates from client environments ($X^2 = 5.6$, $df = 1$, $p = .05$) and associates to client environments ($X^2 = 4.1$, $df = 1$, $p = .05$). There was no significant difference between partners and associates in the coefficients of the other three indicators. The significant effect of firm-specific human capital reduced the sharp distinction between owners' and employees' human capital: the firm-specific human capital of employees also had important survival implications. Hence, Hypothesis 4.4 was partially supported.

We also included variables that were pertinent to Hypothesis 4.5a, which states that firms started as splits are more likely to dissolve than firms founded *de novo*. The significantly positive coefficients of founding type (the omitted category was firms founded *de novo*) in model 3 strongly support the hypothesis. Accounting firms established by splits experienced higher dissolution rates than new foundings. Chi-square results also strongly supported Hypothesis 4.5b. Firms emerging out of acquisitions with name changes showed higher dissolution levels than firms created by acquisitions without name changes ($X^2 = 6.0$, $df = 1$, $p. = .05$) and firms that experienced name changes without acquisitions ($X^2 = 3.9$, $df = 1$, $p = .05$). Acquisitions without name changes had no effect on dissolution, perhaps because the reduction in firm-specific human capital was not as severe in the case of such acquisitions. The insignificant coefficient of name changes implies that the different effects of the two types of acquisitions may not be due to the loss of goodwill from name changes themselves. In contrast, neither the defection of a partner, indicated by the variable for partners leaving firm, or former organization members establishing their own firms, indicated by the variable *split*, had an effect on firm dissolutions. In short, these findings furnish support for Hypothesis 5 and collaterally provide more credence to the earlier hypotheses.

This analysis was replicated on a subsample of single proprietorships, which are common in professional services. In this subgroup, firm tenure equaled firm age. To disentangle the effects of industry tenure and firm tenure, we used an accountant's industry tenure at the time of founding – that is, his or her sole proprietorship's congenital learning (Ingram and Baum, 1997). Although firm tenure is a time-varying covariate, industry tenure at the time of founding is not. The results strongly supported Hypotheses 4.1 and 4.3. Firms whose owners had master's or higher graduate degrees displayed significantly lower dissolution rates. The first-order effects of industry tenure at founding and firm tenure were significantly negative. We included the squared terms of industry and firm tenure to control for the effects of partners' age on firm dissolution because older accountants are more likely to dissolve their offices when they retire or die. The probability of dissolution reached a minimum when a firm's founder had 7.94 [.0103/(2 × .00065)] years of industry tenure at the time of founding and the firm was 8.13 [.0392/(2 × .00241)] years old. A related result from this sub-group analysis indicated that a founder's social capital, for which previous affiliation with client sector firms was the proxy, had the predicted negative coefficient but was not significant.

Figure 4.2 illustrates these effects of industry and firm tenure on the mortality rate of single proprietorships. The vertical axis represents the probability of a single proprietorship's failure in the next two years when other covariates are set to zero. These curves show a difference in elevation. The bottom pair of curves portrays the probability of mortality for single proprietorships in which the founder had either four or eight years of industry tenure at time of founding, and the upper curve depicts the probability of

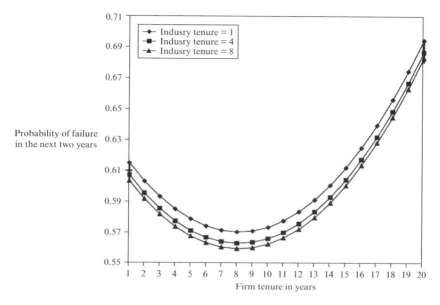

Figure 4.2   *Industry tenure at founding, firm tenure, and the probability*
of single proprietorship failure in the next two years

the failure of entrepreneurs without any industry experience. In addition, a founder's social capital (previous affiliation with client sector firms) has the predicted negative coefficient but is not significant. In short, we can conclude that both firm-specific and industry-specific human capital, as well as social capital, confer distinctive competitive advantages, even when the firm is a sole proprietorship.

Finally, we note the effects of several control variables. Some of the ecological variables included had strong and consistent impacts on firm dissolution. Density at founding had a strong effect on dissolution, but contemporaneous density no longer stood out in predicting dissolution when we included human and social capital variables. Our analysis also showed that the effect of firm age depended on model specification. In line with the liability of newness argument, the natural logarithm of firm age revealed a negative effect on dissolution in model 1. Its effect disappeared in model 3, however, when we included human and social capital variables. Finally, the effect of leverage merits explicit mention. Firms with more associates per partner enjoyed superior survival benefits. This is not a scale effect, as we controlled for firm size. Finally, a number of historical and institutional covariates were significantly associated with firm dissolution.

DISCUSSION AND CONCLUSION

This study produced major evidence for the contention that a firm's human and social capital have important implications for performance. Applying human and social capital theory to firms, we found that the specificity and non-appropriability of such capital diminished dissolutions of professional service firms. Specificity was defined as the degree to which the human capital inside a firm was idiosyncratic and therefore difficult to transfer. Human and social capital were also viewed as non-appropriable, because they are embodied in the individuals who collectively own firms. Results revealed that the industry-specific human capital and social capital of owners (CPA partners) contributed more to firm survival than those of employees (CPA associates) but that the contribution of firm-specific human capital to firm survival did not depend on who held it. Results also indicated that some organizational events, such as acquisition with a name change or an organizational split, unraveled the complementary knowledge and skills held by organization members and thus increased the dissolution rate. We showed these relationships in a dynamic context, thus eliminating doubts about their causal impact on dissolution. This study showed that firm-level human and social capital could be important sources of competitive advantage, especially when the capital was specific to a firm or was held by its owners.

These findings can be juxtaposed against two prominent strands of research regarding firm performance. The resource-based view of the firm (for example, Penrose, 1959; Wernerfelt, 1984) emphasizes the resources held by a firm in explaining firm profitability and population ecology (Hannan and Freeman, 1989) emphasizes population characteristics in explaining firm dissolution. This study used firm dissolution as a dependent variable and included both firm-level resource variables and population (that is, accounting sector) characteristics.

This study has obvious affinities with the resource-based view of the firm, and it should stimulate new studies of intangible capital. In the resource-based view, the tradability, imitability, and appropriability of intangible resources are viewed as jeopardizing a firm's advantage. We were agnostic about the *content* of broadly-defined human and social capital. We did not identify distinct sampling procedures and unusual auditing routines to delineate each firm's unique competencies. Rather, we assumed that the human and social capital that resided in partners or were specific to firms were integral parts of unobservable unique resources that conferred a competitive advantage.

The results provide important evidence against the density-dependence hypothesis (Hannan and Freeman, 1989). The U-shaped relation between density and the dissolution rate found in the model without firm-level human and social capital variables disappeared when we controlled for those variables. We may have obtained this result because firms with high levels of human and social capital generate more competition than firms with low levels of human and social capital (compare Winter, 1990). The present study also provided a finer-tuned perspective on tensions between the firm and population levels of analysis by peeking into firms, rather than treating them as black boxes. For example, we showed that age dependence is actually based on the logic of human capital accumulation: as firms age, they amass human and social capital and thus experience higher survival chances. Age is a rather crude proxy for the firm-specific knowledge that comes with organizational learning. Researchers should substitute another proxy to explore what antecedents (human and social capital) underlie the age dependence phenomenon. The results clearly indicate the need to combine a resource-based view of the firm with population ecology and, if necessary, to revisit the various settings that have been studied (such as newspapers, restaurants, and telecommunication firms) to fully debunk industry density and firm age as precursors of firm dissolution. Clearly, researchers should no longer treat firms as black boxes. Rather, it is the content of those black boxes that yields answers to the question of firm performance.

Weaknesses in this study provide some suggestions for future research. First, prospective research could explore whether and why the density-dependence effect disappeared in this study when important firm-level resource variables were included. Results of this research can explain why many studies have found strong supporting evidence for the liability of newness argument. Stinchcombe (1965) and all the ecologists following in his footsteps (for example, Hannan and Freeman, 1984) argued that newly founded firms face poor survival prospects. Our study shows that many (but not all!) newly founded firms have low levels of human and social capital and thus face a high incidence of dissolution. Conversely, older firms are vulnerable if their stock of human and social capital is low. However, we could not clearly explain why the density-dependence effect disappeared when we controlled for important firm-level human and social capital variables.

Second, researchers also need to shift the focus from dissolution to other performance indexes, such as market share and revenue streams. Although these indexes predict dissolution, they have superior diagnostic value in gauging firm health, and they therefore suggest potential interventions for forestalling untimely death. We assumed that firms with an ability to retain and attract more clients were less likely to dissolve. Sometimes this is not the case. Professionals with that very ability may dissolve an accounting firm when their reputations can secure them better employment opportunities outside the industry. Furthermore, comparing the relative contributions of population characteristics and firm resources to firm profitability may provide more definitive evidence on the relative explanatory powers of the resource-based view of the firm and population ecology.

Third, future research could measure human and social capital variables more germane to the firm level. Although the average human and social capital of partners and associates are important, their distributions should also be explored: the heterogeneity measures of social capital in this study are examples of distributional indicators. For instance, the distribution of employees' firm tenure may influence a firm's ability to transmit firm-specific knowledge, to import new knowledge developed outside, to divide the work according to human capital, and so forth. Future research could explore whether the distribution of that capital is more important than its average. In addition, our measures of social capital were very crude, since we employed long-term historical data. The generally non-significant effects of social capital heterogeneity in this study may be due to the crudeness of the measures. Future research could directly measure the variability of social relationships and explore its effect on firm survival and profitability.

Lastly, future research could uncover the importance of firm-level human and social capital to other industrial settings and to other locations. The present study dealt with a professional service sector in which the organizational form is single proprietorship or partnership (Lee and Pennings, 1998). Human and social capital that are not separable or alienable from individuals might be among the most central resources in accounting for firm performance. Although human and social capital might not be so prominent in manufacturing sectors as in professional service sectors, we think that their weight is increasing as a knowledge society emerges. By exploring other industrial settings, future research could investigate under what conditions human and social capital can be sources of competitive advantage.

NOTES

1. The rationale for using average rather than aggregate industry experience was as follows. Suppose there are two firms, A, with 100 partners, of whom 10 bring in business, and B, with only 20 partners, of whom 10 bring in business. Other things being equal, firm B, with its higher average capital, will perform better and be less likely to be dissolved.
2. For comparison, 5- and 15-year spans were also tested. This sensitivity analysis showed that the results reported here are robust to such changes.

5. Mimicry and the market: adoption of a new organizational form

INTRODUCTION

Why are organizations, occupying the same environmental niche or 'organizational field', similar in structure? Two streams of research have sought to answer this question. Population ecologists (for example, Hannan and Freeman, 1989) suggest that the environment selects firms with structural elements that provide the highest fitness value. The competitive process to which firms are exposed winnows out those that lack an adequate structural template (Hannan and Freeman, 1977, 1984). In contrast, institutional scholars have argued that firms adaptively adopt a certain structure to enhance their legitimacy, thus converging towards a common template in their so-called 'organizational field' or market (for example, DiMaggio and Powell, 1983; Meyer and Rowan, 1977).

The institutional process has been sharply distinguished from the competitive process as shown by earlier institutional studies which sought to explain structural changes and innovation (for example, DiMaggio and Powell, 1983; Meyer and Rowan, 1977). More recently, however, several institutional writers have acknowledged that competitive and institutional processes interact with each other in producing convergence in structure (for example, Powell, 1988, 1991; Scott, 1987; Scott and Meyer, 1991).

While conceding the interaction of the two processes in producing institutional changes, those authors did not clarify the nature of the interaction. The present study proposes hypotheses on that interaction by combining tenets of population ecology and institutional theory. We then test those hypotheses with the partner–associate structure adoption in a population of Dutch accounting firms from 1925 to 1990.

When firms vary in their structural arrangements, their selection environment favors firms having a specific structural arrangement – an observation that is in line with the presumption of competitive isomorphism (Hannan and Freeman, 1977, 1984). Those competitive processes trigger institutional processes. The higher growth and survival rate of those firms amounts to 'market feedback' which shapes managers' cognitive premises – both directly through mere exposure, and indirectly through consultants and other professionals who disseminate that feedback in their rhetoric and in their peddling of the new template (Abrahamson, 1997). In other words, the template gains legitimacy through market feedback favoring adopting firms. That enhanced legitimacy and subsequent changes in a manager's cognition foster mimetic isomorphism (DiMaggio and Powell, 1983).

Though market feedback alone produces organizational change and innovation, several firm characteristics render the firm more susceptible to that information. We propose that a firm's network with adopters, physical location, and clusters of size-equivalent firms filter the information about innovation and its benefits. Those firm characteristics augment the influence of market feedback on the adoption decision.

Our belief is that this study will significantly push the theory of institutional change into new directions by integrating population ecology and institutional theory. This becomes more apparent as we propose and test a very important, but often neglected, aspect of institutionalization – market feedback – and examine how that feedback gets filtered through a firm's specific context.

RESEARCH SETTING

The accounting sector has become an important segment of the ever-growing service sector. This sector has expanded exponentially, and has become increasingly globalized. Before the advent of a partner–associate form (hereafter PA-form) in 1925, the Dutch accounting sector had been composed of either single proprietors or small firms with partners only (hereafter P-form). After the advent of the PA-form, we observe two distinct types of organizational forms: some firms have associate professionals as well as partners (hereafter PA-firms), while others have partners only (hereafter P-firms).

Figure 5.1 shows the number of PA-form adopters in each observation interval and the number of survivors among them. Four comparatively large accounting firms adopted the PA-form in 1925. By 1990, 301 accounting firms had adopted the structural innovation. Figure 5.2 shows the changes in the proportion of PA-firms and their market share or rather their relative 'mass' (Winter, 1990) as measured by the proportion of accountants who were affiliated with PA-firms. PA-firms had gradually increased their collective mass and more than 80 per cent of practicing accountants were affiliated with those firms in 1990.

In PA-firms, partners participate in important strategic decisions and take the profits from operations, while associates receive the command and guidance of partners and usually receive a fixed annual salary

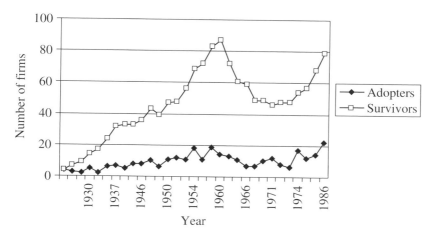

Figure 5.1   Number of PA-form adopters and survivors

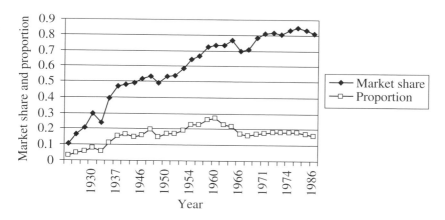

Figure 5.2   Market share and proportion of PA-firms

(Sherer, 1995). In auditing financial statements, a partner forms a team with associates. As 'partner-in-charge' of an audit, the partner signs off the completed audit work and is responsible to the client and the users of audited information for the services provided (Greenwood et al., 1990). Associates in an auditing team attest to the accuracy of financial statements under the guidance of the partner but do not have a formal responsibility for audited results. Accounting firms usually hire freshly qualified accountants as associates, monitor their ability and aptitude for 8–12 years, and promote some of them to partners (compare Galanter and Palay, 1991; Gilson and Mnookin, 1989).

Each partner usually enjoys an equal share of partnership and is entitled to a one person-one vote in strategic matters such as mergers and acquisitions (Greenwood et al., 1994). As PA-firms have grown and become larger, they have evolved into more mechanistic forms and have become less collegial (Hinings et al. 1991; Tolbert and Stern, 1985). Several strategic decisions that had been decided through consensus among all partners are delegated to the managing partners or to special committees.

In P-firms, all participating professionals are partners. A P-firm is very similar to a peer group described by Williamson (1975), since professionals have equal voice and status, and no authority differentiation exists among them. Since all partners share individual and collective unlimited liability, P-firms usually maintain unanimous decision rules in recruiting a new partner. Thus it is very unlikely for professionals to form a large-scale P-firm. It should therefore not surprise us that PA-form advocates (for example, Maister, 1993) would like partnerships to employ associates.

What surfaces from the rhetoric regarding the superiority of the PA over the P-form? The purveyors of the PA-form rhetoric primarily focus on governance structures, as other forms of organizing, for example incorporation, are usually legally blocked. Galanter and Palay (1991) and Russell (1985), for instance, view the PA-form as a condition of firm growth by fostering consensus and trust, while maintaining opportunities for expansion. Trust and homogeneity achieved by the ongoing tournament to partnership decrease the threshold for reaching consensus. Writers and consultants who articulate and embellish the superiority of such governance structures point to the advantages of associates' tournaments, such as screening and socialization, when professional services firms evolve towards large partnerships with a well-established *esprit de corps*, and with a reputation for reliability and reproducibility.

The template is so widespread that we have difficulty envisioning a partnership whose design does not embody this template. The PA-form has emerged as an 'obvious' or natural template for designing professional firms where the law does not allow incorporation, since so many of the large firms in professional services sectors such as accounting, law, and consulting have resorted to it. The form should be viewed as an important structural breakthrough, since, compared to the P-form, this innovation enabled professional service firms to economize on coordination and governance costs when they became large (Galanter and Palay, 1991; Russell, 1985). In a sense, the significance of the PA-form for professional service firms parallels that of the M-form for diversified industrial firms.

This study explores diffusion of the PA-form in the Dutch accounting sector. Its data furnish access to a very unique research setting, where we can explore the effects of population-level selection on the adoption of a new structural template. In most current diffusion studies, sampled actors were not changing over time, nor do they belong to a well-bounded entity. As a result, those studies explored the effect of such actions of other firms in the adoption of new practices and could not incorporate the effect of population-level selection. In contrast, our data provide market selection information such as firm founding and dissolutions, as well as firm growth, and thus allow us to analyze the effects of market selection on the adoption of a new structural template. And we are able to show that spillovers between firms are reinforced by contextual and local conditions.

THEORY AND HYPOTHESES

The historical observation regarding the Dutch accounting industry suggests that institutional changes can happen in the absence of external coercive forces. Population ecology and institutional theory explain why those kinds of institutional changes can happen.

Population ecology emphasized the competitive process as a pre-eminent driver of institutional change and suggested that organizational foundings with a specific form combined with differences in survival rates among firms with different forms produce institutional change. For instance, Hannan and Freeman (1987, 1988) examined founding and mortality rates of American national labor unions in order to explain institutional evolution from craft to industrial union dominance. Here, density – the number of organizations with a specific organizational form in the population – amounts to a critical antecedent of founding and mortality rates. The initial increase of density of firms with a specific organizational form legitimizes that form over others, which in turn boosts founding rates of firms with that form while diminishing their mortality rate. Beyond some threshold, additional density will augment competition within a population, with the result that founding rates decline and those firms' mortality rates go up. Though population ecology acknowledges that growing density of firms with a certain organizational form conveys more legitimacy of the form, its writers have tended to stress the effect of the legitimacy on 'vital statistics' such as founding and mortality rates and have remained silent on its ramifications for organizational changes.

In contrast, institutional theory views organizational transformations and institutional processes as critical precursors of institutional change.

The widespread adoption of a new organizational form will induce changes in norms, beliefs and practices such that the emergent form becomes widely accepted. Institutional writers have focused on the institutional processes that engender the growing presence of new organizational forms. Specifically, they have dealt with the role of peer organizations, nation-states and professionals (for example, Fligstein, 1985; Scott, 1995), though among these writers various sources of legitimacy are distinguished or observed (Ruef and Scott, 1998).

Notwithstanding widely acknowledged interaction between competitive and institutional processes (for example, Powell, 1988, 1991; Scott, 1987; Scott and Meyer, 1991), that interaction has not been explicitly articulated and researched among institutional writers. By way of distinction, we sought to combine population ecology and institutional theory in order to explain the institutional changes by focusing on the role of 'key suppliers' and 'resource and product customers' – which DiMaggio and Powell (1983) considered as important elements of the organizational field. Though the importance of these firms and individuals is recognized by 'new institutionalism', their role has not been clearly articulated and empirically investigated.[1]

The market, which comprises suppliers, customers, and competitors, functions as a contesting arena for competing organizational forms (Nelson and Winter, 1982). When the market favors firms with a certain organizational form, the market feedback furnishes a clue about how private sector firms should be structured. The market as a selection environment significantly influences population-level evolution (Hannan and Freeman, 1989), which in turn has a profound impact on the firm-level choice of structural innovations (Miner, 1994). Figure 5.3 illustrates processes of institutional change, which are not imposed by regulatory agencies. The very first adopters who shifted from the P to the PA-form, might have been influenced by developments of accounting firms in other countries or firms in other sectors – for example law. Or the innovation might have been a chance event, or a response to cope with changes in relative prices of inputs (Leblebici et al., 1991; North, 1990). Given that some firms initially adopted the PA-form, we need a theory of institutional change from a P-form dominated industry to a PA-form dominated one.

The initial adoption of the PA-form creates population-level variation. In other words, there exist P-firms as well as PA-firms. The variation might trigger selection pressures and to the extent that the environment does favor PA-form adopters – for example by superior performance, higher survival and growth rates, and so on – we should observe an increasingly higher market share of adopters relative to non-adopters. In other words, the market for competing organizational forms provides feedback about its

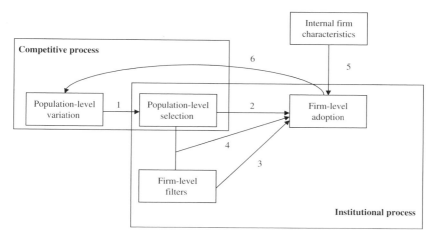

Figure 5.3   Processes of institutional change

preference of the PA-form. Line number 1 in Figure 5.3 indicates this competitive process.

The market feedback – outcome of population-level selection – shapes the views of managers, consultants and writers regarding the superiority of the PA-form and will thus produce a fertile ground for cognitive change. A structural template that the market for competing organizational forms reinforces positively by providing more resources to adopters over not-adopters becomes 'taken-for-granted' and gains a rule-like status. As the form becomes widely accepted, it stands a much higher chance of becoming adopted by peer firms. Line number 2 in Figure 5.3 indicates the direct effect of market feedback on the adoption decision.

Firms imitate peers that are part of their network (Davis, 1991; Palmer et al., 1993), or peers that have similar attributes such as similar-sized firms and geographically proximate firms (Haunschild and Miner, 1997; Haveman, 1993; Strang and Meyer, 1993). Such filters include networks, size similarity and geographic proximity (Benjamin and Podolny, 1999; Greve, 2002). Line number 3 in Figure 5.3 indicates the contextual conditions that produce high spillover levels. Additionally, such mechanisms amplify the effect of market feedback on firm-level decisions not only because that feedback is more likely to be filtered when it travels through channels from donor to recipient organizations but also because the cognitive and network filters help firms make sense of ambiguous market signals. Institutional change is contingent on the sources and paths of influence and sense-making. Line number 4 in Figure 5.3 indicates the effect of the interaction between market feedback and firm-level filters on firm-level adoption. We considered the direct effect of market feedback and its indirect effect through firm-level filters as *institutional process*.

Internal firm characteristics such as firm size also influence the adoption of PA-form when firms reorganize in pursuit of superior efficiency such as the reduction of internal coordination costs. Line number 5 in Figure 5.3 indicates this effect. Finally such institutionally-driven mimicry produces variations that furnish a platform for subsequent negative selection and institutional developments. Line number 6 in Figure 5.3 indicates the effect of adoption decision on population-level variation. Framing of the institutional change in this fashion produces an integration of population ecology, institutional and inter-firm learning theory and leads the way to a fresh perspective on why organizations converge towards a structural standard.

The figure suggests that it is very hard for an organizational form to gain legitimacy and law-like status when market or population-level selection does not favor the form or powerful actors do not coerce organizations to adopt it. Figure 5.3, however, is an ideal-type display of complex institutional changes to illustrate the interaction of the competitive and institutional process in the absence of coercive isomorphism. In reality, the creation of firms with certain forms and associated differential survival and growth rates – population-level selection – affects population-level variation. The population-level variation such as the percentage of adopters also directly influences the adoption propensity. Besides market feedback and firm-level filters, other institutional factors influence adoption behavior. Extant studies on the diffusion of organizational practices extensively explored the effect of population level variation (for example, Davis, 1991; Palmer et al., 1993), firm-level filters (for example, Haunschild, 1993; Greve, 2000) and internal firm characteristics (for example, Davis and Greve, 1997). While controlling for those effects and the direct effect of firm-level filters on the adoption decision, this chapter focuses on effects of market feedback and its interaction with firm-level filters on the adoption of PA-form.

Industry-level Selection

Market feedback   Managers recognize what others are doing and observe how the market responds to their actions – the outcome of market selection. The market as a selection environment provides feedback about these actions by identifying firms that are sub-standard. The feedback is informative to managers especially when the market favors firms with certain attributes; in the present case, the market is conceived as a contesting arena for competing organizational forms (Nelson and Winter, 1982).

Firms tend to adopt a template when the market for competing organizational forms favors extant adopters of the template over non-adopters.

Such mimicry has been widely documented. Firm reaction to the market feedback has been illustrated by the imitation of the Toyota Manufacturing System among American and European automobile manufacturers (Pil and MacDuffie, 1996; Womack et al., 1990). Despite abundant examples of vicarious learning at the firm level and its relevance to mimetic isomorphism (Haunschild and Miner, 1997; Haveman, 1993), vicarious learning or inter-firm knowledge transfer is not explicitly incorporated in institutional theory. We suggest that market feedback favoring structural innovators conditions the cognitive premises of managers and other decision-makers through either direct exposure or through the influence of consultants and other trendsetters.

First, the market feedback leads decision-makers to believe that the adoption of the template enhances organizational performance. When very distinctive and visible templates emerge among organizations in an organizational field, firms will search for market responses to those elements. Market reactions favoring innovative organizations lead people to attribute organizational performance to the innovation and to regard its adoption as legitimate and taken-for-granted (Alchian, 1950; Fligstein, 1991). Such attribution and cognition increase the likelihood of imitation. However, firms adopt the template simply because earlier adopters are successful – not necessarily because they have any concrete, unequivocal evidence that the template would be economically efficient for them (Stearns and Allan, 1996).

Second, idea trendsetters such as academics, writers, consultants, and management gurus exploit the positive market response to innovation adopters to create shared knowledge and belief systems, which new institutionalism has emphasized (Berger and Luckmann, 1967; Meyer, 1994; Meyer and Rowan, 1977; Scott, 1995). Professionals as external consultants or internal experts might play an important role in trendsetting and legitimizing new templates (Abrahamson, 1997; Abrahamson and Fairchild, 1999). Though institutional writers recognize professionals as key agents of social change (for example, Meyer, 1994; Scott, 1995), they have been relatively silent about where such professionals get the idea of what is appropriate and what is not. Advocates of certain management styles, including Peters and Waterman (1982), Hammer and Champy (1993), and Senge (1990) are replete with such implicit and explicit feedback from the market regarding innovation. Managers and other members of the corporate world read those books and are taught or consulted by those professionals. In sum, professionals use information gleaned from market feedback to create a rhetoric justifying and rationalizing the use of the template that receives positive market feedback. Through various media, professionals change the cognitive premises of managers such that they come to believe in the benefits of the template. However, it is more likely to be a rational myth than truth.

Either survival or growth rates indicate market feedback. We choose to consider these two proxies of success because of the limitations imposed on the nature of our study, which extends over one hundred years. We do not know whether growth or survival is more informative or serves to better signal the advantage of a PA-form. Growth could also confound the effect of firm size, which we consider a major inducement of innovation.

Hypothesis 5.1a   The strength of market feedback on firms' survival favoring PA-firms is positively associated with the adoption of a PA-form.

Hypothesis 5.1b   The strength of market feedback on firms' growth favoring PA-firms is positively associated with the adoption of a PA-form.

Conditional Influences

The argument so far assumes that firms are equally exposed to developments and trends in the market. Both the industrial organization and early institutional literature presume such exposure to exist at the industry or population levels. However, several studies have suggested that competitive pressures (for example, Baum and Mezias, 1992; Formbrun and Zajac, 1987; Podolny, 1993) and interorganizational imitations (for example, Greve, 2000; Han, 1994) are localized on the basis of firm size, physical location, reputation, and cognitive identity. We can borrow their line of thinking and treat firm-specific conditions such as social or geographic setting of organizations as rendering institutional processes channeled rather than diluted. Spillovers are conditional upon such contextual factors. As firms are selectively exposed to other firms and their members, behaviors of the select other firms are imitated and used as an anchor in interpreting environments. The implication is that we need to expand our institutional theory to include firm-specific sources and paths of influence.

Foremost, firms are typically embedded in social networks (Granovetter, 1985). The institutional pressures that surface in a market travel more readily through contacts among firms that are somehow bound together through social contacts (Hansen, 1999; Haunschild, 1993). Organizations also interact with one another symbolically. Cognitive categorization theory suggests that firms group other firms on the basis of such attributes as market segment, size, location, labor, and so on and that firms often consider other firms with similar attributes as a reference group (for example, Alpert and Whetten, 1985; Porac and Thomas, 1990; Reger, 1987; Walton, 1986). Firms not only imitate the behaviors of their referent others (Strang and Meyer, 1993), but also interpret ambiguous environmental information such as market feedback on the basis of those behaviors (Porac and Thomas, 1990). Among possible attributes that firms use in their cognitive categorization process, the current study focuses on size similarity and geographical proximity. We extend our framework of institutional change by stipulating that the effect of market feedback on innovation adoption is conditional upon these three firm-specific factors i.e. network embeddedness, size similarity and location proximity.

Network embeddedness Let us first review extensively the interaction hypotheses involving networks. Market feedback does not exert identical influence on all organizations in an organizational field. Rather, organizations linked to innovation adopters are more susceptible to the information, since social networks function both as an information conduit and as channels that embody conformity pressure (Coleman et al., 1966; Mizruchi, 1993). Likewise, network embeddedness exerts greater impact on adoption decisions, as negative selection information gains in strength. In short, networks act as major spillover mechanisms.

First, firms that harbor newly acquired structural arrangements are bound to have members who might share their experiences with other individuals. They stand to transfer market feedback and their experience to people with whom they interact, especially those with whom they have embedded ties – contacts based on trust and mutuality (Levitt and March, 1988; Rogers, 1995). When firms are linked through such personally mediated ties, they are more likely to be the recipient of market information and are bound to give more weight to such information (compare Fligstein, 1991; Haunschild and Beckman, 1998; March, 1994). In other words, information transfer among linked firms strengthens the effect of market feedback on innovation adoption. If social networks function as information conduits in this manner, what matters is the *total number* of innovation adopters with which a focal organization is linked. As the number of relevant contacts increases exposure to market feedback, the number will moderate the effect of market feedback on PA-form adoption.

Second, social networks also influence people in organizations, as individuals in their external networks reveal opinions about appropriate managerial and organizational templates and express salient expectations regarding their compliance (March, 1994). Organizations tied to innovation adopters are more likely to receive conformity pressure, which is created on the basis of market signals favoring innovation adopters. If social networks deliver conformity pressure in this manner, the *proportion* of adopters among firms with which a focal firm has contact is salient (Strang and Tuma, 1993). Using the sheer *number* of adopters in a focal firm's network as an indication of normative influence is inappropriate, since it is assumed that the focal firm is influenced only by adopters in its network, not by non-adopters. If each and every firm in a focal firm's network expresses some normative expectation, it is rather obvious that adopters signal adoption of a novel template, while non-adopters signal the opposite. As the positive market feedback favoring adopters becomes stronger, the proportion of adopters within a focal firm's network will exert a stronger influence on the focal firm's adoption decision. This is because the adopters express higher confidence in the form and exert stronger conformity pressures. This reasoning leads to the following hypotheses.

Hypothesis 5.2a   Market feedback and the total number of direct ties that a focal firm has with adopting organizations will have a positive interaction effect on the adoption of a PA-form.

Hypothesis 5.2b   Market feedback and the proportion of adopters among other firms with which a focal firm has a network tie will have a positive interaction effect on the adoption of a PA-form.

Size similarity   Market feedback about a structural template is more salient if it originates from similar kinds of firms. Such firms would fit the notion of reference groups. The concept has been advanced in the psychological literature and in identity theory (for example, Burke and Reitzes, 1981; Foote, 1951; Stryker, 1968) to describe three functions: a normative function in which individuals rely on norms to evaluate behavior and performance, a cognitive function in which individuals make sense of their world on the basis of what others sharing identity are doing, and a comparative function to furnish a benchmark for making comparative evaluations. The notion could be extended to firms (compare Fiegenbaum and Thomas, 1995; Haveman, 1993; Peteraf and Shanley, 1997).

Because field environments are complex, with heterogeneous firms and a variety of organizational niches, managers sort other firms into groups on the basis of salient traits that differentiate one group from another (Peteraf and Shanley, 1997; Porac and Thomas, 1990). This cognitive categorization allows managers to cope with environmental complexity and uncertainty by restricting their attention to limited neighborhoods of action (Levinthal and March, 1993). As organizations with similar size are likely to compete for the same type of clientele, face similar governance, globalization and expansion challenges and recruit comparable junior professionals (for example, Baum and Mezias, 1992), firms are likely to partition other firms on the basis of size and consider other similar-sized firms as a reference group (Walton, 1986).

Because firms scan and make sense of their environment on the basis of the behaviors of their reference group (Porac and Thomas, 1990), behaviors of similar sized firms can function as a lever that moderates the effect of market feedback on a focal firm's adoption decision. Even when a market has positively rewarded innovation adopters in the past, a focal firm may not perceive the innovation as beneficial or may not recognize the market signals, if similar sized firms have not yet adopted the innovation. In contrast, a firm is likely to be more susceptible to market feedback when more similar sized firms have already adopted the innovation. Such behaviors of similar sized firms function as an anchor when firms seek to interpret market responses to specific innovations. The percentage of adopters among similar sized firms can summarize the average behavioral pattern of the reference group. This reasoning provides the following hypothesis.

Hypothesis 5.3 Market feedback and the percentage of PA-form adopters among firms having a size similar to that of the focal firm will have a positive interaction effect on the focal firm's adoption of a PA-form.

Locational proximity Another important criterion that firms use in categorizing other firms is locational proximity (for example, Porac et al., 1989; Reger, 1987; Walton, 1986). Professional service firms that are geographically proximate are likely to have the same type of clientele and are more like to interact with one another both directly and symbolically. Firms are likely to scan and interpret their environment on the basis of the behaviors of peers who are in their immediate vicinity (compare Jaffe et al., 1993; Podolny and Shepard, 1996). As those regionally neighboring firms are windows through which a focal firm makes sense of environments, it shows greater sensitivity to market feedback when a higher percentage of its proximate firms have already adopted a specific form. In other words, the percentage of adopters among co-located firms moderates the effect of market feedback on adoption decisions. This reasoning leads to the following hypothesis.

Hypothesis 5.4 Market feedback and the percentage of PA-form adopters among firms that are geographically proximate with the focal firm will have a positive interaction effect on the focal firm's adoption of a PA-form.

METHODS

Dependent Variable

We identified the *adoption* of a PA-form by investigating the status of accountants in the firm. If a firm had at least one associate accountant for the first time in its history, we flagged the adoption of a PA-form.

Predictor Variables

1. Market feedback   Two indicators were developed as proxies for *market feedback*. The first is the differential survival rate (*MSSURVIV*) and the second the differential growth rate (*MSGROWTH*). We employed two measures to produce a more robust test of the hypotheses, particularly when doubt existed that the differential growth rate confounded the imitation and size argument.

When calculating the measures, we compounded the survival rate or average growth rate of each observation period of each group, that is, PA-firms and non-PA-firms, from 1925 to the year under consideration.[2] *MSSURVIV* is the compounded survival rate of PA-firms divided by that of non-PA-firms, and *MSGROWTH* is the compounded growth rate of PA-firms divided by that of non-PA-firms. These indicate the degree of survival or growth rate that PA-firms enjoyed over non-PA-firms until the year under consideration. Formally,

$$MSSURVIV_t = \prod_{i=1}^{t} SRPA_i \bigg/ \prod_{i=1}^{t} SRNONPA_i,$$

where i and t are time, $SRPA_i$ is the survival rate of PA-firms during the period of time $i-1$ and i, and $SRNONPA_i$ is that of non-PA-firms.

$$MSGROWTH_t = \prod_{i=1}^{t} GRPA_i \bigg/ \prod_{i=1}^{t} GRNONPA_i,$$

$$\text{where } GRPA_i = \sum_{PA} Size_{k,i} \bigg/ \sum_{PA} Size_{k,i-1}, \text{ and}$$

$$GRNONPA_i = \sum_{NONPA} Size_{k,i} \bigg/ \sum_{NONPA} Size_{k,i-1}.$$

$GRPA_i$ is the average growth rate weighted by the size of PA-firms during time $i-1$ to i and $GRNONPA_i$ is that of non-PA-firms. $Size_k$ is size of firm k measured by the number of accountants who were affiliated with firm k.

In calculating survival rates and growth rates, we excluded firms that changed their organizational structures in a corresponding period.

2. Social networks   We measured the *exposure to adoption norm* by tracing the careers of accountants. One important way in which accountants develop social networks is by changing their organizational affiliations. When two accountants have an affiliation with a firm during any overlapping period, they are assumed to have network ties with each other thereafter. We counted the number of ties ($NTIES_{n,t}$) that accountant n had at time t with accountants in other firms. Among the ties, we also counted the number of accountants who were working for PA-firms at time t ($PATIES_{n,t}$). For each accountant, we divided *PATIES* by *NTIES* to create exposure to the adoption norm at time t. By aggregating individual exposure to the firm level, we developed a proxy for firm level exposure to adoption norm. Formally,

$$EXPOSURE\ TO\ ADOPTION\ NORM_{k,t} = \sum_{n=1}^{Size_{k,t}} [PATIES_{n,t} / NTIES_{n,t}],$$

where n is an accountant and $Size_{k,t}$ is the number of accountants of firm k at time t. Two implications should be noted regarding this measurement. First, we did not consider indirect network ties, not only because direct ties are considered as more important channels through which normative information travels and conformity pressures are activated than indirect ties (compare Palmer et al., 1993), but also because considering indirect ties complicates the measures. Second, any accountant outside a particular firm can contribute more than one tie to the index. For example, if accountant C had network ties with A and B who were at a particular firm at time t, C contributed two ties to the firm at time t. This is also plausible for inferring the presence of conformity pressures.

We measured the *total ties to adopters* by counting the number of ties that accountants at a specific firm have with accountants in PA-firms. It is the summation of $PATIES_{n,t}$ – which is used for measuring exposure to adoption norm – over all accountants at the specific firm.

3. Percentage of adopters among similar sized firms   We defined size similarity in terms of the ratio: size of other office/size of focal office. Firm size was measured by its number of accountants. All values that fell within the range of .5 to 2.0 comprised a size cohort. The cohort was then used to determine which percentage of similar sized firms had a PA-form. We tested other ranges such as 1/3 to 3, 1/4 to 4, and so on. The range of .5 to 2.0 provided the best goodness of fit.

4. Percentage of adopters among geographically proximate firms   We measured the variable by the percentage of PA-form adopters in the province that a focal firm had. We tried other geographic classifications of the Dutch territory including the four largest Dutch cities vs. other regions and west, south, north versus east. The province specification provided the best goodness of fit.

Control Variables

We controlled for the *percentage of PA-firms*, which is measured by the number of PA-firms divided by the number of all firms in the population (Fligstein, 1985; Palmer et al., 1993), since the variable can indicate institutionalization of a PA-form and thus enhance adoption rate of a PA-form.

We controlled for the following firm characteristics: organizational size, age, the number of offices, location and previous organizational changes. We measured *organizational size* by counting the number of accountants who were affiliated with the firm. Size indicates not only the scale and complexity of the organization but also its visibility to external constituencies and, thus, susceptibility to the institutional environment (Dobbin et al., 1988; Edelman, 1990). Larger firms are likely to have stronger motives to create a more efficient governance structure and to endure stronger institutional pressure.

Organizational age was measured by years elapsed after founding. Age has been considered as a key antecedent of organizational change, as age, indicating increased inertia, may have a negative effect on the adoption of the PA-form (Hannan and Freeman, 1984). We controlled the *number of domestic offices*, and the number of establishments in the four largest Dutch cities (Amsterdam, Rotterdam, Utrecht, and The Hague).

Also controlled were the *cumulative number of acquisitions, splits, and name changes* a firm experienced. If organizations have a proclivity toward organizational change, the number of prior changes may be positively associated with their propensity to adopt the PA-form. When two or more firms joined together, the event was coded as an acquisition. When the resulting firm adopted one of the pre-existing names, the event was coded as an acquisition without name change. The firm that maintained its name was coded as an acquirer, whereas the others were treated as acquired firms. When two or more firms joined together and adopted a new name, the event was coded as an acquisition with name change. Continuation of the firm was assigned to the largest of the involved firms and other smaller counterparts were treated as acquired firms. When the size of the involved firms was equal, the new firm was labeled as the continuation of the firm whose name came first in the alphabet.

Organizational splits were coded when at least two partners left and formed a new firm. *Name changes* were coded when the name of a firm differed from its previous one, provided two-thirds or more of its partners continued their affiliation with the firm. The name changes did not include mutations due to acquisition or cosmetic name changes, such as modifications in the order of named partners. Neither did we treat the addition of the Dutch equivalents of 'Accountants' or 'Registered' and 'Limited Liability' to the original as a name change.

Descriptions of the history of the Dutch accounting industry (Zeff et al., 1992) provided important historical changes that may affect adoption rates. We controlled for proxies of 'history', including World War II, Indonesian independence in 1949, and significant changes in regulations that governed the accounting profession and its clients. The effects of World War II and Indonesia's independence are short-lived in this context. World War II was specified as having effects during the period 1941–47, and the independence of Indonesia during the period 1949–51. We also controlled for the two significant regulatory changes the industry experienced. The Act on Annual Financial Statements of Enterprises was approved in 1970 and took effect in 1971. From 1984 onwards, definitive guidelines for auditing were promulgated and enforced by the NIvRA (the exclusive professional association) in collaboration with the Justice Ministry (Zeff et al., 1992).

We also controlled for the length of observation intervals. As mentioned before, the data have non-uniform observation intervals from one to five years. Since the odds of PA adoption may be positively related with the length of the observation interval, we included the natural logarithm of the length of the observation interval (measured in years). We also estimated models with four dummies for each interval length. The results were not substantially different from what we have reported here.

Model and Estimation

Empirical analysis of this study deals with time-varying conditions that lead up to the adoption of a PA-form. Firms that dissolved or were acquired by other firms before adopting a PA-form were treated as right-censored. Firms that were extant in 1990, but did not adopt the innovation, were also right-censored. Having adopted the PA-form, a firm was removed from the data set since it was no longer a candidate for such mimetic adoption. In the event history analysis, we included all P-firms and sole proprietorships, since they were at risk of adopting PA-form. Most firms changed their form from the P-form or sole proprietorship to the PA-form by hiring new associate accountants rather than by reclassifying some existing partners to associates. Single proprietorships were at risk of adopting the PA-form, since they also could hire new associate accountants and thus adopt the PA-form. In other words, single proprietorship at time t can become PA-firms at time $t + d$ by hiring associate accountants during the period d. In fact, our data indicated that 96 single proprietorships adopted the PA-form by hiring new associates.

Since our data involves time aggregation and right-censoring, the estimates from continuous event history analysis are at best biased (Petersen, 1991; Petersen and Koput, 1992). As in Chapter 4, we employed discrete event history analysis. A discrete-time hazard rate is defined by:

$$P_{it} = \Pr[T_i = t / T_i \geq t, X_{it}],$$

where T is the discrete random variable giving the uncensored time of adoption. P_{it} is the conditional probability that firm i will adopt a PA-form at time t, given that it has not already adopted it.

Specifically, we used the complementary log-log function that provides a consistent estimate of the continuous-time, proportional hazards parameters regardless of the interval length or the size of failure rate (Allison, 1982; Petersen and Koput, 1992). The model is expressed as:

$$P_{it} = 1 - exp\ [- exp(\alpha_t + X_{it}\beta)],\ \text{or}$$
$$log\ [- log(1 - P_{it})] = \alpha_t + X_{it}\beta,$$

where α_t is a function of time, X_{it} is a row vector of the firm i's state variable at time t, and β is a column vector of coefficients. In estimating the model, we specify

$$\alpha_t = \alpha_0 + \alpha_1 log(d) + \alpha_2 log(\text{organizational age}),$$

where d is the length of observation interval.

All independent variables were lagged by one observation period. In other words, population-level variables and firm i's state variables at time t were used as independent variables to explain the adoption during time t and $t + d$. Thus, we included firms with a single accountant in the risk set. A procedure with complementary log-log function in SAS (Allison, 1995) was used to estimate the models.

RESULTS

Figure 5.4 illustrates average growth rates of P-firms and PA-firms weighted by their firm size for each observation interval. PA-firms enjoyed higher growth rates than P-firms in every observation interval except for 1982–86.

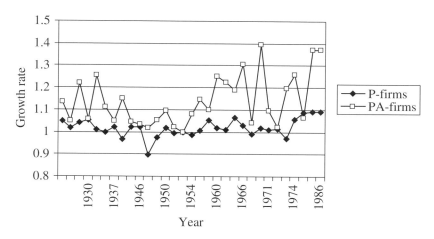

Figure 5.4   Growth rate of P-firms and PA-firms

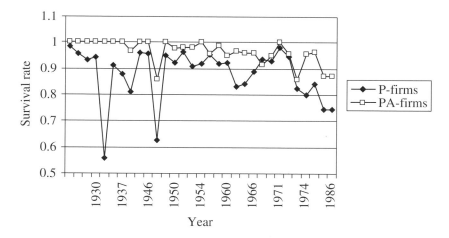

Figure 5.5   Survival rate of P-firms and PA-firms

Figure 5.5 shows survival rates of P-firms and PA-firms for each observation interval. PA-firms enjoyed higher survival rates than P-firms in every observation internal. Both figures suggest that population-level selection has favored PA-form over P-form over a long period of time. It is very likely that the strong market feedback triggered an institutional isomorphic process.

Table 5.1 lists the means, standard deviations, and the correlation matrix of the variables that were used in this study. These statistics were based on

Table 5.1   Means, standard deviations and correlations

Variables	Means	s.d.	1	2	3	4	5	6	7
1. *PA adoption*	0.06	0.24							
2. *Market feedback* (differential growth rate)	7.84	6.67	0.07						
3. *Market feedback* (differential servival rate)	8.13	4.44	0.08	0.95					
4. *Total number of ties to adopters/100*	0.18	0.36	0.08	−0.11	−0.16				
5. *Exposure to adoption norm*	0.26	0.43	0.12	0.19	0.19	0.04			
6. *% Similar-sized firms*	0.08	0.12	0.29	0.04	0.06	0.15	0.16		
7. *% Geographically proximate firms*	0.17	0.10	0.03	0.05	0.15	0.03	−0.02	0.13	
8. *Percentage of PA-firms*	0.18	0.05	0.03	0.11	0.32	0.00	−0.15	0.12	0.47
9. *Organizational size*	1.50	5.80	0.14	0.05	0.05	0.03	0.12	0.32	0.04
10. *Ln* (organizational age)	1.72	1.12	−0.03	−0.05	−0.06	0.17	0.04	0.10	0.09
11. *No. of acquisitions with name change*	0.03	0.30	0.03	0.03	0.04	0.03	0.06	0.24	0.03
12. *No. of acquisitions without name change*	0.06	0.42	0.06	−0.03	−0.03	0.06	0.12	0.18	0.02
13. *No. of splits*	0.01	0.12	0.02	0.00	−0.01	0.01	0.05	0.13	0.00
14. *No. of name changes*	0.09	0.31	0.09	0.00	0.01	0.18	0.10	0.19	0.04
15. *No. of domestic offices*	1.32	1.18	0.19	0.11	0.10	0.07	0.16	0.42	0.13
16. *No. of offices in four largest Dutch cities*	0.54	0.58	0.08	−0.28	−0.28	0.10	0.00	0.19	0.70
17. *World War II* (1 if 1940<Year<1946)	0.02	0.14	0.00	−0.12	−0.15	0.04	0.00	0.00	−0.01
18. *Indonesia's independence* (1 if 1948<Year<1952)	0.06	0.23	0.01	−0.19	−0.17	−0.05	−0.04	0.04	−0.02
19. *Regulation of 1971−73* (1 if Year>1971)	0.25	0.44	0.05	0.87	0.76	−0.07	0.17	0.04	−0.00
20. *Regulation of 1984−89* (1 if Year>1984)	0.05	0.22	0.07	0.56	0.55	−0.04	0.09	−0.02	−0.04
21. *Ln* (length of observation interval)	0.62	0.49	0.06	0.39	0.33	−0.01	0.07	0.03	0.03

961 firms (4456 firm-intervals). Among the statistical findings, a very high correlation between differential growth rate and differential survival rate was observed. Among 301 adopters, 4 firms were omitted from this study because they adopted the structure in 1925. An additional 24 firms were deleted because they were already organized with a PA-structure in the very first year of their observed existence. We could not create firm-level factors

8	9	10	11	12	13	14	15	16	17	18	19	20
−0.01												
0.07	−0.01											
0.00	0.07	0.09										
0.00	0.06	0.25	0.06									
−0.01	0.02	0.12	−0.01	0.42								
0.02	0.04	0.26	0.05	0.17	0.13							
0.00	0.50	0.01	0.19	0.07	0.02	0.12						
−0.07	0.14	0.06	0.05	0.04	0.02	0.08	0.30					
−0.04	0.00	0.05	−0.01	0.00	−0.01	0.02	−0.01	0.04				
−0.08	0.00	−0.12	−0.01	0.04	0.03	0.00	0.01	0.10	−0.03			
0.01	0.04	−0.01	0.02	−0.03	0.00	−0.01	0.09	−0.22	−0.08	−0.14		
−0.03	0.06	−0.09	−0.02	−0.01	−0.01	0.00	0.06	−0.14	−0.03	−0.06	0.40	
0.06	0.03	−0.01	−0.05	−0.01	−0.01	0.02	0.04	−0.07	0.28	−0.22	0.36	0.36

because information was lacking as to whether these firms were actually founded as PA-firms, or whether they were founded without a PA-form and adopted it before they were first observed in the data matrix. The remaining number of adopters in this study was 273.

Table 5.2 presents the results from a regression analysis based on a complementary log-log specification. First, the first two models show the

Table 5.2   Regression analyses of PA adoption (4456 firm-intervals: 273 adopters)

Variables	Model 1	Model 2	Model 3
Intercept	−4.820***	−4.811***	−4.934***
	(.397)	(.399)	(.403)
Market feedback (differential growth rate)	.064***		.067***
	(.025)		(.026)
Market feedback (differential survival rate)		.078**	
		(.031)	
Differential growth rate total number of ties to adopters/100*			.026**
			(.013)
Differential growth rate exposure to adoption norm*			−.012
			(.022)
Differential growth rate% similar-sized firms*			
Differential growth rate% geographically proximate firms*			
Total number of ties to adopters/100	.116***	.114***	.648***
	(.044)	(.044)	(.251)
Exposure to adoption norm	.612***	.624***	.665***
	(.154)	(.154)	(.245)
% Similar-sized firms	1.940***	1.942***	1.896***
	(.715)	(.715)	(.619)
% Geographically proximate firms	2.149*	2.147*	2.237*
	(1.227)	(1.228)	(1.206)
Percentage of PA-firms	7.080***	5.821***	7.782***
	(2.021)	(2.036)	(2.035)
Organizational size	.249***	.245**	.281***
	(.096)	(.096)	(.086)
Ln (organizational age)	−.251***	−.249***	−.263***
	(.059)	(.059)	(.060)
No. of acquisitions with name change	−.172	−.172	−.142
	(.187)	(.187)	(.186)
No. of acquisitions without name change	.189	.185	.201
	(.129)	(.130)	(.130)
No. of splits	−.181	−.155	−.150
	(.352)	(.349)	(.349)
No. of name changes	.372***	.365**	.380***
	(.144)	(.145)	(.145)
No. of domestic offices	.033	.036	.031
	(.043)	(.043)	(.045)
No. of offices in four largest Dutch cities	.323*	.324*	.347**
	(.173)	(.174)	(.168)
World War II (1 if 1940<Year<1946)	.307	.348	.424
	(.463)	(.467)	(.464)

Table 5.2 (continued)

Variables	Model 1	Model 2	Model 3
Indonesia's independence (1 if 1948< Year<1952)	.423*	.398	.413
	(.254)	(.253)	(.256)
Regulation of 1971−73 (1 if Year>1971)	−.530*	−.273	−.460
	(.321)	(.248)	(.320)
Regulation of 1984–89 (1 if Year>1984)	.308	.317	.232
	(.283)	(.283)	(.287)
Ln (length of observation interval)	.178	.203	.104
	(.160)	(.159)	(.161)
Log-likelihood	−935.6	−935.7	−932.9
Degrees of freedom	19	19	21
chi-square test comparing with Model 1 (d.f.)			5.4 (2)*

Variables	Model 4	Model 5	Model 6
Intercept	−4.804***	−4.891***	−4.960***
	(.395)	(.407)	(.409)
Market feedback (differential growth rate)	.060**	.079***	.079***
	(.025)	(.030)	(.030)
Market feedback (differential survival rate)			
Differential growth rate total number of ties to adopters/100*			.021**
			(.010)
Differential growth rate exposure to adopted norm*			−.014
			(.022)
Differential growth rate % similar-sized firms*	.034***		.036**
	(.011)		(.015)
Differential growth rate % geographically proximate firms*		.095***	.107***
		(.030)	(.037)
Total number of ties to adopters/100	.118***	.116***	.600**
	(.045)	(.044)	(.265)
Exposure to adoption norm	.621***	.617***	.694***
	(.154)	(.154)	(.249)
% Similar-sized firms	1.644**	1.934***	1.643**
	(.803)	(.713)	(.671)
% Geographically proximate firms	2.412*	1.151	1.513
	(1.250)	(1.641)	(1.617)
Percentage of PA-firms	7.259***	6.520***	7.275***
	(2.018)	(2.136)	(2.142)
Organizational size	.253***	.250***	.266***
	(.097)	(.095)	(.091)
Ln (organizational age)	−.241***	−.250***	−.250***
	(.060)	(.059)	(.060)

Table 5.2 (continued)

Variables	Model 4	Model 5	Model 6
No. of acquisitions with name change	−.178	−.172	−.155
	(.187)	(.185)	(.186)
No. of acquisitions without name change	.193	.185	.199
	(.130)	(.130)	(.130)
No. of splits	−.181	−.176	−.124
	(.357)	(.349)	(.347)
No. of name changes	.356**	.360**	.336**
	(.144)	(.145)	(.147)
No. of domestic offices	.026	.038	.029
	(.044)	(.043)	(.046)
No. of offices in four largest Dutch cities	.360**	.313*	.394**
	(.176)	(.174)	(.172)
World War II (1 if 1940<Year<1946)	.300	.280	.380
	(.462)	(.465)	(.464)
Indonesia's independence (1 if 1948< Year<1952)	.428*	.416	.403
	(.254)	(.254)	(.256)
Regulation of 1971−73 (1 if Year>1971)	−.550*	−.519	−.469
	(.323)	(.321)	(.322)
Regulation of 1984−89 (1 if Year>1984)	.338	.281	.258
	(.286)	(.286)	(.295)
Ln (length of observation interval)	.183	.187	.121
	(.160)	(.160)	(.162)
Log-likelihood	−932.0	−932.1	−927.3
Degrees of freedom	20	20	23
chi-square test comparing with Model 1 (d.f.)	7.2 (1)***	7.0 (1)***	16.6(4)***

Note:*: $p<.10$; **: $p<.05$; ***: $p<.01$ (two-tailed test); standard errors in parentheses under parameter.

analysis when differential growth rate and differential survival rate are inserted separately in each model. A very high correlation (0.95) between market feedback measures, that is, the growth and survival rate, suggests that the results were not sensitive to the choice of measures. Since model 1 provided a slightly better goodness of fit, we use that model as our baseline model. Models 1 and 2 show the effect of two market feedback indicators while controlling for other variables. In models 3, 4, and 5, we added interaction terms to show their explanatory power for testing hypotheses 5.2a, 5.2b, 5.3, and 5.4. We included all interaction terms in model 6. The chi-square tests at the bottom of Table 5.2 show that the addition of interaction terms, either individually or collectively, significantly improved the goodness of fit.

The coefficients for market feedback support hypotheses 5.1a and 5.1b in all models: the strength of market feedback slanted towards PA-firms was positively associated with adoption propensity. These results indicated that organizational decision-makers are more likely to adopt a PA-form when the market and their customers send a strong signal by shifting their demand to adopters.

Results of model 1 and 2 indicate that all firm-level filters significantly enhance adoption propensity. Firms where accountants had more network ties to adopters and were exposed to stronger adoption norms adopted the PA-form more frequently. The percentage of adopters among similar sized firms, and the percentage of adopters among physically proximate peer firms induce adoption propensity.

The interactions between market feedback and the total number of ties to adopters were also positive and statistically significant for models 3 and 6. Although the incremental chi-square at the bottom of model 3 was significant at $p < .10$, it became significant at the 5 per cent level when the second interaction term from model 3 was omitted. The results supported Hypothesis 5.2a. However the interactions between market feedback and exposure to adoption norm were not statistically significant. The results did not support Hypothesis 5.2b.

The interaction between market feedback and the percentage of adopters among similar sized firms had positive and statistically significant effects on a PA-form adoption in models 4 and 6. The incremental chi-square test as shown at the bottom of model 4, which compares model 4 with model 1, suggested that the addition of this term significantly improved the goodness of fit. The results provided therefore strong support for Hypothesis 5.3.

The interaction term between market feedback and the percentage of adopters among geographically proximate firms also had positive and statistically significant coefficients in models 5 and 6. Incremental chi-square test at the bottom of model 5, which compares model 4 with model 1, suggested that the addition of the interaction term significantly improved the goodness of fit. The results provided strong support for Hypothesis 5.4.

Besides firm-level filters, several control variables had statistically significant effects on PA-form adoption. The percentage of PA-firms in the industry had positive and statistically significant effect on the adoption propensity. In all models, the coefficients of organizational size were positive and statistically significant. The natural logarithm of organizational age had a negative and significant coefficient. This indicates that younger firms are more likely to adopt PA-forms. Among four proxies of prior organizational change, the number of previous name changes was the only variable that was significantly associated with PA-form adoption. The positive coefficient indicates that the number of previous name changes was positively related with

PA-form adoption. The number of offices in the four largest Dutch cities was also positively related with PA-form adoption in all models. Other control variables did not have a consistent effect on the adoption across models.

DISCUSSION AND CONCLUSIONS

To explain institutional changes, the present chapter proposed a framework that combined population ecology and institutional theory by using the concept of market feedback. By analyzing the evolution of the Dutch accounting industry, we showed that population-level or market-level selection has favored PA-form over P-form over a long period of time. This chapter investigated the direct effect of the market feedback and its interaction with firm-level filters on the adoption of PA-form, while controlling for internal firm characteristics, population-level variations, and main effects of firm-level filters. First, we proposed that the market feedback in favor of the new organizational form would positively influence the adoption decision. This prediction was strongly supported by our findings. Second, we hypothesized that social networks, size similarity and physical co-location would interact with market feedback in producing higher adoption levels. This prediction was also strongly supported by our findings.

The implications of the research presented here are broad. First, we investigated a very important but largely neglected mechanism in institutional change – market feedback. That concept enabled us to more meaningfully integrate population ecology and institutional theory for uncovering institutional changes. The results of this study imply that information from population-level selection constitutes an important legitimizing force of an organizational form and leads professionals into creating a rationalized myth. The legitimacy enhanced by positive market feedback in turn stimulates diffusion. Population ecologists (Hannan and Freeman, 1984) have argued that the environment maximizes its ecological rationality by selecting out those firms possessing an ecologically superior form. They later contended that diminished mortality conveys enhanced legitimacy (for example, Hannan et al., 1995), but the primacy for institutional change resides in the environment, not in the strategic choices of managers. The present study, however, shows that both competitive process at the population level and adaptive adoption at the firm level contributed to institutional change as the dominant form evolves from the P-form to the PA-form. More importantly, this study suggests that competitive processes at the population level trigger institutional processes, which in turn change population-level variation. Indeed the observed 'structural' spillovers in our study suggest that the population will be transformed in a way that cannot be captured by the notion of negative selection.

This study invites a new dialogue between institutional theory and population ecology by integrating the two research streams better to capture institutional change. The dialogue so far centers on the issue of whether the density of organizations with an organizational form indicates its legitimacy (for example, Baum and Powell, 1995; Carroll and Hannan, 1989; Zucker, 1989) or whether the adoption of legitimized forms enhances survival chances (for example, Singh et al., 1986). Our study suggests that summary information of market selection in prior time periods conveys legitimacy of organizational forms and thus influences adoption decision by managers.

Second, we incorporated firm-level filters at the firm–environment interface. While most of the previous studies about diffusion filters have investigated their main effect on innovation adoption, we explored their interaction with market feedback on firm-level adoption while controlling for the main effects. The migration of professionals among firms leads to a form of ongoing embeddedness (Granovetter, 1985), in which ensuing network ties function as a route for information transfers and as a normative context for organizational actions. The present study showed that social ties with innovators strengthen the influence of market feedback on adoption. Similar interpretations can be advanced for the role of size similarity and geographical proximity. Because similar sized firms and geographically proximate firms provide windows through which a focal firm interprets population-level selection, that firm is more susceptible to market feedback when a higher percentage of its 'reference group' had already adopted the PA-form. While size similarity and physical proximity are drivers of inter-firm networking and are often linked to networking, we isolated them as a driver of symbolic interactions and documented their main and interactive affects with market feedback over and beyond those of social ties.

Parenthetically, the institutionalization observed in this industry reveals a strong size contingency. The accounting industry is characterized by a duality in that we find a bimodal size distribution. As we have shown, size figures prominently in our results regarding structural innovation. In 1990 more than four-fifths of the sector was without a PA structure, arguably because they are small (mostly single proprietorships), quite distinct from the rest of the sector, and so impervious to the market selection effects experienced by their larger counterparts. Presumably this duality in size also explains the contingent nature of institutionalization as revealed by Figure 5.2 regarding the market share vs. proportion of firms measure. While the market share grows, the number of PA-firms remains flat from 1937 onwards.

Weaknesses in this study provide several suggestions for future research. First, we investigated the diffusion of a PA-form within the Dutch accounting sector. However, as so many network studies, we face the 'boundary specification problem' (Laumann et al., 1989), since institutional processes can operate across borders and industries. For instance, Dutch accounting firms can be influenced by how foreign accounting firms and other kinds of domestic professional firms such as law and consulting partnerships were structured. The present study could not investigate the institutional processes across national and sectoral boundaries due to data limitation. Future research could explore such higher-level processes, especially in this age of technological and market convergence.

Second, we suggested that professionals are likely to exploit market feedback in legitimizing new social arrangements. Due to lack of relevant data, we could not directly test this assumption. Future research might explore whether the level of positive rhetoric around structural innovations is positively associated with the strength of market feedback favoring innovative firms. For instance, content analysis conducted by Abrahamson (1997) and Abrahamson and Fairchild (1999) could be integrated with market feedback information. More generally, future research should investigate what kinds of input professionals are leveraging in justifying new organizational practices.

Third, we assumed that all social contacts are equally influential in disseminating innovation-related information and conformity pressure. An incumbent is influenced by a number of contacts in his environment – 'alters' in the network lingo. A focal firm is more susceptible to external influence coming from a connected alter when the connected alter is similar or is located in the same geographical area. The present study made significant contributions to a firm's innovative receptivity as a function of its network. We partitioned the effects on imitation by uncovering the effects that are due to networks, versus those that are due to size similarity and physical proximity. However, we need to include other significant effects as well – for example strategic similarity and absorptive capacity. We did not use such data because they are hard to come by. However, future research could explore these research questions by using spatial heterogeneous diffusion models suggested by Greve (2000) and Strang and Tuma (1993).

NOTES

1. New institutionalism attends to organizational fields as a unit of analysis, which has been defined as 'those organizations that, in the aggregate, constitute a recognized area of institutional life: *key suppliers, resource and product customers*, regulatory agencies, and other organizations that produce similar services or products' (DiMaggio and Powell, 1983: 148; emphasis added). Though several institutional scholars, such as Meyer and Scott

(1983) and DiMaggio and Powell (1983), have recognized the significance of powerful suppliers and customers in the institutional process, they have ignored the role of small suppliers and customers.

2. The underlying assumption of the market feedback measures is that all information in the past equally contributes to the strength of market feedback. An alternative assumption is that recent market selection outcomes provide more valuable information on the advantage of a PA-form than do older ones. Since we did not have an a priori rationale on how many years we should consider or how much weight we should assign to each year, we tested 60 specifications for this possibility from one year to 60 years. Sensitivity analysis using various time lag specifications shows that specifications of a lag exceeding 18 years brought about the same general pattern of results reported here. Independent of the measurement of market feedback, the other variables related to hypotheses had significant and predicted effect on the PA adoption.

6. Mergers and acquisitions: strategic and organizational fit?

INTRODUCTION

This chapter examines what happens to firms emerging out of a merger or acquisition (M&A). We claim that the match between merging firms, together with their prior acquisitive growth history, are crucial for the fate of the newly created organization.

Organizational founding is typically associated with entrepreneurs, but many firms arise out of existing firms through spin-offs or M&As. What sets the former classes apart from M&A is inheritance: the skills that endow an M&A-based firm originate from the parents, while *de novo* firms have to build capabilities from scratch. Whether new firms formed by the fusion of two existing firms benefit from previously acquired assets hinges partly on the combination and commingling of previously separate bundles of resources. The question that we should ask is: Under what conditions will the combining of such bundles yield distinct benefits for the new firm?

When exploring the fusion of two firms, we should consider a couple of distinct aspects that researchers have addressed. During the 1980s and 1990s much of the concern has been with the degree to which diversification and relatedness prevailed ex ante. Mergers were viewed as an event which could affect the abnormal returns of the constituting firms, depending on whether they belonged to similar or different sectors, for example two, three or four-digit SIC sectors. The greater the relatedness as inferred by the similarity of sectors, the more the two firms could achieve 'synergies' or exploit economies of scope. In those studies, the post-acquisition integration process was presumed to be captured by the expected challenges as inferred by the abnormal returns as manifest in the financial markets, with the greater the unrelatedness, the stronger the complications. Perhaps, if the concern is not with abnormal returns, but with the likelihood of survival, that focus on ex ante conditions might not be so deficient. In the results that we report, the M&As are examined with reference to the survival prospects of the resulting firm. Presumably, if those ex ante conditions bode well for the two firms involved, the post-acquisition process has been well managed by the new firm's management.

However, most of those so-called 'event' studies remained agnostic about the post-acquisition integration process. By the turn of the century, the shift in research from ex ante to ex post inquiries drove researchers towards the blending of the two firms – for example the learning that firms enjoy when they go to successive merger events, thus accumulating a body of routines for integrating the due diligence with assimilation of the two firms. The positive or negative benefits accrue to firms, not only because the due diligence minimizes adverse selection, but also because it assures the likelihood of post-acquisition savings and synergistic benefits. The current research has addressed such questions as illustrated by the work of Zollo and his colleagues (Zollo and Winter, 2002; Puranam et al., 2006). Any M&A combines divergent cultures, strategic orientations and practices into a new configuration and thus creates intra-firm variations. Friction between existing factions is prone to occur (Phillips, 1994; Wulf, 2004). Even M&As that took place many years or even decades ago, like those leading to the creation of RJR-Nabisco and Royal Dutch-Shell still appear to encompass multiple legacies. The magnitude of tensions at these corporations might be a function of the dissimilarity of cultures and practices of their ancestors.

Much of the research on the background of the two merging partners involved in an M&A and their post-merger outcomes resides in the literature on finance and accounting and draws heavily on the capital asset pricing model. For example studies that examine the size equality of merging firms versus those that are unequal in the assets they bring to the M&A table reveal varying aspects of shareholder rights and abnormal returns. A landmark study by Wulf (2004) investigated a sample of 'mergers of equals' (MOEs) in which the two firms are approximately equal. Such events are friendly mergers in which the two firms engage in pre-merger negotiations producing equal board and management representation and more equal sharing of merger gains. The totality of gains, however, does not differ among mergers involving various degrees of equality/inequality, that is, the value created measured by combined event returns is no different between MOEs and a matched sample of transactions. By contrast, the target firm's (rather than the acquirer's) shareholders capture less of the gains measured by event returns in transactions with shared governance. (In the M&A literature the larger of two merging firms is described as the 'acquirer', the smaller as the 'target'.) The conduct of the top management teams in such cases merits further scrutiny; Wulf argues that CEOs trade governance power for premium by negotiating shared control in the merged firm in exchange for lower shareholder premiums.

Ultimately, two firms merge because they anticipate the benefits of joining to outweigh the cost of consolidating the two firms into a single firm – whether loosely or tightly coupled. Mergers sometimes achieve a high level of consolidation whereas in other cases the two firms remain separate, with little effort made towards reaping economies of scope or scale. In the professional service sectors, it is plausible to assume a high level of integration after the merger, particularly if the merger is accompanied by a change in name. The cost of a merger together with expected benefits can be classified into various categories. Within the purview of corporate finance we might decompose them into classes that cumulatively culminate into positive or negative outcomes. The merger is considered a failure when that cumulative outcome does not entail new wealth.

Figure 6.1 suggests that firms may extract cost reductions or achieve revenue enhancements, or both, that outweigh the premia and other charges or opportunity costs that they incur during and after the merger episode. The present data do not permit a fine-grained financial analysis of positive or negative value creation. Rather firms in this study are observed to survive or to exit. And while ample evidence exists in finance regarding flows of negative revenues and bankrupty, this study remains agnostic about such a relationship. Various investigations in finance have demonstrated, however, that dissolution is a likely event whenever the firm's intangible assets, including its human capital, are eroding and financial performance declines (for example, Lev, 2001).

M&As are embedded within a string of historical events, which suggests that firms might learn from the actions required to integrate two different and separate firms. The M&A event that gives rise to a new firm is often sandwiched between previous and subsequent M&As and there is ample evidence that M&As are path-dependent (Amburgey and Miner, 1992). Accordingly we should not examine the outcomes of an M&A in a temporal vacuum.

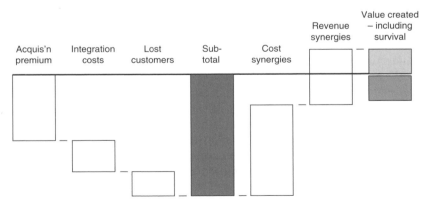

Figure 6.1   Schematic representation of costs and benefits of M&As

Rather we should treat the event as an element in a stream of events by expanding our inquiry to the post-M&A process as it is predicated on the match between suitors. Specifically, that process might be influenced by the firms' previous strategic moves, including prior expansion activities. We perform a longitudinal examination of the matches of firms that participate in M&As. We employ information on 461 M&As involving Dutch accounting firms. Accounting firms are an important part of the 'knowledge economy.' As knowledge-intensive firms, the compatibility and complementarity of their intangible assets and practices can be examined with fine-grained measures. Employing a criterion like 'survival' rather than abnormal returns renders the inquiry all the more immune to the criticism that the post-acquisition process is assumed away as a black box. M&As between accounting firms are widespread and have contributed to high levels of concentration in this sector. The data lend themselves to the execution of the present study: What is the effect of strategic and organizational fit between merging firms on their post-M&A survival chances? Survival as an outcome is invariant across various accounting conventions, jurisdictions or time periods, and remains also otherwise unambiguous in its meaning as a performance proxy. This chapter examines the new firm's odds of survival in relation to 'congruence' – compatability and complementarity – among merging firms, while controlling for their historical and environmental conditions.

LITERATURE REVIEW AND HYPOTHESES

Mergers and acquisitions can be lumped together as the mode through which previously independent firms combine to become a single entity. They may be friendly or hostile. In some cases they involve co-equals, while in other instances one of the two firm dominates. Mergers are distinguished from acquistions in that mergers are assumed to involve two firms of roughly the same size or with equivalent resources. If one of the two firms is much smaller we are inclined to label their fusion an 'acquisition'. The literature, which dates from Berle and Means (1932) onwards, has focused on motives, organizational congruity, relatedness of lines of business, effects on performance, and so on. In this chapter, the attributes of merging firms and their effects on performance are at the center of our inquiry. We draw therefore from those strands of literature that dwell on these issues.

Attributes defining the relationships between the merging firms that stand out in the literature are potential synergy of assets and similarity of cultures and management practices. Scholars have used *strategic fit* or *complementarity* to denote the possibility of synergy and *organizational fit* or *compatibility* to refer to similarity of organizational cultures and management practices (for example, Shelton, 1988; Greenwood et al., 1994). These forms of fit have been examined on the basis of their performance implications.

Three organizational performance categories have received a great deal of attention from M&A studies. One of them is financial performance, such as abnormal return in share price around the announcement of the M&A (for example, Lubatkin, 1987). A second considers the longevity of the expansion following M&A (for example, Pennings et al., 1994). A third class consists of primary data such as interviews and field studies regarding M&A performance, job satisfaction, and employee turnover rate (for example, Greenwood et al., 1994).

The end results of M&As, however, have not yet been fully explored. Among these outcomes is firm survival. Do merging firms enjoy enhanced longevity? There are widely published cases of ill-conceived M&As, ranging from those that were undone to those that culminated in outright dissolution. There are even more examples of M&As, however, such as Unisys (Sperry and Borroughs) and Mattel and the Learning Corporation, that failed by not delivering the income streams expected from them. Further, researchers need to understand what happens to firms that overcome the adverse effects of M&A.

Research on post M&A performance is bifurcated. Some studies investigate the complementarity of the merging firms, while others focus on compatability. Research on complementarity has dwelt on implications for financial performance (for example, Lubatkin, 1987; Singh and Montgomery, 1987). The methodology widely used in these studies is 'event study', which is rooted in the capital assets pricing model of financial economics. Studies dealing with compatibility rely mostly on non-financial performance indices (for example, Buono and Bowditch, 1989; Greenwood et al., 1994; Napier, 1989) and are based on ethnographic methods. Our work suggests that both complementarity and compatibility are germane for the explanation of post-M&A performance. A positive M&A outcome hinges on the presence of complementary capabilities and compatible management practices.

Compatibility

Integration of employees is one of the most critical issues for smooth organizational transition towards a new firm (Buono and Bowditch, 1989). It is particularly crucial in knowledge-intensive firms, including technology-based as well as accounting firms. In a study of large firms' acquisitions of small technology-based firms, Granstrand and Sjolander (1990), for instance, reported that in 60 per cent of cases where key R&D personnel (for example, the general manager) left the firm, the acquisition resulted in subsequent divestment or other manifestations of failure. The possibility of successful integration depends on the pair's structural and cultural similarities, since the integration of like cultures faces lower resistance from organizational members.

Two firms that have similar cultures and routines are defined as compatible. In any M&A, two sets of organizational cultures and routines become unbundled and repacked into the new firm. Thus, an M&A creates more internal diversity and often results in a collision of cultures (Buono et al., 1985; Greenwood et al., 1994; Phillips, 1994). Without some conflict resolution capability, extensive internal diversity would harm organizational functioning.

Attending to M&A-induced conflict and strife distracts management's attention from the firm's productive activities. Incompatible M&As require more attention to conflict resolution and system integration. Consequently, they may harm the firm's ability to compete. In a competitive environment, a firm with incompatible cultures is likely to be selected out. In contrast, firms created by compatible M&As may not experience serious integration problems and can thus capitalize on the M&A experience by building a platform for additional M&As.

Several studies have explored the relation between compatibility and M&A performance. Chatterjee et al. (1992), for example, examined the relationship between top management teams' perceptions of cultural differences and acquirers' stock market gains. They found that cultural similarity had a significant and positive effect on shareholder gains. Datta (1991) reported that differences in top management styles had a negative effect on post-acquisition performance. In a study of a merger of two large accounting firms, Greenwood et al. (1994) found that one firm emphasized the accountant's technical expertise, whereas the other stressed entrepreneurial competence. The difference in core values exacerbated the diffferences between the two former identities and delayed the integration of personnel.

The importance of compatibility depends on the motives of M&As (Napier, 1989). When the acquiring firm leaves the acquired firm alone, because it does not need to integrate cultures and routines, compatibility is not important. In knowledge-intensive sectors, however, compatability is often essential. Most accounting firms, for example, are partnerships with unlimited liability. If one partner brings a loss to the firm, other partners are also responsible for the loss. Consequently, accounting firms want to use a single associate-to-partner promotion rule to preserve the quality of partners. They also want to use an integrated auditing procedure to maintain the quality of auditing services and to minimize auditing risks. The discussion and review of extant literature provide the following hypothesis.

Hypothesis 6.1   Compatibility of merging firms will be negatively associated with organizational dissolution.

Age similarity   Organizations with similar ages usually have similar organizational practices because founders of organizations adopt the best or institutionalized practices at the time of founding. External and internal inertial forces perpetuate and solidify those practices. Stinchcombe (1965) showed that industries established at the same period exhibit similar organizational demographies. Other evidence for age dependence has been generated by Eisenhardt (1988), who reported that the age of a store chain is a significant predictor of the compensation system used. Boeker (1989) found (i) that founding time shaped an organization's proclivity to become marketing or finance-driven and that (ii) the patterns of influence set at founding persisted over time. The findings provide evidence of both the adoption of institutionalized practices at founding and their retention. Since firms with similar ages are likely to have similar organizational practices they should be more compatible.

Hypothesis 6.1-1   Age similarity of firms involved in an M&A will be negatively associated with organizational dissolution.

Size similarity   The relationship between organizational size and structure is a central topic in organizational theory. Research has shown that organizational size is a key driver of bureaucratic features such as greater formalization and an extensive division of labor (see, Kimberly, 1976 for a review). Organizational size is also related to culture. Small firms tend to have entrepreneurial and participative cultures, while large firms are more rigid and bureaucratic (Sales and Mirvis, 1984). The correlation between size and bureaucratization suggests that size similarity may be positively related to the combined returns of the firms involved in M&A.

Empirical studies on size similarity and M&A performance produced inconsistent results. Shelton (1988) reported that size similarity has positive associations with the combined abnormal returns. Singh and Montgomery (1987) showed that the relation was positive in related M&As but negative in unrelated M&As. Cheng et al. (1989), however, found that the target–bidder asset size differential was positively associated with 'merger premium'. Bruton et al. (1994) did not find a significant relationship between size similarity and performance judged by academic evaluators. Despite these inconsistent results, the logic of compatibility provides the following hypothesis.

Hypothesis 6.1-2   Size similarity of involving firms will be negatively associated with the possibility of organizational dissolution.

Structural similarity   While size is related to various attributes of organizational structure, we should also consider structural similarity in its own right. Organizational structure delineates how the organization's members should coordinate and divide their responsibilities. When precursors have the same structure, organizational members may not experience difficulty in working under the 'new' structure since the new structure is likely to be similar with that of the precursor. A new firm created by an M&A of firms with differing structures must establish a coherent structure for efficient functioning. The structure adopted will be new to at least some of the organization's participants. Consequently, they will have to adjust or modify their activities and this adjustment and learning may not be easy to some members. Therefore, M&As of firms with similar structures will outperform others.

Professional service firms (PSF) display distinct structural arrangements. The leverage ratio – the number of associates divided by the number of partners – has been conceptualized as a key structural element in the professional service industry (Sherer, 1995). The leverage ratio is closely related to the extent of division of labor, possibility of promotion, and degree of competition among associates (Galanter and Palay, 1991). It also influences the organizational cultures. Low leveraged firms tend to be more collegial and less bureaucratic than highly leveraged firms (Starbuck, 1992).

An M&A of two firms with differing leverage ratio, consequently, would create adjustment problems for some organizational members. An extreme case is a merger between a highly leveraged firm and a firm consisting of partners only. Partners of the latter would experience difficulty in handling associates – for example, training and socializing them and delegating some decisions to inexperienced associates. When merging firms had similar leverage ratio, and thus similar routines and cultures, organizational members would be easily integrated into a new firm.

Hypothesis 6.1-3   Structural similarity of involving firms will be negatively associated with organizational dissolution.

Familiarity   Familiarity through organizational members' network ties can facilitate the post-merger integration process for various reasons. A pair of firms whose members are densely tied to each other will have similar cultures and routines before the M&A. First, they will have similar frame of reference and cultures. Many theorists agree that people influence and are influenced in forming their perception or attitude by those with whom they interact (for example, Salancik and Pfeffer, 1978). People with network ties may have similar views on how the organization should be structured and managed. Two firms of which members are densely tied, therefore, will have similar cultures and routines.

Second, they are likely to share managerial practices even before the merger. Information transfer through network ties will increase the similarity of networked firms (DiMaggio and Powell, 1983). Since interpersonal ties facilitate information transfer, organizations tied to each other will have the same information on viable routines available in their societies and thus will exhibit similar managerial practices (Haunschild, 1993; Palmer et al., 1993).

Furthermore, members of previously well-networked firms may experience less conflict after M&A. Two firms tied through extensive webs of social connections are in a better position to evaluate the possibility of successful integration before the M&A decision, since those ties render information between the two firms more symmetric. Familiarity does not breed contempt; rather it produces positive attitudes (Zajonc, 1968). Employees already familiar with each other are likely to show positive affection. Accountants who were the linking pins between the two firms could function as the liaison in forging a smooth transition. This line of reasoning provides the following hypothesis.

Hypothesis 6.1-4   Familiarity through the network ties based on the firms' employees is negatively associated with organizational dissolution.

Complementarity

Apart from compatibility, M&A outcomes hinge on the complementarity of the two firms. The argument of complementarity is that firms that have balanced bundles of resources across resource dimensions will perform better since they may not have under-utilized resources (Black and Boal, 1994). As a result, an M&A of two firms that are complementary in their resources will perform better than non-complementary M&As. This logic of complementarity has been tested in studies on the relationship between 'relatedness' of merging firms and M&A performance (for example, Lubatkin, 1983; Salter and Weinhold, 1979).

Empirical studies on the complementarity–performance relationship, however, produced inconsistent findings. Singh and Montgomery (1987) reported that abnormal returns of related targets were significantly higher than those of unrelated targets. Bruton et al. (1994) and Shelton (1988) also reported that related acquisitions were more successful than the unrelated acquisitions. Lubatkin and O'Neill (1987) found that related mergers significantly decreased systematic and total risks of acquiring firms. Lubatkin (1987) and Seth (1990), however, did not find significant relationships between M&A relatedness and performance.

In horizontal M&As, creating monopolistic power will be a major M&A

motive (Copeland and Weston, 1988). Nonetheless, complementarity can exist in horizontal M&As (Chatterjee, 1986), because firms within an industry vary in their capabilities across diverse resource dimensions. For instance, some firms are strong in technology while other firms excel in marketing and distribution. The logic of complementarity leads us to the following hypothesis.

Hypothesis 6.2 Complementarity of involving firms' resources will be negatively associated with organizational dissolution.

Geographical complementarity Specific hypotheses on Hypothesis 6.2 can be developed by considering the characteristics of the research setting because rent-generating resources differ across industries. Accounting firms provide auditing, tax consulting, and/or management consulting services to their clients. Providing these kinds of services usually requires face-to-face interaction between accountants and clients.

Geographical proximity, consequently, has been a key factor for clients in selecting their service providers. Due to the importance of this professional–client interface, multi-establishment firms are likely to favor PSFs that have multiple offices and thus are physically close. In other words, PSFs that have offices in multiple cities are better positioned to serve multi-establishment clients. Two observed correlations provide suggestive evidence for this argument. First, an accounting firm's size, as proxied by the number of offices a given PSF has, is highly correlated with the number of publicly traded firms the PSF has as clients (*Public Accounting Report*, 1994). Secondly, Spurr (1987) reported that there exists a high correlation between the PSF's size and the client's size.

Clients with multi-establishments provide a larger revenue stream and also tend to pay higher hourly fees to accounting firms. Large and multi-office accounting firms get premium fees not only for auditing services (Firth, 1993; Francis and Simon, 1987) but also for compilation and review services (Barefield et al., 1993). As a result, accounting firms that are geographically diversified are likely to perform better.

This evidence suggests that an M&A will be more successful when the M&A partners cover different territories. This geographical complementarity was undoubtedly a key motive in the globalization of consulting and accounting firms. We thus hypothesize that the merger of firms that occupy differing geographical niches is more likely to be successful than the merger of firms with overlapping niches.

Hypothesis 6.2-1 Geographical complementarity will be negatively associated with the possibility of organizational dissolution.

Human and social capital complementarity   To be successful, organizations should have access to both production and marketing capabilities. Firms can internalize those capabilities or outsource them from the market. When outsourcing incurs a great deal of transaction costs or increases the uncertainty of operation, firms have the incentive to internalize those capabilities through vertical integration (Caves and Bradburd, 1988; Williamson, 1975) or to semi-internalize through strategic alliances (Teece, 1986).

Among the inputs of accounting firms, the professional's capability often outweighs financial capital and physical investments because most of the production and marketing capabilities are carried by professionals. A firm consisting of accountants capable of conducting high quality services can be defined as a firm that has production capabilities. We adopt the term 'human capital' for those capabilities. Even though human capital is originally defined as an individual's attribute (Becker, 1975), we define a firm's human capital as the aggregation of human capital of accountants who are affiliated with the firm.

A firm having many ties with potential clients can be defined as a firm that has marketing capabilities. We use the term 'social capital' for representing such marketing capabilities. Firm-level social capital can be inferred from the number of external ties to potential clients that organizational members have (Burt, 1992).[1] The salience of network ties in obtaining clients comes from the difficulty in measuring the quality of the services (Burt, 1992). In fact, the quality of intangible professional services is very hard to measure. In those settings, network ties are likely to come into play for the clients in selecting their service providers.

The social capital is essential for the conversion of production capabilities into organizational returns. A firm can be unbalanced in its human and social capital. If a firm has more production capabilities than it can sell, it has under-utilized production capabilities. Likewise, if a firm has more marketing capabilities than it can produce, it has under-utilized marketing capabilities. A merger of the two firms will be beneficial since it allows them to use their previously under-utilized capabilities. In the same vein, the merger of an accounting firm endowed with under-utilized human capital with another firm endowed with under-utilized social capital will be more successful than the others. This reasoning leads us to the following hypothesis.

Hypothesis 6.2-2   Human and social capital complementarity will be negatively associated with the possibility of organizational dissolution.

CONTROLS

In addition to conventional controls such as regulation, economic or political shocks and time, we need to be alert for rival plausible alternative hypotheses. Foremost among these controls are acquisitive learning and size.

Organizations learn from relevant prior experiences. M&A experiences, specifically, provide valuable lessons about post-acquisition integration (Fowler and Schmidt, 1989; Pennings et al., 1994). A firm with a great deal of M&A experience will know how to integrate the firm and capitalize on that knowledge by seeking additional M&As (Amburgey and Miner, 1992). Existing studies have reported the positive performance effects of M&A experience. Cumulative M&A experience is positively related with returns on equity (Fowler and Schmidt, 1989), performance judged by academic evaluators (Bruton et al., 1994), and their persistence (Pennings et al., 1994).

The stock of M&A experiences should be positively associated with organizational failure. Firms emerging out of a string of mergers have comparatively high levels of internal variations. They encounter conflict across routines and people. People socialized by diverse firms have divergent organizing views. Without successful integration of chafing cultures and routines, they are unable to render reliable services and thus would be outcompeted by other firms. Firms that have overcome the integration problems are likely to re-engage in more M&As to maintain their growth momentum (Amburgey and Miner, 1992) or to take advantage of their knowledge regarding post-M&A integration. The growth motive can be justified because large professional firms can generate higher revenue per partner (*Public Accounting Report*, 1994. Thus it is plausible to expect that M&A-specific knowledge accumulated during a firm's history will be positively associated with the possibility of dissolution.

Large PSFs are better positioned to serve multi-establishment clients (*Public Accounting Report*, 1994; Spurr, 1987) and also get premium fees (Barefield et al., 1993; Firth, 1993; Francis and Simon, 1987). Furthermore, larger firms command more resources, enjoy superior economies of scope and scale, and should therefore face a better post-acquisition process. Through growth, they signal success and accumulation of good will. It is therefore plausible to expect them to be an attractive M&A partner in the population. Following the merger, up to the year of censoring, we expect large firms to face better M&A outcomes than do smaller firms – in our case survival.

DATA AND METHODS

Sample

We sampled the firms created by M&As from the population of accounting firms, since we were only interested in what happened to those specific firms. However, we also used the relevant population data for measuring our variables. Our initial sample consisted of 516 M&As in the history of the Dutch accounting industry.

Among the 516 M&As, we deleted 44 that happened during the period 1986–90. The deletion was unavoidable because we did not have the outcome information regarding those M&As; these new entrants were right-censored. We also deleted an additional 11 in which 3 or more firms were involved in an M&A during an observation interval. Applying the notion of compatibility and complementarity to more than two involved firms is very difficult, if not impossible. If firm A acquired firm B and C during an observation period, we can create two observations: A with B and A with C. No information exists as to whether firm A acquired firm B earlier than firm C. Even if we were to randomly assign a sequence, the resulting data would suffer dependence problems among observations. Thus our final sample consists of 461 M&As. For longer than one year length of observation interval, we divided the number of M&As during the interval by the length.

Figure 6.2 illustrates how we constructed our sample. To simplify this explanation, we will assume the presence of yearly data. In Case 1, we had two M&As. The first M&A was consummated during the period 1935–36. We had 14 non-events (1936–49) and one additional M&A (1950) between the first M&A and the second M&A. We constructed compatibility and complementarity measures by using both firm A and B's information in 1935. Those measures were used as independent variables for the 15 firm-years. After A's acquisition of C, we had 39 non-events (1951–89). As in the first M&A event, the compatibility and complementarity, calculated by using two firms' 1950 profiles, were used as independent variables for the 39 firm-years.

In Case 2, A acquired C and D during the period 1950–51. We did not have any information about whether A acquired C first or not. Firm-years of 1951 onwards, consequently, are not included in the sample. Case 2 contributed 14 non-events and one M&A. In Case 3, C contributed 13 firm-years: 12 non-events (1938–49), and one acquisition (1950). Firm A contributed 54 firm-years: 52 non-events, 1 M&A, and 1 dissolution. B and D did not contribute any firm-years in our setting.

Applying the sampling procedure to our population data produced 1186 firm-intervals. We treated our data as if one observation interval is a year.

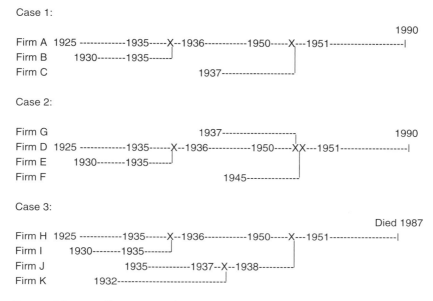

Figure 6.2   An illustration of sample composition in a repeated hazard model

Among them, there are 838 non-events, 48 dissolutions, and 300 involvements in additional M&As.

Measures

Individual-level data were aggregated to produce firm level information. We coded organizational foundings, deaths, and changes by examining the changes of an accountant's organizational affiliation. Organizational changes examined in this study included M&A and name change. In identifying M&As, we used the criterion of two-thirds of partners. That is, two-thirds or more of the partners should join a new firm to be considered as a counterpart of the M&A. One of the difficulties in selecting a criterion is that we did not know whether other accountants left the firms before the M&A or after the M&A. We also used more than half, and more than three-fourths criteria to ensure the robustness of our results. The sensitivity analysis revealed that our results were not sensitive to the criterion.

We coded name changes when a firm's name differed from its previous one, provided two-thirds or more of its partners continued their affiliation with the firm. We did not include name changes due to M&A or cosmetic name changes such as modifications in the order of named partners, or additions of the Dutch equivalents of 'Accountants' or 'Registered' and 'Limited Liability' to the firm's original name. We coded organizational founding when a new name was listed in the directories for the first time without an M&A or name change. Dissolution was flagged when a firm's name was permanently delisted from the directories without an M&A or name change. We measured previous M&A experience by the number of M&As conducted by the involved firm before the particular M&A.

To measure compatibility and complementarity, we used the firm-level information in the last observation period before a particular M&A. For instance, if both firm A and firm B were listed in the directory of 1974 and if a firm resulting from A and B's M&A was listed in the directory of 1978, we used the firm-level information of 1974 for creating compatibility and complementarity measures.

Compatibility   We measured firm age at M&A by subtracting the founding year from the last observation year before the M&A. We divided the younger firm's age by the older firm's age to measure age similarity. Maximum of the measure was 1 when the involving firms were founded in the same year. A number close to 1 indicates that the firms were similar in age. We did not use the absolute difference between the age of two firms. Two firms of 90 and 60 years old are likely to be more similar than two firms of 32 and 2 years old since the first two firms have experienced the same selection environment for 60 years.

Firm size at M&A was measured by the number of CPAs affiliated with the firm in the last observation year before the M&A. To measure size similarity, we divided the smaller firm's size by the larger firm's size. We measured structural similarity by the absolute difference of two leverage ratios. Leverage ratio is the number of associates divided by the number of partners. Since some firms did not hire any associates, we could not create a ratio measure analogous to age or size similarity.

We measured familiarity between involving firms by considering the network ties among their CPAs. Ties between accountants were measured by tracing the careers of accountants. Accountants developed social networks by changing their organizational affiliations. When two accountants had an affiliation with a firm during any overlapping period, we assumed that they had network ties with each other thereafter. If firm i and j had 10 and 20 accountants respectively before the M&A, there were 200 (10*20) possible ties. We counted the actual number of ties that firm i's CPAs had with firm j's CPAs. We divided the actual number by the possible number of ties to measure familiarity of two firms. We assumed that the higher the number, the higher the familiarity.

Complementarity   We developed three competing measures for geographical complementarity. The degree of non-overlap between two firms' market niches indicated geographical complementarity. Geographical complementarity, consequently, is the degree of market extension in terms of FTC categorization. Differing rules to define market niche provided differing measures for the variable. We developed three kinds of categorization to divide the market. The first had three categories: the set of the four largest Dutch cities (Amsterdam, Rotterdam, Utrecht and The Hague), other domestic areas, and foreign markets. Geographically, the Netherlands bifurcates into a large conurbation in the west, called 'De Randstad' versus what the French might call the 'Province'. De Randstad comprises the four largest cities, has a population of about 10 million people, and is the center of the Netherlands' economic gravity. The second measure for geographical complementarity was based on six categories: each of the four cities, other domestic areas, and the foreign market. The last measure was based on 13 categories: each of the 12 Dutch provinces with the foreign market. For each categorization, we used the following formula,

$$Geographical\ complementarity = \sum\nolimits_{k=1,n} |DI_{ik} - DI_{jk}|,$$

where n is the number of categories, DI_{ik} is the number of firm i's offices in kth market divided by the total number of firm i's offices, and DI_{jk} is the number of firm j's offices in kth market divided by the total number of firm j's offices. The value of the measure ranges from 0 to 2. Zero indicates that two firms' market niches are perfectly overlapping. A value of two indicates that two firms' market niches do not overlap at all.

We measured human capital by using two variables, general human capital and industry-specific human capital of the firms. General human capital was measured by the proportion of CPAs among all CPAs who possessed a master's or higher degree. Industry-specific human capital of a firm was measured by the average of CPA's industry-specific human capital. We measured the CPA's industry-specific human capital making use of the natural logarithm of tenure in the accounting industry. To avoid Ln(0), which is negative infinity, we added 1 for the tenure of all accountants. We assumed that the speed of industry-specific knowledge accumulation decreased over the career of the CPA.

We measured social capital with two measures. One was the proportion of CPAs among all CPAs in the firm who had worked in other industries or government. The other was the proportion of accountants among quitters who left the firm within the previous 10 years to work for other industries or government but never came back to the accounting industry. We used a ten-year span not only because the strength of network ties decreases with the decrease of interaction, but also because the quitters retired from the business world and no longer provided any value to the firm. For comparison, we also tried 5 and 15-year spans. The sensitivity analysis showed that the results reported here were not significantly different.

We standardized the human and social capital score by using means and standard deviations of each resources dimension. Means and standard deviations were calculated by using 7027 firm-intervals (that is, the population firm-intervals during the period 1880–1986). On the basis of the standardized scores, we created a global human capital score by adding the standardized educational level score and the standardized industry-specific human capital score. Likewise we added two standardized social capital scores to create a global social capital score. Our reason for collapsing the categories was that they may not be complementary. For instance, having both a high educational level score and high industry-specific human capital would not produce any synergistic effect on organizational performance. If one party had more resources in both of the dimensions, we assigned 0. If not, we multiplied the absolute difference of the two firm's human capital scores and the absolute difference in their social capital scores.

Control Variables

We controlled for proxies of 'history', including World War II, Indonesian independence in 1949, and significant changes in regulations that governed the accounting profession and its clients (1971–73 and 1984–89). Specifying the length of the effects of these events, especially those for regulations, was not easy. We specified World War II as having effects during the period 1941–46 and Indonesian independence during the period of 1949–51. The effects of those historical events would be short-lived. Significant changes in the regulations such as the mandatory auditing of all listed firms, which changed the demand for audit services, would have persistent effects on the industry until the abolition of the regulation itself. For that reason, we specified that the regulation would have its effect during the entire period following the onset of the regulation. Size, another important control variable was captured by the number of professionals in the firm.

The sector in which the firm is embedded represents an important background for M&A. We controlled for the number of peer firms (that is, density), which signals both the level of competition and the availability of potential merger partners. The density of the industry may influence the incidence of dissolution of firms created out of an M&A. We also controlled for the number of M&As in a previous year (total number of M&As in previous observation interval divided by the length of the interval). High M&A levels also affect concentration ratio and force ill-conceived mergers out of the market. Conversely, as we argued, the number of prior M&As at the firm level confers learning benefits and affects dissolution negatively.

We also controlled for the length of observation intervals as a time-varying covariate. As before, we have non-uniform observation intervals from one to five years. Since we expected that the odds of events may be positively related with the length of the observation interval, we included the natural logarithm of the length of the interval (in years). In estimating the model, we lagged time varying covariates, firm size, and all control variables one observation period.

Model

The events we are interested in here are dissolution or additional M&As. We adopted a multinomial logit model to estimate the effects of our independent variables on the probability of an event. The decision was made on the following basis. First, firms could not experience those events simultaneously. Applying competing risk models, consequently, was adequate to our setting. Second, Cox's proportional hazard model (Cox and Oakes, 1984) was not appropriate since we had non-uniform observation intervals and many ties of a events. Third, discrete time event history could be used instead of a continuous event history model (Allison, 1982). As binomial logistic regression could be used to analyze repeated event history (Allison, 1982), a multinomial logit model could be used to analyze repeated and multiple types of events. The logit model is expressed as follows.

$$Log[P_{ij}/P_{i3}] = X_i\beta_j, J = 1, 2,$$

$$P_{ij} = P(C_i = j|X_i) = e(X_i\beta_j)/\left[1 + \sum_{k=1}^{2}e(X_i\beta_k)\right], J = 1, 2,$$

$$P_{i3} = P(C_i = 3|X_i) = 1/\left[1 + \sum_{k=1}^{2}e(X_i\beta_k)\right],$$

$$\beta_3 = 0,$$

where, C_i is consequence category that firm i experienced,
X_i = a row vector of firm i's independent variables,
β_j = a column vector of coefficients, and
P_{ij} = probability that the firm i experiences consequence j where j is in a set of (1 = dissolution, and 2 otherwise).

Non-event ($C_i = 3$) was used as a reference category. The parameters estimated in this model could be interpreted only in reference to the non-event category. For instance, a positive coefficient of a variable in category 2 (additional M&A) indicated that the increase in the variable increased the ratio of the probability of engaging in additional M&As to the probability of non-event. In estimating the model with SAS, we lagged all independent variables one period.

RESULTS

Table 6.1 provides the results of multinomial logit regression. The analysis is also based on 461 M&As and 1186 firm-intervals. In the present study, firms established by M&As may dissolve. We also compared the predictive power of the three geographical complementarity proxies. Even though we could not compare the results with formal statistical procedures, comparisons of three log-likelihoods favored the simplest categorization of geographical niches (that is, the four '+' cities, other domestic areas, and foreign countries). The results reported in Table 6.1 are based on this simplest categorization.

Age similarity significantly enhances the probability of the merged firm engaging in additional M&As (vis-à-vis the status quo). It does not, however, have any significant effect on the probability of dissolution. Size similarity does not have any effects on dissolution and additional M&As. Structural similarity has positive and significant effects on the M&A probability (p < .01). It does not, however, significantly influence the probability of dissolution. Contrary to our prediction, familiarity through CPAs' direct network ties significantly decreases the probability of engaging in additional M&As (p < .01). A firm created by an M&A of two firms whose members were densely tied before the M&A is less likely to initiate additional M&As than a firm created by an M&A of two firms whose members were weakly tied before the M&A.

The two complementarity hypotheses received rather strong support. Geographical complementarity significantly decreases the probability of dissolution (p < .01). Geographically overlapping M&As were more likely to dissolve than geographically non-overlapping M&As. In other words, the merger of firms with differing geographical niches is more viable than the merger of firms with geographically overlapping niches. Geographical complementarity, however, does not have a significant effect on the probability of the new firm engaging in additional M&As (vis-à-vis the status quo). Human and social capital complementarity significantly enhances the probability of engaging in additional M&As (p < .01). If the two

Table 6.1   Multinomial logistic regression results for the consequences of M&As (461 M&As; 1186 firm-intervals)

Variables	Dissolution	Additional M&A
Intercept	−43.394***	−2.396**
	(15.260)	(1.134)
Compatibility		
Age similarity	−.470	.403*
	(.531)	(.242)
Size similarity	.525	−.213
	(.638)	(.295)
Structural similarity	−.228	1.521***
	(.936)	(.374)
Familiarity via CPAs' direct network ties	−.021	−.405**
	(.415)	(.193)
Complementarity		
Geographical complementarity	−.864***	−.180
	(.270)	(.116)
Human and social capital complementarity	.031	.168***
	(.166)	(.047)
Resources accumulation		
Previous M&A experience	.312***	.086***
	(.099)	(.030)
Firm size (time-varying)	−.076***	.004*
	(.020)	(.002)
Controls		
Logarithm of interval length	2.436***	.522*
	(.801)	(.282)
Government regulation 1971–73	−.038	−.093
	(.289)	(.121)
Government regulation 1984–89	5.706***	.507
	(1.846)	(.350)
World War II (1941–45)	.708	.346
	(.802)	(.287)
Indonesia's independence (1949)	1.043**	−.475*
	(.417)	(.271)
Density	.337***	−.001
	(.124)	(.008)
Density squared/100	−.061***	.001
	(.023)	(.002)
M&A levels in prior year	.275***	.098***
	(.102)	(.037)
Number of events	48	300
Log-likelihood	−1383.09: −2294.08	

Notes: Standard errors are in parentheses. *: p < .10; ** p < .05; *** p < .01 (two-tailed test).

involving firms were complementary in their human and social capital, a firm created by the M&A of the two was more likely to engage in additional M&As (vis-à-vis the status quo).

Supporting Hypothesis 6.3, previous M&A experiences have positive and significant effects on both types of events. If the pair of firms had conducted many M&As before the current merging, a firm created by an M&A of the two was more likely to dissolve (p < .01) and to engage in additional M&As (p < .01). Firm size also has the predicted effect on dissolution and on involvement in additional M&As. Large firms were less likely to dissolve (p < .01) and more likely to engage in additional M&As (p < .05). The parameters support Hypothesis 6.4.

Table 6.1 also shows the effects of the various control variables on post-M&A outcomes. The governmental regulation of 1984–89 significantly increased the probability of dissolution and of being an M&A target. The regulation involved the mandatory external audit and financial disclosure of small and medium-sized firms. The previous regulation, that is the one of 1971–73, pertained to large firms and had a much milder effect on M&A outcomes. We note that Indonesia's independence in 1949 increased the possibility of dissolution, and diminished the propensity to acquire other accounting firms. The density has an inverted U-shaped relation with the dissolution: positive first-order effect and negative second-order effect. The positive effect of density on dissolution reaches a maximum, when the density is 275.57 [0.3366/2*(0.061/100)]. The density does not have any effect on the involvement in additional M&As. The level of acquisitive activities in the sector during the previous year has a positive relation with dissolution and additional M&As.

DISCUSSION

This study has shown that M&A outcomes can be traced to the 'chemistry' of the merging firms. The evolution of a firm that emerges out of two previously independent firms is conditioned by their compatibility and complementarity. Furthermore, the prior expansion activities and growth/decline of the merging firms appears to be an important determinant of post-M&A outcomes. Several things can happen to a firm founded by an M&A. A somewhat unlikely event is dissolution. More common is the scenario that firms will persist over time, although their evolutionary processes after the merger diverge. In this study we differentiated between firms that simply continued versus those that were drawn towards acquisitive opportunities and actually implemented other M&As. The study also stands out in that we trace the trajectories of firms through successive mergers and the divergence in outcomes: dissolution or subsequent merger. The advantage of centering the analysis on such outcomes does not only render arbitrary the idiosyncracies of the financial criteria such as 'abnormal returns' but also frees the analysis from assuming that abnormal returns somehow capture the post-M&A integration process in some state of equilibrium.

The effects of preconditions vary by type of outcome. The most important and only significant predictor of dissolution was geographical complementarity. In contrast, proxies of complementarity and resources accumulation had strong, hypothesis-consistent effects on the new firm to engage in additional mergers. The results indicate that environmental selection favors compatible and complementary M&As.

It is crucial to view M&A conduct in a dynamic perspective. As the findings in this study demonstrate, many mergers are sandwiched between other M&A activities. Having prior M&A experience is a predictor of both firm dissolution and additional M&As. The findings indicate that M&A experience does not automatically make firm accumulate acquisitive knowledge. Firms that dissolved despite a great deal of acquisitive experience may be firms that could not handle immense internal variations brought about from joining separate entities. Firms that were involved in additional M&As may be the firms that had the capability to handle merger-induced internal diversity. Those firms tried to take advantage of that capability or to retain their strategic momentum (Amburgey and Miner, 1992).

We have also included the new firm's size as a time-variant covariate to obtain an additional grasp on this post-acquisition process. If the firm shrinks, perhaps through attrition, through a split, or by breaking up, it evidently is not undergoing a positive post-acquisition process. However, if the firm remains stationary in size or grows, its life after the merger is very much assured. We should therefore not be surprised that resource accumulation either through internal growth or M&A makes such firms prone to continue with an acquisitive expansion strategy.

M&As and Compatibility

The ability to sustain acquisitive behavior appears to be conditioned by the ability of the pair of merging firms to be compatible, while dissolution is only marginally affected by the pair's harmony. In other industries, it has been found that flawed mergers are rarely so disastrous that the new firm meets an untimely death. Quinn (1988) examined the Mellon and Girard bank merger and found them to be so incompatible culturally (although they were geographically complementary), that the post-acquisition process drained significant resources from the new firm. From our findings, one would conjecture that other banks are unlikely to seek Mellon out as an M&A partner.

According to our results, incompatibility is not a good predictor of M&A failure! One might speculate that in face of divergent structures and cultures, the individual professionals are not strongly affected by the reality of the post-acquisition era. While the fusion of the two firms' governance structure requires significant efforts, the day to day operations might remain loosely coupled. Each CPA serves his or her roster of clients, and apart from changes in auditing procedures, the professional continues with business as usual.

A different interpretation should be advanced for the expansion conduct of the firm whose partners were incompatible. As a 'two for one', it comprises two entities rather than one. Such targets might be shunned by other firms. The situation is analogous to a collective bargaining stalemate where one of the parties is divided regarding some settlement. In the case of M&As, the suitors are in fact quite selective in the choice of partners. The accounting sector comprises firms with an emphasis on reliable, reproducible performance of auditing services. When a marriage partner comprises incompatible factions, the negotiation of additional M&As might degenerate into a *menage à trois*. The ensuing uncertainty is incongruous with the nature of the accounting industry and probably in other sectors as well. The results of this study suggest that among accounting firms, the choice of mates with an M&A history is hardly 'a-select'. Peer firms are either drawn to those firms that display a better than average fit, or disharmonious firms have little inclination to grow through acquisition.

It was assumed that firms benefit from having intelligence about possible merger candidates, including of course, their level of harmony. However, the results on familiarity, as measured by CPAs' direct network ties, do not corroborate this view. Network ties were negatively related to the possibility of engaging in additional M&As. One plausible reason is that firms may have some risk-taking tendency in selecting M&A partners. Merging with a familiar firm is less risky than merging with an unfamiliar firm, as spelled out when we developed Hypothesis 6.1. If firms are risk-averse and if risk-aversion is retained in a new firm, the firm created by a merger of two familiar firms may not consider unfamiliar firms as a target of additional M&As. This tendency decreases the number of possible targets and thus decreases the probability of engaging in additional M&As.

M&As and Complementarity

Two complementary measures have differing effects on post-M&A outcomes. Creating a stronger presence in a single locale increases the likelihood of dissolution compared with firms that spread their presence over several

locales. Human and social capital complementarity does not affect the likelihood of dissolution, but it creates a much higher propensity in the new firm
to seek out and merge with other firms. Such complementary mergers foster
a growth strategy through additional M&As.

As Black and Boal (1994) have indicated, it is not the sheer accumulation
of those intangible assets, but rather the relationships among bundles of
assets that produce a sustainable competitive advantage. The architecture
of those resources, or what they call factor networks with specific inter-
resources relationships, confer an edge over the competition. Our findings
can be fitted into the Black and Boal framework: it is the bringing together
of under-utilized human and social capital through a merger that generates
a renewed proclivity towards M&As. It also suggests that the maintenance
and enhancement of strategic fit provides a potent inducement for further
expansion initiatives. Future research should reveal whether in fact firms
build up a trajectory of merger activity in which each and every merger is
either complementary or supplementary.

Limitations

We should acknowledge, once more, that the present study is based on a
sample of a single industry, which provides some very strong advantages,
as well as some limits in generalizability. Among the advantages we
mention are the avoidance of aggregation bias (Schmalensee, 1985), the use
of fine-grained data to measure compatibility and complementarity, the
avoidance of classifying mergers as 'horizontal' or 'vertical', and the focus
on a service sector which is part of the growing 'knowledge' economy.
Disadvantages include the lack of financial measures of performance, the
absence of data on M&A with firms outside the audit industry (for
example, diversification towards management consulting and headhunt-
ing), which *The Economist* (1995) signals as important trends. While the
data are fine-grained, and single industry studies are becoming the norm
(Rumelt et al., 1991), additional studies would further enrich the insights
of this chapter. Ideally these studies should include both manufacturing
and service sectors, as well as EU and non-EU settings.

Like any study, this combines limitations with important strengths that
should inspire others to develop additional theory and collect data on the
interaction between organizational strategy and firm and industry evolution. The strategy of a firm exists neither in a temporal vacuum, nor is it
disjointed from its ecological context. M&As are a major punctuation in a
firm's history, and give rise to changes in industry structure. The resources
that the two firms bring together and rebundle in the subsequent
implementation process inform us about the future prospects of the firm.

CONCLUSION

This chapter has explored M&As from an evolutionary perspective. M&As, as very important strategic decisions, were conceptualized as a key factor that influences organizational evolution. M&As increase intra-firm variations and change firm's resources configuration. As the effects of compatibility and complementarity show, finding the 'right' partners allows a firm to engage in a future growth race through additional M&As. Finding a good 'match' not only frees the new firm from expending important resources to solve internal conflicts, but also permits utilization of previously under-utilized resources. The effects of previous M&A experience and firm size suggest that firm capability to integrate internal diversity created by M&As is important as well.

NOTE

1. Burt (1992) himself seems to define firm-level social capital two ways. In defining firm-level social capital, he uses the aggregation of organizational members' network ties. In the discussion of structural autonomy, firm-level social capital is inferred from the structure of inter-organizational transactions and competition. Here we use the former definition for social capital.

PART III

The role of individual mobility for organizational behavior and performance

7. Spatial and temporal heterogeneity in founding patterns

INTRODUCTION

The study of the relation between organizational dynamics and geography has a long tradition that traces back to research on human ecology (Park, 1926; Hawley, 1950). Human activities assume an orderly arrangement in space resulting in the formation of 'human ecologies' whose boundaries are spatially or geographically delimited (see McKenzie, 1968). Spatial considerations have been the object of growing interest in fields such as strategic management, sociology and economics (see Sorenson and Baum, 2003). Yet, the conditions under which local interactions shape industry evolution have received scant attention.

Density-dependence theory, at least in its original formulation (Hannan, 1986), shares a similar limitation. Although a large body of empirical evidence has been collected in support of this theory (for a comprehensive review see Baum, 1996 and Carroll and Hannan, 2000), some of its basic assumptions have been questioned. Two recurrent criticisms revolve around (1) choice of the unit of analysis for studying ecological processes (Singh, 1993), and (2) dearth of evidence regarding micro behaviors which engender legitimation of new organizational forms (Hedström, 1994; Baum and Powell, 1995).

The development of this discussion has drawn growing attention to the degree of heterogeneity as a precondition for the emergence, rise and decline of organizational populations. Spatial considerations have gained momentum (Lomi, 1995; Greve, 2002; Sorenson and Audia, 2000) and geography is now widely acknowledged to condition founding patterns. Although the effects of density-dependent legitimization have been found to span national boundaries (Hannan et al., 1995; Wezel and Lomi, 2003), other studies have shown that ecological processes originate from smaller geographical areas within national organizational populations (Lomi, 2000; Greve, 2002). Similarly, time has come to be seen as an important source of heterogeneity because the intensity of legitimation and competition is a function of the age of the industry (for example, Hannan, 1997) and selection pressures vary over time (Sorenson, 2000; Barnett et al., 2002). A joint examination of the spatial and temporal dimensions of legitimation and competition, therefore, is 'important because processes, structures and functions of organizational populations are defined by time and space' (Lomi and Larsen, 1996: 1289).

Building upon this stream of research, the purpose of this chapter is to investigate evolutionary patterns of spatial and temporal heterogeneity. Our contribution is threefold. First, we argue that local density-dependent processes occasion organizational foundings on the grounds that proximity facilitates communication and stimulates the diffusion of information (Rogers, 1962; Bala and Goyal, 1998). Second, since industries undergo significant transformations as they age (Hannan, 1997; Hannan et al., 1998), we show how multiple local rather than national evolutionary clocks affect organizational foundings. Third, we provide empirical evidence on social contagion that produces diffusion of new organizational forms.

To this end, we examine founding rates in the Dutch accounting industry during the period 1880–1986, both at the population and the subpopulation levels of analysis. The natural division of the Netherlands into provinces which represent important administrative and political units (for example, de Pree, 1997; Lee and Pennings, 2002; Boone et al., 2002) allows us to consider the pools of potential entrepreneurs to be geographically embedded in such institutional and socio-economic identities. Furthermore, the choice of a professional service industry, where local relationships with clients and competition for labor stand out (Maister, 1993), is consistent with our theoretical assumption that organizations depend upon local demand and supply.

THEORY

Spatial Heterogeneity in Organizational Foundings

Organizational ecologists have developed a theory of industrial evolution based upon the concept of density-dependence (Hannan, 1986). Density conditions both mortality and founding rates through legitimation and competition. A new organizational form acquires legitimacy when it displays a template or architecture that becomes socially recognized (Meyer and Rowan, 1977). At the time of its first appearance, an organization with a new form generally lacks this kind of recognition. Customers and suppliers need to be cultivated, and employees socialized into new roles. Institutionally, we observe time compression diseconomies because some period elapses before the preponderance of a new form becomes apparent. In the early stages of the industry life-cycle, higher density enhances social recognition (that is, legitimation) of the new organizational form, with the effect of attracting additional entrepreneurs and reducing the risk of mortality of incumbents. Eventually, the industry becomes unable to accommodate a growing number of organizations. Competition intensifies as organizations draw from the same set of resources (Hannan and Freeman, 1977; Hawley, 1950), depressing their growth and survival rates, while diminishing the motivation of others to enter the industry.

A large body of empirical evidence supports density-dependence theory (see chapter 10 in Carroll and Hannan, 2000). Yet, some of its assumptions have been challenged. The industry is rarely homogeneous. The neglect of local differences in density and associated founding or mortality rates results in imprecise estimates of the effect of legitimation and competition (Baum and Amburgey, 2002; Lomi, 1995). Carroll and Wade's (1991) study of the American brewing industry is compelling and has drawn renewed attention to the 'spatial dimension' that is so central in the work of human ecologists (for example, Hawley, 1950). Researchers have begun to investigate boundary-spanning processes across nations. In their study of the European automobile industry, Hannan et al. (1995) showed that legitimation spills over to other countries while competition remains largely domestic. Empirical support for the multi-level density-dependence theory of evolution, however, is still scant and limited to the European auto industry (Hannan et al., 1995; Hannan, 1997; Dobrev et al., 2001). To clarify the unit of analysis, some ecologists have focused on the relative influence of smaller geographical areas (for example, regions, states, provinces). Bigelow et al. (1997), for example, argued that geography and physical distance 'account for the different scale of effects of legitimation and competition rather than nation-state political boundaries' (1997: 394). This echoes Lomi's (2000) findings for the core–periphery relationship between commercial banks in Copenhagen and in the rest of Denmark.

Different arguments have been advanced for the local nature of both legitimation and competition. Consider first legitimization. According to ecological theories, the lack of cognitive legitimation significantly constrains the action of potential entrepreneurs. The contextual factors that render a novel form increasingly acceptable and cognitively appropriate require visibility. The new form also requires acceptance in the minds of founders and their stakeholders (Lee et al., 2001). As Aldrich and Fiol put it, '[C]ognitive legitimation refers to the spread of knowledge about a new venture' (1994: 645) such that it becomes so familiar that it is taken for granted, with the effect that 'attempts at creating copies of legitimated forms are common, and the success rate of such attempts is high' (Hannan and Freeman, 1986: 63).

Entrepreneurs as boundedly rational actors (March and Simon, 1958; Cyert and March, 1963) seek new market opportunities mainly locally. Founding a new venture requires the mobilization of various resources – such as human and physical capital, goodwill, reputation and social capital (Lee et al., 2001) – many of which are accessible primarily at the local level. Coping with these problems requires cooperation and interaction between different individuals, groups and organizations (Aldrich and Fiol, 1994; Lee et al., 2001). Social interaction (for example, Festinger, 1953; Sorenson and Stuart, 2001) and network ties emerge among actors who are spatially co-located (Park, 1926; Hawley, 1950), as the relative costs increase with geographical distance (for example, Lazarsfeld and Merton, 1954). Proximity stimulates information exchange (for example, Saxenian, 1994), knowledge circulation through personal contacts (Scherer, 1984), and localized knowledge spillovers, with the associated economies of agglomeration (see Marshall, 1922; Arrow, 1962; Romer, 1986).

Competition, too, might vary by geography. Rivalry is a small number phenomenon and the number of competitors a firm recognizes is mediated by local information (Baum and Lant, 2003). Proximity intensifies rivalry for local buyers and suppliers as shown in the study by Carroll and Wade (1991). In the service sector, physically proximate firms also vie for local human capital (Cattani et al., 2002). Dependence on a local resource pool fosters greater mutual awareness and rivalry among firms (Hawley, 1950; Sørensen, 1999b). We hold, therefore, that local rather than national competition shapes founding activity (Sorenson and Audia, 2000).

Actually, both legitimization and competition are subject to geographic variations within nationally defined industries. The studies by Lomi (1995) and Greve (2002) addressed the local nature of these evolutionary phenomena explicitly. Lomi (1995) discovered how different groups of rural cooperative banks in Italy reacted differently to the same national competitive and institutional pressures. His results suggest an asymmetric influence of local and non-local density. While no real 'difference in legitimation was found across models based on local and non-local specification of density, competition is seven times stronger at the regional than at the national level' (Lomi, 1995: 137). Greve (2002) showed that local density occasioned the evolution of a population within a given geographical area. His findings demonstrate how 'density dependence operated locally within small areas and spilled over from neighboring areas' (2002: 870).

Summarizing, the effects of density-dependence should be stronger at the local than national level. Cognitive legitimacy and competitive constraints are proportional to the degree of physical proximity among organizations (Baum and Mezias, 1992). We thus hypothesize:

Hypothesis 7.1 Founding rates in a given population of organizations are more strongly affected by local rather than national density-dependence processes of legitimation and competition.

The bifurcation of populations into 'national' versus 'local' presents boundary definition issues: foundings occur in neither purely local nor national space. Rather, they occur along a geographic gradient ranging from focal and proximate, to neighboring and more distant contexts. Along this gradient, we might observe physical, institutional or cognitive discontinuities. To date, however, 'neighbor effects are rare in regional founding studies (but see Wade Swaminathan and Saxon, 1998), since they have not been made the focus of theory yet' (Greve, 2002: 861).

The existence of these neighbor effects is consistent with the presumption in biology that the environment is divided into *adaptive zones*. An adaptive zone is an ecological space or niche comprising a unique set of resources that a given species can exploit (Ridley, 1999; Schluter, 2000). Since adaptive zones constitute discrete clusters, the members of the same species are exposed mainly to the selection forces within their specific zone. However, ecological processes are never entirely discretely clustered. Only in the presence of discontinuities in the environments, as when natural gaps or barriers (for example, a mountainous chain) keep different zones completely separate, can clusters actually develop. Resources are distributed along a continuum and proximate adaptive zones tend to overlap to some degree. The absence of natural gaps or barriers allows for some level of interaction among individuals coming from proximate areas. It is the presence of boundary permeability that renders the local evolution susceptible to the development in adjacent areas.[1] Just as in nature, competition for scarce resources is more frequently intra-specific (that is, within the same adaptive zone) and less frequently inter-specific (that is, among proximate adaptive zones), so organizations are likely to be affected by the behavior of firms from proximate rather than more distant sub-populations.

Interactions among firms across neighboring sub-populations further legitimize a new organizational form and stimulate its spatial diffusion (for example, Hedström, 1994; Hannan et al., 1995). Mitchell's (1969) classic study on the Huk rebellion in the Philippines was among the first to document the social influence of neighboring areas on the focal area. His research on spatial diffusion of the guerrilla ideology against the Philippine Republic's government is germane to our assumption that density-dependence unfolds along a geographic gradient. The interest in geographic diffusion goes back to Hägestrand's *Innovation Diffusion as a Spatial Process* (1953) which showed how contagious behavior enhanced the adoption of agricultural innovations (for example, vaccination against bovine tuberculosis) by

Swedish farmers. Contagion represents the transmission of practices, beliefs and attitudes through direct or indirect contacts whose presence is moderated by the physical environment. A growing body of literature on contagion has examined the spatial nature of diffusion in such fields as geography (for example, Cliff et al., 1981), epidemiology (for example, Bailey, 1976) and sociology (for example, Rogers, 1962).

Social interaction among actors fosters diffusion, but also raises the level of competition (see Lomi and Larsen, 1996). Whenever boundaries have diminished political and institutional saliency, the separation among subpopulations hinges on the sheer permeability of their boundaries. Under such conditions transportation costs represent the main constraint to the spread of competitive forces. Greve (2002) followed such a train of thought in his study of the Tokyo banking industry. The author investigated the impact of changing number of competitors in neighboring areas on the local founding rate and demonstrated how 'competition should also have non-local effects such as those posited by spatial competition theory. Taking spatial density-dependence to be the result of the joint effect of spatial competition . . . suggests that the effect of a given sub-population's density gradually weakens as the distance from that sub-population increases, but it retains the same inverted-U-shaped effect on founding' (Greve, 2002: 854).

These observations lead us to qualify the first hypothesis and further elaborate on the notion of localness and associated spatial heterogeneity. We now argue that legitimation and competition affect new entries along a geographical gradient and, therefore, we hypothesize:

Hypothesis 7.2   Founding rates in the focal area are more strongly affected by local rather than neighboring density-dependence processes of legitimation and competition.

Time Heterogeneity in Organizational Foundings

A recurrent criticism of ecological theories holds that they do not account for the historical dynamics of organizational populations. Perhaps density-dependence is a mere reflection of timing effects (Zucker, 1989). Legitimation and competition, however, are not timeless as 'the effects of density rates on founding and mortality change systematically as organizational populations age' (Hannan, 1997: 193). A Darwinian perspective on evolution in fact assumes that it is more difficult to enter a mature than a young population. Over time, surviving organizations increase their average fitness and spread out across the resource space with the effect of deterring new entries (Sorenson, 2000). Temporal variations in selection thresholds thus condition entries and organizational life chances (Barnett et al., 2002). However, as a population ages, the perceived risk of founding a new venture declines: employees, customers and investors become more readily available to potential entrepreneurs. Cognitive legitimacy improves with time when the cumulative number of organizations entering a population grows.

Since aging industries undergo significant transformations, it is paramount to specify at which level of analysis they take hold. A national perspective on industry evolution might overlook differences in (i) resource endowments and (ii) timing of diffusion among geographical areas. The observed heterogeneity in the development of regional economies hinges upon intra-national differences in resource endowment (Sabel, 1989). Shifting the level of analysis from the population to the sub-population predicated on the spatial heterogeneity hypothesis leads us to consider inter-temporal patterns of change. As noted before, the idea that the environment comprises distinct adaptive zones implies that peer organizations belonging to the same sub-population are predominantly exposed to selection pressures within their specific zone. Such local variations constitute the basis for claiming temporal heterogeneity. While one region might experience severe competition – with the effect of discouraging new entries – the same industry in another region might still be in its formative stages and attract prospective entrepreneurs. But even when ecological clocks were to be initially synchronous, regional differences might produce different evolutionary patterns over time. Within the same industry, opportunities and constraints are spatially and temporally uneven in their distribution. Under the assumption that local more than national evolutionary clocks condition organizational foundings, we hypothesize:

Hypothesis 7.3   Founding rates are more likely to be affected by the age of the local population than by the age of the national population.

Over time, information about new organizational forms spreads across geographical boundaries through networks of people and organizations (for example, Hedström, 1994). As the industry matures, its cultural image becomes crystallized and is diffused through several avenues. These include media, transportation and telecommunications, and mobility of individuals (for example, Hannan et al., 1995).

Knowledge spillovers are not confined to firms co-located within the same geographical area. When organizational knowledge diffuses across geographical boundaries it becomes available to other – more distant – firms (see Powell and Brantley, 1992; Jaffe et al., 1993). Tacit knowledge (see Polanyi, 1967; Winter, 1987), such as the governance of new organizational forms, spreads more gradually than articulate knowledge because its trans-fer requires social relationships that typically concentrate more tightly in space (Sorenson and Baum, 2003). The same argument holds for the diffusion of a new organizational form that depends critically on the pres-ence of social contagion.

To date, ecological research has devoted only scant attention to social contagion spanning distinct sub-populations and their amalgamation into a single national industry. We infer such micro-behaviors from the migra-tion of individuals across geographical areas. Interregional mobility results in the creation and breaking of social ties that constitute avenues for infor-mation and knowledge dissemination. Webs of relationships form and evolve by dint of the movements of potential 'entrepreneurs' across distinct geographical areas, so reducing local variation in organizational forms. In their study on the locational incidence of contacts between biotech firms and university-based scientists affiliated with them, Audretsch and Stephan (1996) found that older scientists were affiliated with spatially more distant firms than their younger peers and that their social networks were less geo-graphically bounded. Such movements produce contagion from distant to more proximate areas. Social contagion ultimately affects the scope of diffusion through both the atomistic behavior of adopters and contacts, 'between members of the population who have and have not yet adopted' (Strang and Tuma, 1993: 614).

Social contagion reduces the sparseness of ties among localized clusters. Interaction across neighboring areas generates new chains of connection and concatenates them into a single national or contextual industry. The migration of individuals across different locations significantly affects the adoption of a new organizational form. In the Paris Commune of 1871, overlaps in National Guard battalion enlistments played a crucial role in establishing 'a stable network of social links among neighborhoods, bridg-ing the insularity of the *quartier* that predominated in political activity during the siege' (Gould, 1995: 184). By stimulating cross-neighborhood exposure, overlapping enlistments proved to be a conduit for communica-tion and social interaction among otherwise sparse urban areas that significantly shaped the mobilization of the insurgent forces. Another com-pelling case is the study of Hedström et al. (2000) on the diffusion of the Swedish Democratic Party during the period 1894–1911, which showed how visits of political agitators from neighboring areas had the effect of establishing 'bridges' between geographically distinct locations and speed-ing up the overall diffusion. These meso-level networks proved to be impor-tant not only for 'recruiting members to *existing* movement organizations, they [were] important for understanding the process that generates *new* movement organizations as well' (2000: 149).

Just as contagion engenders the spread of an epidemic, so it drives diffusion of innovations. Individuals often function as traveling salesmen or brokers carrying information from one area to another and making distant imitation possible. The migration of knowledgeable individuals across geographical areas facilitates the diffusion of a new organizational form through social contagion. By 'word of mouth' communication new adopters can access the experience of early adopters, especially that part of their knowledge that is tacit and therefore difficult to transmit (Geroski, 2000). Local interaction generates positive feedback, with the adoption of a new form depending on its frequency of adoption by proximate organizations. Cognitive legitimacy increases with the cumulative number of organizations so that the incentive to adopt a new organizational form rests largely on the number of previous adopters.

Social contagion figures prominently across local sub-populations having their own local clocks. Contagion across boundaries is important during the early stages of the evolution when individuals from neighboring areas contribute to spreading relevant information in the focal area. We expect their impact to diminish as local evolutionary time passes and organizational sub-populations gravitate towards a national form. We thus hypothesize:

Hypothesis 7.4   Inter-local mobility, more than the intra-local one, positively affects local founding rates during the early periods of population development. As local evolutionary time passes, the opposite relationship holds true.

EMPIRICAL SETTING

To test our hypotheses we traced founding patterns within the Dutch accounting industry during the period 1880–1986 at the population and the sub-population levels of analysis, respectively. Previous studies using the same data (see Boone et al., 2000: 372; but also Chapter 4) found statistically insignificant findings about density-dependence in their analyses. We argue that one of the possible explanations for this is the absence of any control for the geographical heterogeneity of this population. In line with more recent studies using data on Dutch industries (see, for example, the resource partitioning study by Boone et al., 2002 on the Dutch newspaper industry), we studied the impact of the temporal and spatial dimensions on founding rates after dividing the overall population of accounting firms into 11 sub-populations, each corresponding to a different province. Our basic assumption is that each province represents a distinct selection environment (or adaptive zone) where legitimation and competition processes take place. In the next section we briefly explain why provinces are the appropriate unit of analysis to study how spatial heterogeneity affects founding rates within each sub-population.

The Geographic Location of the Study

When considering geography, we should ask not only whether 'mere' distance matters, but also, and more importantly, whether 'borders' matter. It is not in fact the mere proximity that determines the spatial heterogeneity of organizational founding rates. Entrepreneurs are embedded in geographic entities that have more or less well defined boundaries, comprise institutional and socio-economic identities and are endowed with distinct bundles of resources. Geographic entities within a country include Standard Metropolitan Statistical Areas (SMSAs), provinces or states, counties, industrial districts and autonomous regions. They are distinct for historical as well as developmental and administrative reasons. The study by Pennings (1982) found sharp differences among SMSAs in entrepreneurial activity within specific 4-digit SIC codes because SMSAs vary considerably in relevant resource endowments. Other studies show the existence of significant geographical differences, as illustrated by Putnam's (1996) classic study on social capital (for example, with some exaggeration, Alabama is a world of loners, while Minnesotans are well endowed with social capital), and by Linz and de Miguel's (1966) famous paper on Spain in which they identify the existence of eight Spains. As spelled out in Chapter 2, we could likewise and with confidence assume that the eleven provinces of the Netherlands constitute distinct, institutionally differentiated environments.

Data

The Dutch accounting industry shares many of the features of those industries that Porter (1980) defines as fragmented; where no single firm has a dominant position, entry barriers are low and services are differentiated. Furthermore, the capital investments to start up a new venture are low. Given their small size, firms tend to operate at the local (province) level and their critical resources (for example, clients) tend to be local as well. This is particularly relevant in service industries where the client–firm relationship – especially for small, individual firms – as well as competition on the labor market are more likely to be local (Maister, 1993). The accounting service industry is in fact 'entirely a personal service industry' (Benston, 1985: 47). It is worth noting that although the scope of the activity of some firms spans several provincial boundaries, the province is still the relevant environment for most of the firms.

Variables

In our model the independent variables include spatial, non-local density-dependence, temporal heterogeneity, and migration of professional accountants. With respect to spatial density-dependence, we tested our first Hypothesis (7.1) by creating two variables, focal provincial density (*FocalPrDensity*) and focal provincial density squared (*FocalPrDensity2*), to estimate the impact of processes of legitimation (through the linear effect) and competition (through the squared effect) at the province level. We also accounted for the influence of density-dependence processes measured at the national level (*NationalDensity* and *NationalDensity2*).

As to our second Hypothesis (7.2), the influence of neighboring sub-populations was measured by a variable – *NearPrDensity* – computed as the sum of the density values of neighboring provinces. The variable is meant to capture the influence from these areas. We also squared the same variable – *NearPrDensity2* – to verify the non-linear effect of this influence.

We tested our third Hypothesis (7.3) regarding the effect of temporal heterogeneity among different sub-populations on founding rates, by including in the model a variable – *ProvAge* – that measures the age of the industry at the province level, and comparing it with a similar variable at national level – *IndustryAge* – that controls for the age of the entire industry. Building on previous work (Cattani et al., 2002), we tested the effect of the migration of professional accountants across geographical provinces in diffusing the new organizational form by reconstructing the histories of individual organizations. To this end, we kept track of the geographical movements of 4272 accountants during the overall study period, that is, 1880–1986. More specifically, for each year we established whether during the year before the foundation of a new venture the founder worked: (i) within the same geographical area (*Local Founders*); (ii) in any of the neighboring provinces (*Neighboring Founders*); (iii) in more distant provinces (*Distant Founders*); or (iv) in no province because s/he is new to the industry and therefore was not in our database the year before (*New-to-Industry Founders*).

By way of an example, suppose a new firm is founded in a given year in Noord Brabant, a southern province of the Netherlands (see Figure 2.2). The founder might be a professional accountant who used to work for a firm located within the same province or a different one. In the latter case, if the firm is located in Zeeland, Limburg, Gelderland or Zuid Holland, the professional accountant is coming from a neighboring province, otherwise from a more distant one. By contrast, when the founder was not working for any firm, we could not establish the geographical area of origin. To avoid using the same-year founders, for every province we lagged the sum of the values in each of these categories. We test our fourth Hypothesis (7.4) by interacting each of these categories with the local evolutionary time – that is, *ProvAge*.

Drawing from Pennings et al. (1998), several control variables were also included in the model to control for changes in the environment at the national level. In particular, two dummies were created for the occurrence of *World War I* (1914–18) and *World War II* (1941–46). Since *Indonesia's independence* was supposed to have a persistent effect due to the shrinkage of the market for auditing services, we used a dummy taking on the value of 1 if year > 1949, 0 otherwise. The government *Regulation of 1929*, in the wake of the Great Depression, was presumed to have most impact during 1929 and 1930 (1 if year = 1929 and = 1930, 0 otherwise). Another institutional event was the emergence of a *Single Association*, NIvRA, which represented the collective interests of all Dutch accounting firms and was established in 1966 (1 if year > 1966, 0 otherwise). The industry also experienced two regulatory changes in 1971 and 1984. In the former case, the Act on Annual Financial Statements of Enterprises required annual audits. In the latter, definitive guidelines for auditing were promulgated and enforced by NIvRA in collaboration with the Dutch Ministry of Justice. Both regulations significantly heightened the demand for audit services. Two variables were then used, namely *Regulation of 1971* (1 if year > 1971) and *Regulation of 1984* (1 if year > 1984). We included *C4* – a measure of concentration of the market share of the four largest firms – to control for the influence of concentration on foundings. Finally, to capture diversity in growth opportunities at the province level, we used a time-varying variable – *ProvInhab* – that measures the number of inhabitants in each province. More densely populated areas are expected to generate more entrepreneurs. Table 7.1 provides evidence of the temporal asymmetry in the starting time of different provinces, whereas Table 7.2 presents the descriptive statistics and the bivariate correlation of our covariates.

MODEL AND METHOD OF ANALYSIS

As is common in studies of organizational foundings, we assume entries to be a realization of an arrival process. In these cases, the Poisson regression represents the most appropriate solution for studying dependent variables that take on only integer values. Under the assumption that the process of founding follows a Poisson distribution, the main problem to deal with is

Table 7.1 Year of first founding of accounting firms among Dutch provinces

Area	Province	Year of first founding
Mid West	Zuid Holland	1880
Mid West	Noord Holland	1890
Mid West	Utrecht	1901
Center	Gelderland	1916
Mid East	Overijssel	1921
South West	Zeeland	1921
South East	Limburg	1921
South	Noord Brabant	1925
North East	Drenthe	1928
North	Groningen	1906[a]
North	Fryslan	1934

Note: a. This province is an exception. In fact, the second firm that entered this area was after 19 years, in 1925.

overdispersion – that is, the tendency of the variance of the founding rate to increase faster than its mean. To correct for overdispersion and time dependence in the rate of foundings – our data set is a pooled cross-sectional/time series – we used a negative binomial regression model. Thus, we inserted a stochastic component – ε_{it} – to account for this problem. Using z to denote a vector that controls for the geographical origin of nascent entrepreneurs and w to denote a vector that contains controls measured at different levels of aggregation, we estimated the following regression model:

$$r_i(t) = \exp(\alpha_1 NationalDensity_{t-1} + \alpha_2 NationalDensity2_{t-1}$$
$$+ \beta_1 FocalPrDensity_{it-1} + \beta_2 FocalPrDensity2_{it-1}$$
$$+ \gamma_1 NearPrDensity_{it-1} + \gamma_2 NearPrDensity2_{it-1} +$$
$$+ \delta IndustryAge_{t-1} + \zeta ProvAge2_{it-1} + z'_{it}\theta + w'_t\delta)\cdot\varepsilon_{it}$$

where $\exp(\varepsilon_{it}) \sim \Gamma [1, \alpha]$. In this formulation of the negative binomial model, the parameter alpha, estimated directly from the data, captures overdispersion. More precisely, we used a variant of the negative binomial estimator that allows correcting for the interdependence among observations due to the presence of multiple observations within each geographical area. To correct for the bias resulting from the fact that founding rates systematically vary among provinces, we employ the fixed effect version of

Table 7.2 Means, standard deviations and correlations

Variable	Obs	Mean	s. d.	1	2	3	4	5	6	7	8	9	10	11	12	13
1. *ProvInhab*	583	770488.30	643767.50	1.00												
2. *NationalDensity*	583	157.15	107.51	0.33	1.00											
3. *NationalDensity2*	583	36235.75	32356.74	0.30	0.97	1.00										
4. *FocalPrDensity*	583	14.42	28.07	0.79	0.35	0.34	1.00									
5. *FocalPrDensity2*	583	994.28	2811.10	0.67	0.30	0.30	0.96	1.00								
6. *NearPrDensity*	583	63.74	62.96	0.41	0.70	0.68	0.48	0.39	1.00							
7. *NearPrDensity2*	583	8019.86	11590.18	0.33	0.60	0.62	0.42	0.34	0.94	1.00						
8. *IndustryAge*	583	51.82	30.56	0.41	0.69	0.65	0.25	0.17	0.49	0.39	1.00					
9. *ProvAge*	583	25.72	26.31	0.72	0.59	0.56	0.59	0.47	0.52	0.47	0.68	1.00				
10. *Local Founders*	583	0.85	2.30	0.67	0.10	0.07	0.53	0.46	0.19	0.13	0.28	0.54	1.00			
11. *New-to-Industry Founders*	583	1.69	4.27	0.50	0.06	0.02	0.48	0.41	0.18	0.12	0.14	0.36	0.55	1.00		
12. *Neighboring Founders*	583	0.49	1.35	0.62	0.09	0.06	0.47	0.40	0.24	0.19	0.25	0.52	0.66	0.54	1.00	
13. *Distant Founders*	583	0.31	0.86	0.35	0.07	0.01	0.15	0.08	0.06	0.00	0.37	0.41	0.41	0.21	0.23	1.00

the negative binomial model proposed by Hausman et al. (1984) which conditions the estimation on the total count of events in each area. Since we assume that important factors shaping founding activity are geographically grounded, the fixed effects are defined at the province level. The different length of the intervals has been controlled by creating a variable accounting for diverse time spans and using it into the OFFSET option. We estimated the final model using STATA.

RESULTS

Table 7.3 presents the estimates obtained from a conditional fixed effect negative binomial model. The first model in Table 7.3 tests the classical population ecology Hypothesis on density-dependence processes at the national level. Both the linear effect of density – *NationalDensity* – measuring legitimation, and the quadratic effect of density – *NationalDensity2* – measuring competition are statistically significant, though opposite to those predicted by ecological theory. In their analysis of the exit rates within the same population, Boone et al. (2000) found a similar inverted pattern of density-dependence. They concluded that 'the parameters of the contemporaneous density variables show the opposite signs of what has usually been found in ecological studies . . . That is, exit first rises and then declines with density. Apparently, density-related legitimation processes did not occur at the onset of the Dutch audit industry' (2000: 372). This result confirms the limited explicative power of national ecological models for this industry. Market concentration – measured using the *C4* index – is significant and, on average, has a negative impact on foundings. The Act of Financial Statement – *Regulation of 1971* – and the regulation of 1984 have a similar effect. On the other hand, the benefit of a single association representing the collective interest of all Dutch firms is evident. These results are by and large consistent with those obtained by Pennings et al. (1998).

The second model tests H7.1 – that is, how density-dependence, measured at national level, hides unobserved spatial heterogeneity. The value of the log likelihood in model 2 shows that the model with the variables measuring local legitimation – *FocalPrDensity* – and local competition – *FocalPrDensity2* – fits the data better than the previous one ($\chi^2 = 2[L_2 - L_1]$ = 17.66 with p-value < .0001 for 2 d.f.). The results support our hypothesis on spatial density-dependence. This is consistent with previous works (Lomi, 1995; Greve, 2002) and suggests that geographical heterogeneity significantly affects both legitimation and competition.

Following recent developments in ecological theories (for example, Wade et al., 1998; Greve, 2002), we explored whether the evolution of neighboring

*Table 7.3   Conditional fixed effects negative binomial regression
models for the founding rate of Dutch accounting firms,
1880–1986*

Variables	Model 1	Model 2	Model 3	Model 4	Model 5
Constant	−.95**	−.87**	−1.50**	−1.70	−1.79**
	(.33)	(.32)	(.39)	(.47)	(.49)
ProvInhab (in millions)	−.54**	−.80**	−.93**	−.38*	−.35*
	(.15)	(.17)	(.17)	(.22)	(.22)
World War I	−.81**	−.64*	−.71**	−.59*	−.49
	(.32)	(.33)	(.34)	(.34)	(.36)
Regulation of 1929	.84**	.92**	.78**	.60	.63*
	(.42)	(.40)	(.39)	(.39)	(.37)
World War II	−.09	.06	.07	.18	.21
	(.46)	(.45)	(.44)	(.43)	(.42)
Single association	1.57**	1.59**	1.58**	2.50**	2.12**
	(.30)	(.29)	(.27)	(.33)	(.35)
Indonesia's independence	1.62**	1.71**	1.85**	2.64**	2.56**
	(.30)	(.29)	(.26)	(.28)	(.28)
Regulation of 1971	−.69**	−.67**	−1.12**	−1.22**	−1.08**
	(.21)	(.21)	(.26)	(.25)	(.27)
Regulation of 1984	−.40**	−.45**	−.44**	−.06	.14
	(.17)	(.18)	(.18)	(.19)	(.21)
C4	−2.70**	−2.71**	−1.94**	−1.96**	−1.77**
	(.48)	(.49)	(.56)	(.60)	(.61)
NationalDensity	−.01**	−.01**	−.01**	−.003	−.003
	(.00)	(.00)	(.00)	(.003)	(.003)
NationalDensity2	.003**	.004**	.003**	.001	.001
(in hundreds)	(.001)	(.001)	(.001)	(.001)	(.001)
FocalPrDensity		.03**	.03**	.03**	.03**
		(.01)	(.01)	(.01)	(.01)
FocalPrDensity2		−.012**	−.014**	−.014**	−.017**
(in hundreds)		(.006)	(.006)	(.006)	(.006)
NearPrDensity			.01**	.02**	.02**
			(.00)	(.00)	(.00)
NearPrDensity2			−.005**	−.006**	−.006**
(in hundreds)			(.001)	(.002)	(.002)
IndustryAge				−.01	−.01
				(.01)	(.01)
ProvAge				−.04**	−.02*
				(.01)	(.01)
Local Founders					−.18**
					(.09)

Table 7.3 (continued)

Variables	Model 1	Model 2	Model 3	Model 4	Model 5
New-to-Industry					.04
Founders					(.03)
Neighboring Founders					.44**
					(.12)
Distant Founders					.44**
					(.15)
*Local Founders * ProvAge*					.002*
					(.001)
New-to-Industry Founders					−.0003
* ProvAge					(.0005)
Neighboring Founders					−.01**
* ProvAge					(.001)
Distant Founders *					−.01**
ProvAge					(.002)
Log likelihood	−887.36	−878.53	−870.70	−859.07	−839.28

Note: *: p<.10; **: p<.05; ***: p<.01 (two-tailed test); standard errors in parentheses under parameter.

provinces affects the evolution of a given sub-population. We estimated a model including the linear and the quadratic term of *NearProvDensity*. Not only does model 3 better fit the data ($\chi^2 = 2[L_3 - L_2] = 15.66$ with p-value <.0001 for 2 d.f.), but both coefficient estimates for *NearPrDensity* and its squared term are statistically significant as well. The effect of local density-dependence remains highly significant. Furthermore, the magnitude of *FocalPrDensity* and its squared term (*FocalPrDensity2*) is three times as large as the estimates of the corresponding density measures in contiguous provinces and in both cases the difference is statistically significant (p-value <.10 with 1 d.f.). The relationship is represented graphically in Figure 7.1. The numeric values used to plot the graph were generated from the coefficient estimates of the variables in model 3.

Based on these estimates, the multiplier[2] of the curvilinear founding rate for focal provincial density, *on average*, reaches its maximum (λ^*) when the density of the average sub-population is at N = 88. At that value, the founding rate is about 3 times larger than the same rate when N = 0 – that is, when no firm has been founded as yet. This value is similar to that found by Lomi (1995) in his study on rural cooperative banks in Italy. Put differently, the rate at which new organizations are created initially increases with the level of density due to the provincial legitimation effect. However, beyond a

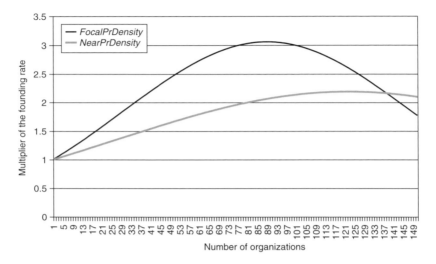

Figure 7.1   *Multiplier of the founding rate for density at the focal province*
            (FocalPrDensity*) and contiguous provinces (* NearPrDensity*)*
            level

certain level, which corresponds to a sub-population's carrying capacity, the
rate of founding declines as higher levels of density entail more competition.
For the average sub-population of our sample this threshold is reached
when density is equal to 88. This finding confirms the importance of the
local legitimation and competition processes for each sub-population. The
difference in magnitude between the maximum values of the multiplier of
the founding rate for focal and neighboring provincial density, respectively,
suggests that local density-dependence effects dominate those from contiguous provinces. The maximum value of the multiplier of the founding
rate for neighboring provincial density is reached when $\lambda^* = 2.19$. The same
value obtained at the local level of analysis is 50 per cent larger.

Whereas all these models have been estimated to test whether spatial
dimension represents a source of heterogeneity among sub-populations, in
model 4 we included age or duration of the industry – *IndustryAge* – and a
variable – *ProvAge* – that accounts for differences in age among sub-populations and was created to test the temporal dimension of organizational heterogeneity (Hypothesis 7.3). Identifying the unit of analysis of temporal
evolution of a population is critical to understanding at which level of analysis selection processes take place. The model shows that local clocks more
than the national one shape the evolution of the Dutch accounting industry.
In particular, for each 1-year increase in the age of the sub-population, the

number of new foundings decreases by approximately 4 per cent (exp 0.04). Thus, these results support Hypothesis 7.3.

The logic behind Hypothesis 7.4 is that migration of individuals from established organizational populations facilitates the diffusion of a new organizational form across geographical areas. But we also argued that the effect of these movements in the focal area diminishes over time. Model 5 tests this hypothesis by including both the main and the interaction effect between founders' geographical origin and local evolutionary time – *ProvAge*. As the coefficient estimates indicate, the impact of movements of professionals from neighboring and more distant provinces on founding in the focal area diminishes over time. As time passes, however, local dynamics – mostly in the form of spin-offs – become increasingly important in driving entries. It is worth noting that adding these variables improves the fit of the model with our data ($\chi^2 = 2[L_5 - L_4] = 39.59$ with p-value $< .0001$ for 8 degrees of freedom). This pattern of results is consistent with Hypothesis 7.4.

DISCUSSION AND CONCLUSIONS

Two recurrent criticisms of the density-dependence model (Hannan, 1986) refer to the choice of the proper unit of analysis and the neglect of micro-behaviors leading to legitimation. While a growing body of research has stressed the neglect of unobserved heterogeneity, and the corresponding misrepresentation of the significance of ecological processes, a main challenge has been the decomposition of national populations into sub-populations (Baum and Amburgey, 2002; Lomi, 1995). Understanding the geographical sources of heterogeneity has both theoretical and normative consequences for entrepreneurs and policy-makers alike.

We have therefore advocated a perspective on organizational foundings that focuses on the spatial and temporal sources of heterogeneity in new entries within a population of organizations. We first explored organizational foundings as a function of spatial density, showing that local, more than national, density-dependence processes help explain industry evolution. Second, we demonstrated how multiple, heterogeneous local clocks shape density-dependence processes unfolding in different geographical areas. Third, we showed how spatial diffusion unfolds through inter-local mobility. In this regard, the migration of individuals across geographical areas is an important micro-mechanism for the spreading of new organizational forms.

One of the most interesting implications of the present analysis is the identification of micro-mechanisms driving macro-evolutionary processes

(Schelling, 1978). The existence of distinct sub-populations of organizations exhibiting idiosyncratic evolutionary trajectories suggests that a more fine-grained examination of the forces shaping the evolution of an industry can be obtained by shifting the level of analysis to that of the sub-population. Local entrepreneurial deeds have repercussions beyond the boundaries of the geographical area in which a given sub-population is residing. Yet, the overall spectrum of these deeds – entry, competition or collaboration – cannot be fully captured by simply looking at entries. A multi-level analysis therefore endorses our contention for studying mortality rates within populations.

We believe that our findings improve knowledge of ecological processes. It is worth noting that most of the findings on multi-level density-dependence have been anchored in manufacturing industries, if not solely in the automobile sector (Hannan et al., 1995; Hannan, 1997; Dobrev et al., 2001; but see Wezel and Lomi, 2003). By contrast, for service industries results are still scant (Greve, 2002; Lomi, 2000), in spite of their growing importance in the modern economy. The nature of the service sector partly explains some of the inconsistencies of results observed in the multi-level density-dependence literature. By showing the existence of spatially heterogeneous density-dependence processes, our findings have interesting implications for research dealing with resource partitioning (Carroll, 1985). In their analysis of the dynamics of resource partitioning among Italian rural cooperative banks, Freeman and Lomi (1994: 291) noticed that this process is observable only when regional fixed effects are not introduced into the model. Their results hint at the possibility that resource partitioning might be geographically distributed or simply the byproduct of spatial and temporal heterogeneity. Boone et al. (2000) found strong evidence for resource partitioning within the same industry especially during the years before 1971 – that is, when the concentration of the industry was still low, small provinces like Groningen, Overijssel and Limburg were still growing, and one of the biggest provinces (North Holland) had just reached its density peak. The importance of legitimation and competition at a less aggregate level than the entire industry should thus be considered to fully understand the firm's environment and its impact on organizational creation and dissolution.

Ecological theories dwell on the evolution of organizational populations. The study of their evolution concerns six main sub-processes, each characterized by its own vital rate: (i) creation of new organizational forms (speciation rates), (ii) founding of new organizations (founding rates), (iii) growth and contraction of organizations (growth rates), (iv) change in the existing organizations (rates of change), (v) disbanding of organizations (failure rates), and (vi) extinction of populations (rates of extinction). While organizational ecologists have widely studied foundings and failures, and have extensively investigated the organizational processes related to change and growth, scant effort has been devoted to understanding extinction events (for two noticeable exceptions see Lomi et al., 2005; Wezel, 2002) and, in particular, organizational speciation – that is, the emergence of a new organizational form (see Rao and Singh, 1999). Dealing with the emergence and diffusion of new organizational forms, institutional theorists emphasize the influence of social and governmental institutions – for example, regulatory and professional organizations (DiMaggio, 1991). Besides such normative and regulatory effects, however, cognitive legitimacy can spread through the movement of individuals across geographical areas. Our study provides an illustration of how the migration of professional accountants has directly conditioned the diffusion of new organizational forms. Similar considerations are consistent with recent developments in organizational theory that explore the relevance of personnel turnover in diffusing new social movements (Hedström et al., 2000), and influencing organizational innovation (Rao and Drazin, 2002) and performance (Cattani et al., 2002; Phillips, 2002).

The choice of the province as a meaningful social entity might be questioned on the grounds that social contagion significantly reduces the cognitive distance among separate geographical areas and renders administrative boundaries less salient. Yet, our findings on the relative importance of ecological processes observed at different levels of analysis signal that geography should not be disregarded. As implicit in the hypothesis on spatial heterogeneity, competition among firms tends to be local. More distant firms are less likely to compete for the same pool of resources or to interact with one another. The intensity of the interaction among new and existing organizations is proportional to their degree of physical proximity (Baum and Mezias, 1992; Sorensen and Audia, 2000). In professional services sectors, with a preponderance of personal (that is, based on trust and reputation) and local (that is, embedded in the existing social fabric) relationships, the possibility of starting a new venture, and its subsequent survival are primarily – though not exclusively – geared to garnering locally available resources. Firms acquire and retain such resources by offering customized services and adapting their practice to the special needs of local clients (see Smigel, 1969; Porter, 1980; Maister, 1993).

Finally, by showing how local, rather than national, ecological processes shape organizational foundings in different geographical areas, we believe that the results of our chapter offer a new perspective on entry decisions. The existence of spatial and temporal sources of heterogeneity suggests that industries comprise distinct sub-populations, each experiencing distinct and non-synchronous evolutionary phases. Similar considerations suggest that opportunities and constraints for entrepreneurs are asymmetrically distributed in space. A deeper understanding of the conditions affecting vital processes should thus consider spatial dynamics when investigating patterns of industrial evolution.

NOTES

1. Similarly, Levin argues that 'ecological communities and ecosystems are heterogeneous in space and time, and this heterogeneity affects diversity and the evolution of life histories. Such biotic heterogeneity reflects underlying heterogeneity in the abiotic environment, frequency-dependent habitat and niche partitioning, and the stochastic phenomena associated with disturbance and colonization' (1989: 248).
2. The multiplier is found by computing $\exp[(\xi_i^*N) + (\omega^*N^2)]$ based on the estimates of Model 3, where N is equal to the density of organizations, N^2, and the subscript i refers to the fact that we are comparing two measures, namely the *FocalPrDensity* and the *NearPrDensity*.

8. Heterogeneity shifts due to member mobility: new insights on demographic diversity and organizational survival

INTRODUCTION

The study of organizational demography in general, and that of top management teams in particular, has often been examined as a major precursor to strategic positioning and organizational outcomes (for example, Finkelstein and Hambrick, 1996; Hambrick et al., 1996). Past research has investigated the short-term performance consequences of top management entries and exits at the firm or at the individual level of analysis (Harris and Helfat, 1997; Groysberg, 2001). The consequences of inter-firm mobility for different outcomes of the source and of the destination firm (for example, Agarwal et al., 2004; Madsen et al., 2003; Rao and Drazin, 2002; Rosenkopf and Almeida, 2003) have been likewise explored. Demography and inter-firm mobility have rarely been combined to explain organizational long-term performance. The investigation of the survival implications of diversity at firm and inter-firm levels due to mobility is the theme of this chapter.

Specifically, we focus on three under-explored issues in organizational demography research: (i) the dynamics of demographic diversity *variations* within firms, (ii) the influence of demographic variation on the *competitive overlap* among firms, and (iii) the survival consequences of (i) and (ii), the intra- and inter-firm demographic variations. First, empirical research has focused on the study of the *levels* (that is, stock) of diversity, estimating the 'average effects' of diversity changes on performance. Moving beyond this static approach to explore the dynamic impact of diversity *variations* on organizational performance, researchers have noticed that focusing on such variations produces a direct investigation of the underlying mechanisms of the theory (see Carroll and Harrison, 1998). We examine here the impact of mobility of key members (for example, top managers) as shocks to the level of diversity. The concern with diversity variations also permits a test of symmetric consequences: the same marginal impact of increases and decreases on performance.

Second, recognizing organizational demography as a precursor to strategic decisions requires that we acknowledge that firms do not exist in a vacuum but rather are embedded in a sector or specific region. Research on inter-firm mobility has rarely been paired with demographic aspects even as one would presume that shifts in heterogeneity would have implications beyond their consequences for internal group processes (Sørensen, 1999b). As 'managers operate on mental representations of the world and those representations are likely to be of historical environments rather than current ones' (Kiesler and Sproull, 1982: 557), overlapping demographic attributes reveal strategic similarity among competitors. For instance, if managerial teams are similar in terms of gender or seniority, their incumbents are likely to converge in decision-making (Pegels et al., 2000). The presence of demographic variations *within* firms could lead to investigations regarding the impact of overlap changes *between* them. In this case too, the consequences of increases and reductions of overlapping managerial characteristics due to mobility might reveal a symmetric effect.

Third, top management-team research has mainly focused on short-run outcomes as proxied by accounting measures such as ROI, failing to include long-run organizational performance measures such as growth (for an exception see Sørensen, 1999a, 1999b) and survival. To move towards a dynamic theory of demographic diversity, longitudinal research designs capturing long-term implications of changes in demographic heterogeneity are needed (Boone et al., 2006). Although Hambrick and Mason's model (1984: Figure 2, page 198) speculated on within-firm diversity and long-run performance, the research to date has rarely investigated this issue (for two partial exceptions see Hambrick and D'Aveni, 1988 and 1992). Note that diversity might hamper either current coordination and alignment of members seeking a common frame of reference or joint decisional commitment. That may also have long-term repercussions in that heterogeneous rosters of people are unlikely to settle into a set of lasting, persistent routines, practices and a collectively ingrained body of knowledge. From an inter-organizational standpoint, shifts in demographic diversity shape organizational survival chances by reducing or augmenting competitive overlap. Survival is jeopardized when overlap (measured along different characteristics, including socio-demographics, for example, Rotolo and McPherson, 2001) increases.

This chapter elaborates on these three points to propose a multi-level approach to the survival consequences of demographic variations in Dutch accounting firms.

THEORY

Organizational Implications

Firm membership embodies a configuration of skills, experience, and social contacts that are specialized towards the market segments or sectors in which a firm operates. Differences among members partly reflect differences in their backgrounds, such as prior career development across firms. This diversity matters because it can at once hinder or enhance organizational performance. For example, demographic differences among the members might challenge the alignment to such a degree that much energy gets diverted from the tasks at hand, and substandard outcomes on a variety of performance criteria ensues. Diversity challenges coordination and alignment of the membership. Diversity also produces differences in cognitive perspectives and behavioral dispositions that render the firm strongly embedded in its strategic position and long-term trajectory.

Research on upper echelons (Hambrick and Mason, 1984) has elaborated on the diversity–performance link under the assumption that organizations mirror the values, goals, and experiences of their pre-eminent members. Managers' demographic profiles enter into the performance argument because their characteristics are presumed to occasion psychological dispositions and subsequent strategic choices (for example, Hambrick and Mason, 1984). Characteristics such as gender, age, and tenure affect managers' decisions and actions through three different screens (see Hambrick and Mason, 1984). First, their background delimits the problems and information by which their attention is attracted. Second, selective perception occurs because managers devote disproportionately more attention to the stimuli in their field of vision. Finally, the information they receive is filtered through their cognitive lenses. The degree of heterogeneity in demographic characteristics typically amounts to a 'proxy for cognitive heterogeneity, representing innovativeness, problem-solving abilities, creativity, diversity of information sources and perspectives, openness to change and willingness to challenge and be challenged' (Finkelstein and Hambrick, 1996: 125). As a result, teams with high variability in their demographic attributes typically have different schemata or ways of seeing the world (for example, Michel and Hambrick, 1992).

The managerial cognition literature supports this conjecture, as evidenced by studies on managerial cognition and strategic decision-making (for example, Tripsas and Gavetti, 2000), which support the conclusion that 'managerial work experience shapes managerial cognition' (Adner and Helfat, 2003: 1022). Demographic heterogeneity contributes to this argument as divergent mental frames produce cognitive heterogeneity by alternatively interfering with intra-group communication (for example, Lawrence, 1997; Zenger and Lawrence, 1989); strengthening internal conflict (Jehn et al., 1999); increasing the time for reaching consensus (Hambrick et al., 1996); lowering adherence to budget and schedule (Ancona and Caldwell, 1992) or undermining strategic consensus (Knight et al., 1999) and stimulating framing contests. Since tenure heterogeneity hampers social integration, organizations endure higher turnover rates (for example, O'Reilly et al., 1989; Wiersema and Bird, 1993).

Some reviews of the literature stress the multifaceted nature of the relationship between heterogeneity and performance (Guzzo and Dickson, 1996). A positive outcome is observed when tasks are complex and uncertain – for example those faced by top management teams, for which 'informational diversity should theoretically be more beneficial than in routine tasks' (Barsade et al., 2000: 809). Other studies stressed the positive externalities associated with demographic heterogeneity when groups are faced with creative problem solving and innovation (for example, Bantel and Jackson, 1989; Eisenhardt and Schoonhoven, 1990). While this seemingly discordant finding reflects the more general issue of whether demographic variables inform about cognitive proclivities in predicting team outcomes (Lawrence, 1997; Kilduff et al., 2000), the specific outcome might partly explain these discordant findings. The literature seems to center on the negative impact of demographic – and implied attitudinal or cognitive diversity (see Boone et al., 2004; Jehn et al., 1999; Harrison et al., 2002).[1]

An important but as yet unanswered question concerns, therefore, the impact of variations in the demographic composition of groups (see also Williams and O'Reilly III, 1998). Answering this question should elucidate the relation between demographic heterogeneity and performance, whether at the group or the firm level. Although empirical inquiries have involved *levels* (stock) of heterogeneity, its harmful effects pertain to the costs of recruitment into the firm (that is, *inflows*) (see Pfeffer, 1983). We agree with Carroll and Harrison (1998: 658) that 'a major source of this diversity comes from the disruption by newly entering individuals'. As demographic variation spells differences in social cohesion, communication, and strategic consensus, the recruitment of new members winds up affecting (increasing or reducing) such differences. Such staffing effects occur because of the correspondence between demographic and cognitive heterogeneity. A recruit's propensity to embrace the firm's values and norms is proportional to the demographic fit with the recipient organization. Unless newcomers overlap demographically with the roster of people they are joining, their collective ability to function effectively becomes compromised.[2]

Theoretical and empirical research in organizational demography of top management teams has already pointed out that demographic diversity engenders a downward spiral of failure (Hambrick and D'Aveni, 1992; Stewman, 1988). Departing from the above evidence that membership heterogeneity reduces short-term performance, compositional deterioration will follow due to the inability of attracting new talents. Retaining valuable executives becomes increasingly difficult because stars are likely to exit when organizations perform poorly (Groysberg and Nanda, 2002). Increases in demographic diversity severely threaten a firm's long-term effectiveness. It is conducive to framing contests in that executives with divergent demographic profiles are bound to exhibit divergent strategic preferences that lead them to frame strategic directions in often opposite or contrarian ways. Within-group cooperation around strategic choices and their implementation is sustainable when people trust each other and deviance from reciprocity can easily be monitored and sanctioned (Campbell, 1994). Group heterogeneity however impedes trust and reciprocal altruism in groups (Ruef et al., 2003; Boone et al., 2006). Last but not least, a 'team of divergent composition may be seen as incompetent or ill-suited [. . .] causing stakeholders to withdraw or restrict their support for the organization' (Hambrick and D'Aveni, 1992: 1463). Rises in demographic diversity may trigger a cascade of unforeseeable events that increase the risk of organizational failure. This line of reasoning remains consistent with the insights of Hambrick and Mason (1984: see Figure 2, 198; see also the recent review of Carpenter et al., 2004: 751). As socialization processes or communication hinge on the fit between new entries and the roster of exiting membership, new member inflows augmenting group heterogeneity would increase the risk of organizational failure. In line with our approach regarding the symmetry of this effect, we also hypothesize that inflows which further homogenize firm membership enhance its survival chances. Accordingly, we hypothesize:

Hypothesis 8.1a   When key member inflows raise demographic heterogeneity, the hazard of organizational failure increases.

Hypothesis 8.1b   When key member inflows decrease demographic heterogeneity, the hazard of organizational failure declines.

Competitive Implications

Demographic variables inform us of the mental models of decision-makers which factor into competitive relationships and the likely framing towards which a group evolves, if such evolution can be observed. Mental models condition managerial perceptions of their markets (for example, Porac et al., 1989; Reger and Huff, 1993) as well as their commensurate strategic actions (Thomas et al., 1993). These 'models' are inferred from demographic attributes as managerial knowledge structures are formed on the basis of differences in origins – for example, experiences (Walsh, 1995). Pfeffer (1983) holds that individuals belonging to similar age cohorts exhibit identical values and beliefs. Demographic profiles inform about the strategic positioning of their firms (Finkelstein and Hambrick, 1990); their strategic diversification (Michel and Hambrick, 1992) and internationalization (Carpenter and Fredrickson, 2001; Sanders and Carpenter, 1998); and scope of their competitive response (Hambrick et al., 1996). Long-tenured managerial teams persist in entrenched strategies and favor courses of action that mirror the status quo (Hambrick et al., 1993; Finkelstein and Hambrick, 1990). In short they are often precursor to their firms' prevailing patterns of actions, because their demographic characteristics 'provide vital information on a firm's gravitation towards certain segments, or towards niches to compete and on the likelihood of success in the chosen market niches' (Pegels et al., 2000: 914).

A theory concerned with the impact of inter-firm mobility on demographic diversity and firm performance should then take into account that firms are embedded in webs of competitively interdependencies. Firms do not operate in a social vacuum, 'organizational demographers attribute no causal or mediating force to the demographic characteristics of other organizations' (Sørensen, 1999b: 714). As a result, the transfer of people inevitably affects the degree of demographic similarity among firms.[3]

Several studies have pointed to the inter-firm implications of demographic heterogeneity (Boone et al., 2004; Keck and Tushman, 1993; Lawrence, 1997). Managers with equivalent demographic characteristics typically exhibit 'attentional homogeneity' – that is, similarity in the mental models regarding their sector and its incumbents (Abrahmson and Hambrick, 1997). Convergent and analogous views of the competitive environment in turn affect resource allocation and other strategic decisions (Sørensen, 1999b). Demographically akin managers among peer firms express higher levels of mutual awareness, and tacitly or explicitly mimic their strategic choices (see Pegels et al., 2000; Skaggs and Youndt, 2004). Firms with demographically similar team members exhibit higher levels of strategic similarity and hence competitive interdependence. That is because 'a cohort is the societal experiences that have been imprinted on its members and have helped to shape their values and perceptions' (Hambrick and Mason, 1984: 202), and cohorts of managers exposed to similar historical environments share identical mental models (Kiesler and Sproull, 1982).

The argument, therefore, takes on a different line here because inter-firm demographic differences also matter. Consider research on organizational ecology and niche overlap (McPherson, 1983; Hannan and Freeman, 1989). A vast literature in organizational ecology demonstrates how competitively interdependent firms act locally on some specific dimensions, with intensity being greater at larger levels of overlap. McPherson (1983) argued that the competition between two voluntary organizations for new recruits is proportional to their socio-demographic similarities. Baum and Singh (1994) showed that overlap between segments of the child-care population produced higher failure levels. Similar findings have been found regarding technological (Podolny et al., 1996) and geographical (Baum and Mezias, 1992) overlap. As firms with demographically similar members share similar strategic orientations (for a review see Carpenter et al., 2004), we expect them to vie for the same resources and to face more rivalry. In contrast, dissimilarity produces divergent mental dispositions among them and results in divergent strategic pursuits (Pegels et al., 2000). Thus, ensuing increases in demographic similarity produce identical strategic frames of reference (Sørensen, 1999b). Conversely, mobility events that result in firms becoming demographically more unique also render them less interdependent strategically. As before, we test for the existence of symmetric consequences of overlap variations by suggesting that increases in inter-firm demographic similarity raise the risk of organizational failure, whereas the opposite holds true for drops in similarity:

Hypothesis 8.2a   When key member inflows raise demographic similarity among firms, the hazard of organizational failure increases.

Hypothesis 8.2b   When key member inflows decrease demographic similarity among firms, the hazard of organizational failure declines.

DATA

Data consist of information about individual professional accountants and their organizations and were collected from the membership lists (or directories) of accountant associations with one- to five-year gaps or intervals.

The concern here is with the survival implications of hiring new members as partners rather than associates. Accounting firms have a dual stratification with the top echelon endowed with superior human and social capital. The effects of member entry on strategic conduct should be higher when the recruitment of new organizational members involves partners. Partners are the owners of the firm. As such they have a greater incentive to use their human capital for the growth of an organization than do associates. Partners are more critical for a firm's performance and survival as they have greater influence on organizational outcomes (Galanter and Palay, 1991). Partners are responsible for the overall management of accounting firms. Their decision-making power extends to the task of building/changing routines, such as those dealing with hiring and firing policies, procuring work and deploying junior professionals, differentiation (that is, to hedge against market shrinkage), investment, personal financial planning, and liability insurance premium decisions (for more details see Maister, 1993). The partners' social capital is thus more germane to the organization's profit potential than that of the associates (see Pennings et al., 1998). Thus, the recruitment of new partners often entails a shift in the competitive landscape within which firms compete.

Independent Variables

The inflow of key members (here, partners) affects the level of demographic heterogeneity of the recipient firm. Due to the critical role of localized networks and experience in this industry (see Smigel, 1969), we measured the heterogeneity of values and goals in the firm in terms of *local* tenure. As mentioned before, the province constitutes the main locale for these professional services firms. The length of service within the focal 'province' thus serves as the demographic attribute of choice in testing our theory. This measure captures the putative propensity toward certain strategic commitments. The presumption is that partners or managers with equivalent bodies of experiences exhibit similar mental models. In fact, '[M]easures based on team tenure therefore potentially underestimate the extent to which managers are similar' (Sørensen, 1999b: 727) – whenever senior decision makers move towards a peer firm, that variable would take on the value 0, regardless of their level of prior experience, implying that entering partners exhibit identical experience and, thus, ignoring the differences along this dimension – each time they begin a new stage in their career when joining a different firm.

Nevertheless, local tenure as main dimension of demographic heterogeneity remains anchored in the theoretical argument. As 'managers operate on mental representations of the world and those representations are likely to be of historical environments rather than current ones' (Kiesler and Sproull, 1982: 557), managers exposed to similar historical environments share equivalent mental predispositions. Tenure signals socialization and cognitive programming, and the longer its duration, the stronger its mental and attitudinal end will result. Local tenure, and by implication indigenous or 'native' experience, makes the peer firms' members more knowledgeable about current market conditions and future trends, and by derivation instills competitive awareness among them.

When staffing involves such local occupational seniority and equivalence in experience and socialization, the stronger the mutual awareness, the higher the intensity of rivalry between firms. Moreover, an important strength of this measure is its focus on the survival consequences of demographic equivalence among peer firms. Long-tenured managerial teams in fact have been shown to engage in persistent strategies and to select policies more committed to the status quo (see Hambrick et al., 1993; Finkelstein and Hambrick, 1990).

Organizational demographers measure the level of tenure heterogeneity employing the coefficient of variation – that is, the ratio of the standard deviation of tenure to its mean. By aggregating this measure, however, two main problems emerge. First, while this standardization improves comparability across organizations, it comes 'at a minimum price of interpretive ambiguity' (Sørensen, 2002: 478). Models that use the coefficient of variation alone risk confounding the differential effect that the mean and the standard deviation might have on social processes. Second, when averages are computed using lower-level (for example, managers) data, researchers implicitly adopt an 'additive' model – that is, the aggregate or higher-level measure is just a summation of the lower-level units regardless of the variance among these units (see Chan, 1998). By contrast, the standard deviation is a more appropriate measure of heterogeneity because it overcomes the aggregation bias by computing the distance between individuals, irrespective of the mean (Barsade et al., 2000).[4]

To test hypotheses 8.1a and 8.1b, the variations in the value of the standard deviation for local tenure was adopted. For each firm we first calculated the standard deviation of the number of years the partners spent within the focal province. In particular, we captured the evolving nature in local tenure heterogeneity by creating a time-varying variable – *Tenure Heterogeneity Flow* – which measures the change in the value of the standard deviation in tenure that can be attributed to the entry of new partners only. We excluded endogenous diversity shifts – for example, changes due to partner death, retirement or simple exit. We calculated the variable net of the natural increase (that is, due to the mere passage of time) in tenure between two consecutive time periods as well as any other variation due to the departure or death of partners over the same period.

To test hypotheses 8.2a and 8.2b, we created the variable *Demographic Overlap Flow* that measures the degree of overlap change in the average stock of provincial experience (due to partner inflows) between the recipient and its competitors located within the same geographical province. We chose an average measure because both quantitative (Finkelstein and Hambrick, 1990; Sørensen, 1999a, 1999b) and qualitative research (Tripsas and Gavetti, 2000) suggests that average team tenure profoundly affects strategies and performance. The overlap measure varies over time as a result of recruiting new partners, again net of the natural increase in tenure between time t and time $t-1$ as well as any other variation due to the departure or death of partners over the same period. First, for each firm we computed the maximum and minimum values for the provincial tenure range by adding and subtracting 10 per cent to (from) the mean value of firm tenure.[5] We quantified the degree of niche overlap by counting the number of firms falling within the same tenure range in a given year. Since the inflow of key members can affect the degree of demographic similarity between the recipient and its competitors by increasing or decreasing their mean tenure overlap, the number of firms falling within the new range is likely to vary accordingly. To measure changes in demographic overlap among firms, we calculated the difference between the numbers of firms in two consecutive time periods, respectively. To make sure this effect was solely due to new entries, we restricted the variation of this variable to the cases in which at least one new partner entry in a given year is observed.

A strict test of the theory implies checking the symmetric impact of the counteracting forces behind, within and between firm differences. From earlier research it has been observed that both heterogeneity and overlap are harmful to the firm. With the variables, *Tenure Heterogeneity Flow* (*TH*) and *Demographic Overlap Flow* (*DO*), we model their effect through a 'spline' function. In a spline specification a variable is allowed to have slopes that differ depending on whether its values lie above or below a given cut-off point (Greene, 2000: 322–4; see also Greve, 2003). More specifically, we fitted a model that estimates the risk of dissolution of the organization i at time t as follows:

$$Exit_{it} = F(\alpha_1(TH_{t-1})D_{TH_{t-1}\leq 0} + \alpha_2(TH_{t-1})D_{TH_{t-1}>0} +$$

$$\beta_1(DO_{t-1})E_{DO_{t-1}\leq 0} + \beta_2(DO_{t-1})E_{DO_{t-1}>0} + \delta X_{t-1}),$$

where separate variables are entered to model the positive and negative effects. More precisely, α_1 is the coefficient that refers to tenure heterogeneity decreases (H1b); α_2 is the coefficient that refers to tenure heterogeneity increases (H1a); β_1 is the coefficient that refers to demographic overlap decreases (H2b); and β_2 is the coefficient for demographic overlap increases (H2a). Furthermore, δ is a vector of coefficients for the controls, and D and E are variables that take on the value 1 if the subscript condition is true, 0 otherwise. To facilitate an intuitive interpretation of the opposite direction of the coefficients and to allow us to log-transform the variables, diversity decrements are measured in absolute values. Thus, while we expect α_1 (H1b) and β_1 (H2b) to be negative, α_2 (H1a) and β_2 (H2a) should be positively related to organizational failure. Such a model specification allows us to appreciate the different slopes exhibited by the decline and the increase coefficients as conditional on the aforementioned change due to members entering the partnership team. Their entry serves as a demography-altering event having negative or positive long-term performance consequences.

Control Variables

Besides our variables of theoretical interest, we included in the final model several control variables at the historical, provincial and organizational levels to rule out a number of competing hypotheses.

Historical controls The history of the Dutch accounting industry has been marked by many important events that might well affect organizational survival chances in specific years. In particular, we created two dummy variables for the governmental regulations dealing with *World War I* (1914–18) conditions and the occurrence of *World War II* (1941–46). Since the 1960s, the Dutch accounting industry has witnessed several fundamental regulatory changes. More stringent requirements – for example, the need for higher levels of education and experience, and the examination to become CPA – have over time restricted the entry of potential competitors. As mentioned in Chapter 2, several major regulatory changes have encompassed both the supply and the demand of professional accounting services. We then created a variable – *Single Association* – which takes on the value 1 if year > 1966, 0 otherwise. In 1970 the Act on Annual Accounts of Companies (which took effect in 1971) expanded the number of firms required by law to disclose audited annual accounts by including large private firms and cooperative societies in addition to public companies. We also captured the effect of the regulatory changes enforced in 1971 and 1984, which significantly heightened the demand for audit services, with two dummy variables – *Regulation of 1971* (1 if year > 1971) and *Regulation of 1984* (1 if year > 1984), respectively.

Provincial controls We included the linear and quadratic effects of density measures at the provincial level – *Focal Province Density* and *Focal Province Density2* – to estimate the extent to which more general ecological phenomena affect organizational survival. In the presence of high levels of concentration, just a few organizations control most of the available resources. We thus controlled for concentration of the industry – *C4* – given by the total market share of the top 4 firms.

The risk of organizational failure also depends on how many firms were founded or disappeared each year, which reflects both the degree of munificence of the environment and the extent to which ecological conditions affect inter-organizational mobility by creating/destroying new job opportunities. Accordingly, we created two variables – *Firms Entering Province* and *Firms Exiting Province* – to account for the number of firms founded and dissolved during the previous year within a given province. We proxied the variations in carrying capacity (for example, number of potential clients) over time with the number of inhabitants – *Provincial Inhabitants* – in each province for each year. We accounted for other systematic geographical differences by introducing provincial fixed effects.

Organizational controls   We controlled for size and age – *Size* – as the logarithm of the annual number of professional accountants (partners and associates) while age was proxied by number of years since inception. We also controlled for *level* (that is, the stock) of diversity and overlap at $t-1$ – that is, *Demographic Heterogeneity Stock* (log) and *Demographic Overlap Stock* (log), respectively. Thus, our modeling design provides a stricter test of the 'acceleration' in the rate of organizational failure due *solely* to further increases above the existing level of diversity.[6] We expect both these variables to be positively related to organizational failure. Additionally, we controlled for the leverage of the firm absorbing new partners – *Recipient Leverage* – that is, the number of associates per partner for each year. Firms with low leverage enjoy higher survival chances. Many firms in this sector are single proprietorships and because of such preponderance, we created a dummy variable – *Single Proprietorship* – taking on the value 1 if size is equal to 1, otherwise 0. Although it may seem strange for a study on teams to include individual firms in the sample, we opted for a control variable, instead of deleting observations, to avoid adding any bias due to censoring. (However, in the last column of Table 8.2 below we present the estimates obtained by eliminating individual firms from the risk set.) We aim at capturing part of endogeneity, by controlling for a few other firm characteristics. First, for each year, we also computed a ratio where the numerator is the *sum* of years of provincial experience of all organizational members before the inflow of new members, and the denominator is the mean value of provincial experience – that is, *Relative Position*. The rationale is that competitively stronger organizations are less exposed to the hazard of failure. Such an advantage guarantees the selection of inflows from a larger pool of applicants. Second, failing to control for team size is likely to bias the estimation of team heterogeneity effects (Carpenter et al.,

2004). We avoid this bias by adding a variable that counts the number of partners that compose the team – *Team Size*. Third, we control for the degree of demographic turbulence of the firm by counting the number of members (associates and partners) entering and exiting the organization – *Member Entries* and *Member Exits*. Last, as the impact of a standard deviation is critically affected by the mean of the same variable (Sørensen, 2002), we control for the mean of team local experience – *Average Team Experience.*

Finally, to ensure exogeneity with respect to the dependent variable, we lagged all our covariates by one period. In Table 8.1 we report the descriptive statistics and the correlation values for the variables used in the analysis.

MODEL AND METHOD

Following a standard procedure, the life of each organization was partitioned into organization-years (Tuma and Hannan, 1984). Since our data were collected at irregular intervals, the use of continuous event history analysis would bias our estimates (for a discussion see Allison, 1982). As in chapters 4 and 5, we employed discrete event history analysis. The complementary log-log specification provides consistent estimates of the continuous time irrespective of the interval lengths and/or the size of the survival rate (Allison, 1982). The final model formulation is similar to that used in Chapter 5.

As mentioned before, one potential concern involves the endogeneity problem due to self-selection among firms and their incoming partners. In other words, the entry of partners observed may be systematically biased – that is, not random. Literature in labor economics indicates however that matching is difficult and a great deal of uncertainty accompanies the hiring of a new member (see Jovanovic, 1979). Usually, high levels of short-term turnover suggest matching uncertainty (for example, Belzil, 2001). Therefore, we computed the number of years elapsed between individual movements. The findings obtained (not reported here) suggest that in this service sector, partners on average stayed put for eight years. Considering the time gaps in our data, we interpret this high mobility frequency as further confirming the existence of substantive uncertainty in the job-search process. That led us to consider self-selection on recruitment not to be a serious problem in this study. We controlled for the different length of the intervals by creating a variable accounting for them and using it into the 'offset' option. All the estimates were obtained with Maximum Likelihood Estimation method using version 8 of STATA.

Table 8.1 Descriptive statistics and pairwise correlations

Variable	Mean	Std. Dev.	1	2	3	4	5	6	7	8	9	10
1. Age	12.77	12.22	1.00									
2. Provincial Inhabitants	1723102	659750.7	0.05	1.00								
3. C4	0.23	0.12	-0.21	0.15	1.00							
4. Firms Entering Province	13.53	11.44	0.08	0.39	0.04	1.00						
5. Firms Exiting Province	12.89	12.43	0.04	0.50	0.14	0.50	1.00					
6. Provincial Density	67.42	37.86	0.20	0.60	-0.42	0.28	0.40	1.00				
7. Individual Firm	0.69	0.46	-0.10	-0.09	-0.04	-0.05	-0.07	-0.05	1.00			
8. Size (log)	0.44	0.83	0.13	0.12	0.10	0.09	0.11	0.06	-0.78	1.00		
9. Leverage	0.15	0.48	0.06	0.10	0.04	0.03	0.06	0.05	-0.46	0.55	1.00	
10. Relative Position	0.91	0.84	0.36	-0.00	-0.05	-0.00	-0.01	0.03	-0.21	0.26	0.11	1.00
11. Team Size	2.41	7.86	0.02	0.09	0.14	0.09	0.11	0.01	-0.27	0.66	0.20	0.15
12. Member Exits	0.13	1.53	0.06	0.03	0.04	0.01	0.03	0.02	-0.08	0.21	0.09	0.07
13. Member Entries	0.22	2.48	0.06	0.04	0.05	0.01	0.04	0.02	-0.11	0.28	0.12	0.10
14. Average Team Experience	3.02	5.80	0.09	0.10	0.01	-0.03	0.06	0.09	0.04	-0.05	-0.05	0.19
15. Demographic Heterogeneity Stock	-1.75	1.44	0.02	0.06	0.06	-0.01	0.06	0.03	-0.41	0.39	0.18	0.14
16. Demographic Heterogeneity Increases	0.02	0.47	-0.02	0.00	-0.02	0.01	-0.00	0.01	-0.01	-0.08	-0.04	-0.02
17. Demographic Heterogeneity Decreases (absolute value)	0.01	0.57	-0.02	-0.01	-0.02	-0.01	-0.01	0.01	0.01	-0.07	-0.02	-0.02
18. Demographic Overlap Stock	1.77	1.39	-0.14	0.19	0.13	0.07	0.14	0.12	0.11	-0.03	-0.00	-0.07
19. Demographic Overlap Increases	0.47	1.06	-0.07	0.03	-0.02	-0.08	-0.01	0.03	0.02	-0.03	-0.02	-0.06
20. Demographic Overlap Decreases (absolute value)	0.21	0.67	-0.01	-0.01	-0.00	0.02	-0.01	-0.02	0.09	-0.10	-0.03	-0.03

Variable	Mean	Std. Dev.	11	12	13	14	15	16	17	18	19	20
1. Age	12.77	12.22										
2. Provincial Inhabitants	1723102	659750.7										
3. C4	0.23	0.12										
4. Firms Entering Province	13.53	11.44										
5. Firms Exiting Province	12.89	12.43										
6. Provincial Density	67.42	37.86										
7. Individual Firm	0.69	0.46										
8. Size (log)	0.44	0.83										
9. Leverage	0.15	0.48										
10. Relative Position	0.91	0.84										
11. Team Size	2.41	7.86	1.00									
12. Member Exits	0.13	1.53	0.31	1.00								
13. Member Entries	0.22	2.48	0.41	0.50	1.00							
14. Average Team Experience	3.02	5.80	-0.02	0.03	0.03	1.00						
15. Demographic Heterogeneity Stock	-1.75	1.44	0.18	0.08	0.06	-0.04	1.00					
16. Demographic Heterogeneity Increases	0.02	0.47	-0.09	-0.10	-0.07	0.06	-0.07	1.00				
17. Demographic Heterogeneity Decreases (absolute value)	0.01	0.57	-0.07	-0.04	-0.04	-0.00	0.07	0.00	1.00			
18. Demographic Overlap Stock	1.77	1.39	0.03	0.00	0.00	0.01	-0.03	-0.01	-0.01	1.00		
19. Demographic Overlap Increases	0.47	1.06	-0.02	0.04	0.03	0.12	-0.07	0.04	-0.02	0.03	1.00	
20. Demographic Overlap Decreases (absolute value)	0.21	0.67	-0.05	-0.06	-0.09	-0.13	-0.02	-0.03	-0.00	0.03	0.10	1.00

RESULTS

Table 8.2 presents the maximum likelihood estimates for the complementary log-log models of organizational failure. Model 1 includes the control variables. In model 2, we introduced the variables *Tenure Heterogeneity Decrease* and *Tenure Heterogeneity Increase* to test hypotheses 8.1a and 8.1b. In model 3 we test the hypotheses by adding the stock of heterogeneity – *Demographic Heterogeneity Stock*. Then we repeat the same logic for the overlap measures. In models 4 and 5 we tested hypotheses 8.2a and 8.2b by entering the variables *Demographic Overlap Decrease* and *Demographic Overlap Increase* with and without the stock measure – *Demographic Overlap Stock*.

In the baseline model (model 1) all variables accounting for provincial effects – that is, births, deaths and densities – are in the expected direction and statistically significant, supporting our choice of the unit of analysis.[7] At the organizational level, the controls point to the existence of a curvilinear age effect: accounting firms are more likely to dissolve when very young or old (the minimum risk of dissolution is set at 28 years). A stock of human capital above the provincial average (*Relative Position*) significantly reduces the risk of dissolution. As expected, the larger the number of departures, the greater the hazard of failure, whereas the bigger the partnership, the greater its survival chances. The single proprietorship dummy is not statistically significant, suggesting that no systematic bias ensues in our results due to the inclusion of single proprietorships in the risk set.

Interestingly enough, the coefficient measuring the impact of *Tenure Heterogeneity Flow* is not statistically significant. We interpret this finding as suggesting the existence of a potential asymmetry between the positive and the negative effects. We test for this speculation by splitting the variable across positive and negative variations. Model 2 also presents the coefficient estimates for change in tenure heterogeneity *due to new inflows*. The findings obtained seem to run against the original theory (Hambrick and Mason, 1984). While formulating hypotheses 8.1a and 8.1b we argued in fact that the impact of key member inflows on the risk of organizational dissolution depends on the shift they produce in tenure heterogeneity. Once controlling for the stock of diversity (model 3), however, the positive and negative effects of demographic variations on survival gain statistical significance. We interpret these results as suggesting that the impact of diversity variations changes according to the level of its stock. Notice also that the *asymmetry* between the positive and negative coefficients also becomes evident – and it is confirmed by a chi-square test. The inclusion of these variables in model 3 improves significantly the fit of our model, so providing strong support for hypotheses 8.1a and 8.1b.

As for the competitive implications of inter-firm mobility, we expect the hazard rate of dissolution due to new entries to be a function of the increase in the demographic similarity to its competitors. Model 4 presents the estimate of the overlap shifts associated with *new entries*, without controlling for the existing level of overlap. Adding these variables significantly improves our model's goodness of fit. An increase in demographic overlap due to inter-firm mobility has the hypothesized effect on organizational dissolution – as the coefficient of the *Demographic Overlap Increase* variable indicates. Conversely, recruitments that result in diminished overlap (*Demographic Overlap Decrease*) enhance organizational survival. The positive and significant estimate of the *Demographic Overlap Stock* variable in model 5 confirms the competitive effects of similarity, but does not influence much the magnitude of the (overlap) variation coefficients. It is worth noticing, however, that in the same model, the coefficient measuring the impact of within-firm diversity-increases loses statistical significance. This result supports the main thrust of our chapter: the consequences of intra-firm diversity cannot be grasped unless we consider the demographic make-up of competitors. We view these findings as providing support to hypotheses 8.2a and 8.2b, and, by and large, to our reasoning.

Robustness Tests

We tested the robustness of the results to alternative model specifications. First, although we did our best to control for potential endogeneity problems, this is still an issue that may affect our findings. To control for further unobserved firm-level effects, we re-estimated our models adopting a two-stage specification (Heckman, 1979). We first estimated a probit model measuring the *organizational probability* of experiencing one new entry (including all the controls presented in model 1). Then, we used the estimates obtained from this model as a control in the dissolution-rate specification. Because of our binary dependent variable in the second step, we created a probit specification with self-selection, following the approach of Van de Ven and Van Praag (1981). The results, available from the authors upon request, confirm that endogeneity is not a serious concern.

Second, while the way we operationalize organizational dissolution does not coincide with 'failure', it is nevertheless consistent with previous research (for example, Boone et al., 2000; Phillips, 2002), which defines failure as exit from the market, without distinguishing between bankruptcy and merger or acquisition. But mergers or acquisitions are quite distinct from exit due to failure or extremely poor performance. For this reason, since the M&A activity in the Dutch accounting industry was mainly, if not exclusively, concentrated in more recent years, especially after 1966, we

Table 8.2 Complementary log-log models for the failure rate of Dutch accounting firms, 1880–1986

	Model 1		Model 2		Model 3		Model 4		Model 5		Model 6 No single prop.	
	Coef.	Std. Err.	Coef.	Std. Err.	Coef.	Std. Err.	Coef.	Std. Err.	Coef.	Std. Err.	Coef.	Std. Err.
Age	-.096	.008**	-.096	.008**	-.084	.007**	-.080	.007**	-.073	.007**	-.051	.012**
Age2	.002	.000**	.002	.000**	.001	.000**	.001	.000**	.001	.000**	.001	.000**
WWI	.498	.199**	.495	.199**	.492	.197**	.474	.198**	.508	.197**	.256	.605
WWII	-1.454	.155**	-1.451	.156**	-1.449	.156**	-1.438	.156**	-1.450	.158**	-1.441	.319**
Single Association	1.019	.168**	1.020	.168**	.836	.171**	.747	.172**	.828	.172**	.541	.277
Regulation 1971	-1.293	.170**	-1.292	.170**	-1.205	.168**	-1.130	.168**	-1.125	.172**	-1.727	.260**
Regulation 1984	-.833	.144**	-.833	.144**	-1.061	.156**	-1.033	.155**	-1.071	.155**	-.564	.219**
Provincial Inhabitants	-.000002	.000001*	-.000002	.000001*	-.000001	.0000001	-.000001	.0000001	-.000001	.000001	.0000007	.0000003**
C4	-.506	.855	-.518	.853	-.681	.908	-.576	.899	-.941	.925	2.349	1.166**
Firms Entering Province	-.033	.004**	-.033	.004**	-.029	.004**	-.027	.004**	-.028	.004**	-.024	.008**
Firms Exiting Province	.065	.003**	.065	.003**	.062	.003**	.062	.003**	.062	.003**	.049	.005**
Provincial Density	-.014	.007**	-.014	.007**	-.013	.007	-.015	.007**	-.014	.007**	.000	.016
Provincial Density 2	.000114	.000047**	.000114	.000047**	.000096	.000046**	.000099	.000046**	.000091	.000045**	.000029	.000097
Individual Firm	.011	.109	-.002	.108	.117	.112	.116	.112	.159	.113	.130	.086
Size (log)	.218	.088**	.236	.087**	.099	.089	.071	.089	.065	.090	-.086	.072
Leverage	-.076	.073	-.083	.073	.005	.070	.016	.070	.011	.070	-.434	.079**
Relative Position	-.523	.055**	-.516	.056**	-.502	.054**	-.499	.055**	-.505	.056**	-.012	.006
Team Size	-.015	.007**	-.015	.007**	-.012	.006	-.011	.006	-.012	.007	.023	.012
Member Exits	.046	.019**	.049	.022**	.045	.010**	.042	.010**	.040	.010**	.016	.009
Member Entries	.007	.015	.016	.016	.018	.008**	.017	.008**	.019	.007**		
Average Team Experience	.066	.004**	.066	.004**	.067	.004**	.064	.004**	.064	.004**	.074	.009**

	(1)		(2)		(3)		(4)		(5)		(6)	
Demographic Heterogeneity Flow	.018	.012										
Demographic Heterogeneity Stock					.319	.018**	.337	.019**	.337	.019**	.141	.023**
Demographic Heterogeneity Increases – H8.1a			.036	.056	.127	.027**	.092	.023**	.085	.054	.040	.026
Demographic Heterogeneity Decreases (absolute value) – H8.1b			−.039	.028	−.065	.024**	−.058	.024**	−.055	.025**	−.047	.028*
Demographic Overlap Stock									.266	.033**	.420	.060**
Demographic Overlap Increases – H8.2a							.128	.022**	.129	.022**	.108	.039**
Demographic Overlap Decreases (absolute value) – H8.2b							−.081	.013**	−.072	.003**	−.042	.014**
Constant	−2.842	.264**	−2.945	.255**	−2.563	.258**	−2.700	.259**	−3.075	.263**	−5.115	.467**
Log-likelihood	−4492.31		−4492.12		−4349.53		−4328.50		−4301.47		−1299.89	
Provincial fixed effects	Included		Included		Included		Included		Included		Included	
Offset	Included		Included		Included		Included		Included		Included	

Notes: ** p<0.05; * p<0.10. Two-tails tests.

double-checked the robustness of our results by running the analysis on a sub-sample that includes firms from 1880 to 1966. Although the statistical significance of the within-firm diversity measures appears to be weaker, the results are consistent with those presented here.

Finally, although our models control for single proprietorships, our results might be driven by the preponderance of these cases. Although the dummy variable flagging individual firms never reaches statistical significance in the results presented in Table 8.2, we further checked for this problem by fitting a model that excluded sole proprietorships from the risk set. Model 6 of Table 8.2 reports the results for the models estimated, empirical findings being qualitatively similar to those reported before. A significant discrepancy involves local density-dependence: both its linear and curvilinear effects disappear, suggesting that small firms (those excluded from the risk set) are disproportionately exposed to such negative selection. Altogether these results led us to conclude that inclusion of single proprietorships does not alter the main results.

DISCUSSION AND CONCLUSIONS

Drawing from organizational demography theories and the class of studies involving upper echelons, in this chapter we sought to explore new ground in diversity and long-term firm performance. We also considered the role of managers in shaping organizational outcomes. As managers are the 'guts' of organizations, their mobility shapes organizational behavior, which in turn conditions the competitive interactions among the firms in a sector. Empirically, we tested our ideas using a sample that coincides with the entire population of the firms belonging to a professional services sector, and we longitudinally traced the movements of professionals between firms across geographical space. Therefore, we proposed a multi-level theory on the survival consequences of demographic diversity variations. The inflow of members alters the demographic make-up of firms, both internally and externally. Mobility changes internal diversity but alters the degree of similarity between firms as well. We were able to distinguish between mobility events that augment or reduce heterogeneity, thereby implementing a more robust test of the theory.

Our findings suggest that uncovering such relationships is very much dependent on a joint consideration of intra-firm and inter-firm levels of analysis. By delving into the specific conditions under which the entry of key individuals produces beneficial or detrimental consequences, the chapter has shown that personnel inflow should be framed as a multi-level phenomenon. Instead of investigating each level in isolation, our study is among the first to analyze their dynamic interactions in a longitudinal setting. While the degree of fit between new recruits and the recipient firm conditions the performance consequences of hiring new members, those consequences are not confined to the recipient firm. As demographic characteristics are also critical in influencing the strategic positioning of firms (see Carpenter et al., 2004 for a review), the new members affect the degree of similarity between donor and recipient firm. We believe that the present chapter shows how personnel inflow constitutes an important force in strategy convergence/divergence within industries. The performance implications of recruiting new members, thus, depend critically on changes in competitive overlap among firms.

The present study adds significantly to the body of literature on upper echelons. First, by modeling both the increases and decreases in tenure heterogeneity, the methodology adopted here permits us to decompose the positive and negative changes in demographic diversity both within and between firms. Such episodes in the firm's life are bound to be associated with volatile framing contests, that is, episodes during which the choice of strategic direction becomes smooth; or the opposite, the deliberations among the top decision-makers evolve into a 'framing contest' in which the firm might run amok, if not worse. The asymmetric effects of heterogeneity variation due to member inflows call for further investigations. Our findings demonstrate that the existing stock of demographic heterogeneity of a team may influence the positive impact of a diversity reduction on survival. We have followed the putative assumption regarding demography and cognition, arguing that demographic heterogeneity is predictive of mental and attitudinal diversity. Mental diversity shapes the threshold for reaching consensus in beliefs and attitudes and, if that threshold rises, the risk of disbanding grows, while lowering the threshold should have had opposite consequences. Virtually all the pertinent literature assumes, at least implicitly, diversity to have a symmetric relationship with performance, but as diversity is not constant but alters with the recruitment of members, significant alterations in the composition of top management teams might ensue. The asymmetric effects we found might be attributed to increases producing disproportionately harmful effect, taxing the firm beyond the diversity level at which it has settled. By contrast, a decline in diversity, while theoretically beneficial, might not register much of an effect as the firm has already achieved a level of competency in dealing with diversity. It might have inoculated itself against the adverse and dysfunctional effects of current diversity and have arrived at a modus operandi for dealing with the current level of demographic heterogeneity. A firm characterized by some divergence in membership, facing challenges towards the creation of what Nelson and Winter (1982) call 'truce' might therefore quite easily disintegrate, thus showing a much sharper elasticity of disbanding. The observed asymmetry points here to the absence of 'God as geometer' (Stewart and Golubitsky, 1992).

Second, we created significant additions to the recent cross-sectional findings concerning inter-firm dynamics of tenure heterogeneity (Pegels et al., 2000). The evidence presented here shows that demographic overlap changes significantly affect organizational performance. We consider especially intriguing the finding obtained by model 5 in Table 8.2: after adding the overlap related variables, the coefficient measuring the impact of the level of within-firm diversity loses its statistical significance. In this respect, our results provide further support to the work of Sørensen (1999b) and suggest that the consequences of intra-firm diversity cannot be fully grasped without considering the demographic characteristics of competitors. The results of this study provide a first hint at the strategic convergence or divergence between firms due to executive migration and the subsequent effects on firm survival. We found evidence of asymmetric effects also while examining demographic differences between teams. More research is needed to shed light on this issue. However, we may speculate that an increase in demographic overlap occurring when a firm poaches people from peer firms in the same strategic domain will further intensify competition and result in lower levels of performance. Conversely, when inter-firm demographic overlap declines, its effect on rivalry might not be salient or might translate into diminished competitive awareness. Compared to intra-firm variations, this effect is 'pure': the asymmetry between positive and negative variations does not depend on the value of the stock – that is, the marginal impact of increases is always larger than that associated with decreases. More research is needed to clarify whether such a cognitive inertia is at work.

A persistent concern in the literature on organizational demography is the ambiguity regarding demographic characteristics matching cognitive ones (for example, Finkelstein and Hambrick, 1996). The research to date assumes that tenure diversity produces divergent mental frames without substantiating this claim – it is just assumed that this is what it might be. By no means is our study immune to such criticism. We likewise assumed that managers with comparable demographic traits should exhibit similarity in their mental models and, by implication, convergence in strategic decisions and behaviors. Unfortunately, our data do not allow us to establish an empirical link between demographic characteristics and mental proclivities. However, among all possible demographic attributes, tenure, and especially local tenure is defensible as a precursor to cognitive dispositions. By contrast, attributes such as ethnicity, age and gender are much more tenuous when assuming a demography-cognition connection, especially when invoked to impute mental dispositions around strategic and market conditions. In knowledge-intensive industries such as the accounting sector, with close ties between professionals and their clients, local and lasting exposure to local conditions appears more germane to the acquisition of common perceptions and attitudes. The implied socialization within geographical markets is bound to instill commonality in beliefs and values compared to other settings where propinquity is not paramount.

The accounting sector is relatively static and persistent in its compliance with widely accepted standards. Individual firms possess distinctive qualities and reveal varying degrees of rents (The Accounting Reporter, 2004). Demographically homogeneous partnerships are prone to higher degrees of compliance and strongly ingrained norms and values but when jolted by misfit and divergent members joining they become dangerously exposed to bankruptcy or industry exit. Particularly in this type of sector, the heterogeneity–performance relationship comes sharply into focus when recruitment draws a firm into a more disjointed and divergent membership and preservation of well-ingrained routines and practices is jeopardized. Recall that the diversity–performance relationship takes on a negative or positive aspect depending on the complexity of task, and the uncertainty and ambiguity of markets. The accounting sector strives towards reliability and replicability, both for individual firms and their industry. Innovation and adaptation occur slowly and are subject to stringent regulation and standard-setting. This industry would therefore be expected to witness strong harmful effects of diversity and equally strong benefits of homogeneity since these conditions impede or facilitate the compliance with accounting rules and conventions, and even more so today as the corporate world is fraught with numerous accounting scandals which necessitate further elimination of ambiguity in corporate disclosure. We should press for additional research in high technology and other emerging or novel industries, where the findings on diversity might be contrary to ours.

The results on diversity and performance as decomposed here should motivate researchers to link demographic with cognitive variables at the individual, team or organizational levels so that the researcher can peek more successfully into the decision-making taking place within companies. Similarly the cognitive framing of markets and strategic groups and firm performance would benefit from data that more tightly connect demographics with mental proclivities.

NOTES

1.   Although other literature conversely suggests that functional diversity is beneficial for organizational performance.

2. A vast literature initiated by Schneider (1987) examines how top management teams – through 'cycles' of attraction, selection and attrition – become increasingly homogeneous. That is because social groups, such as top management teams, have the tendency to reproduce themselves by the selective recruitment of similar people and by facilitating the turnover of dissimilar ones, a process labeled 'homosocial reproduction' by Kanter (1977). Adopting this perspective, Boone et al. (2004) for instance have shed light on the short-run negative consequences of avoiding this social norm.

3. Inter-firm mobility, of course, is not the only mechanism stimulating the emergence of shared perceptions of the competitive environment. As Reger and Huff (1993: 106) note, however, hiring from the same labor pool is an important avenue through which company managers interact with each other, besides participation in industry associations and other gatherings, access to similar sources of information such as trade publications, or employment of the same consultants.

4. In analyses not reported here we controlled for the stock of mean tenure due to new entries. It turned out that mean increases were positively related to organizational dissolution. This finding is in line with recent findings (for example, Sørensen, 1999b) and may be interpreted as an indicator of the risks associated with strategic persistence (Finkelstein and Hambrick, 1990). The qualitative conclusions of this chapter remained unaffected by the inclusion of this additional control.

5. Other studies define an organizational niche using a two standard deviation window centered on the mean (for example, Sørensen, 1999a, 1999b). To reduce the bias of the 10 per cent band, we also applied a 20 per cent and a 30 per cent band and the results, though not reported here, were not significantly different from those presented in this chapter. However, Williams and O'Reilly (1998: 120), after reviewing about 80 articles, concluded that 'the preponderance of empirical evidence suggests that diversity is most likely to impede group functioning.' Their interpretation of the discordant findings relates to 'the failure to distinguish between idea generation (or "creativity") and its implementation. To perform successfully, groups in fact "must have both the ability to develop creative solutions and to implement or execute these ideas"' (Williams and O'Reilly, 1998: 119).

6. This becomes clear when considering that, algebraically, our model resembles a restricted distributed lag regression without the lagged dependent variable as covariate.

7. Analyses not reported here confirmed that the linear and quadratic effects of local density are prevalent on that of national density. This result is consistent with that obtained by Cattani et al. (2003) for entry rates.

9. Competitive consequences of routine spillovers due to inter-firm mobility

INTRODUCTION

The recruitment, development and retention of employees are central factors for organizational survival. While the focus on people as a source of superior performance is hardly new (for example, Penrose, 1959; Pfeffer, 1994; Grant, 1996), the importance of people has recently become even more salient on the grounds that a firm's stock of routines is enacted by its members (Cyert and March, 1963; Nelson and Winter, 1982; Coff, 1997). Not surprisingly, recruiting individuals from rival organizations has been increasingly used to access resources and routines not available in-house (see Rao and Drazin, 2002). Likewise, firms attempt to limit outbound movement of members to competing firms (see for example, Coff, 1997).

Much of the theory and research to date has focused on the antecedents of turnover with general inquiries on voluntary turnover (for a review see, for example, Williams and O'Reilly III, 1998). Inquiries on possible turnover consequences have revolved around the impact of the transferring member's performance (Harris and Helfat, 1997; Huckman and Pisano, 2006). Another subset of research studies has examined cases of turnover limited to inter-firm mobility, and their consequences for the source firm (Sørensen, 1999b), the destination firm (Agarwal et al., 2004; Rao and Drazin, 2002; Wezel and Saka, 2006), or both the source and destination firms (Phillips, 2002). Evidence suggests that spin-offs are speedier than *de novo* firms in mobilizing resources (Ruef, 2005), and tend to replicate or modify an idea encountered through their previous employment history (Bhide, 1994). In their study of the US commercial laser industry, Klepper and Sleeper (2005) further confirmed that spin-offs inherit knowledge from their parents. The rationale of these studies is that members moving to a peer firm bring along not only their skills and experience (McKelvey, 1982; Boeker, 1997; Rao and Drazin, 2002), but also those organizational routines in which they have played a part (Phillips, 2002).

Despite this large body of research, several issues remain unresolved. Many studies assume that inter-firm mobility entails the transfer of resources and routines without any further qualification. However, resources and routines are distinct and so are the conditions under which they can be successfully transferred. As they move from firm to firm, members bring along their human and social capital. But the extent to which they can replicate existing routines in the destination firm is less obvious because routines are less dependent on single individuals. Previous studies treat such behavioral templates as homogeneous and do not distinguish between high-order and operating routines. This distinction is particularly important for explaining the competitive implications of inter-firm mobility. Lower-order routines are decomposable and portable (Baldwin and Clark, 2002) and readily replicated across time and space. By contrast, higher-order routines attend to the creation and coordination of lower-level routines as well as organizational resources (Dosi et al., 2000; Winter, 2000; Zollo and Winter, 2002) and it remains unclear whether their value can be captured in the destination firm (see Edmondson et al., 2001).

This chapter explicitly studies the competitive implications for the donor organization of higher-order routine replication due to inter-firm mobility. Our theoretical argument rests on the premise that recruiting key organizational members from rivals is a critical mechanism by which firms can appropriate routines, but also resources (for example, Rao and Drazin, 2002). Prior research has also suggested how the consequences of personnel mobility are not confined to the recipient firm because inflows and/or outflows may eventually increase the competitive similarity between donor and recipient organizations (Sørensen, 1999b; Phillips, 2002; but see Boone et al., 2006). We argue that a critical condition for inter-organizational similarity can be attributed to the transfer of higher-order routines due to personnel outflows. Since these routines govern processes of resource acquisition and allocation, their successful replication is a source of competitive interdependence. A review of the conditions facilitating higher-order routine replication, therefore, helps understand when inter-firm mobility produces competitive consequences that undermine the donor's survival chances. It is worth noting that whether or not the recipient benefits from this routine transfer remains a separate issue. Our main concern is with the competitive interdependence between the donor and the recipient produced by increased similarity. That is why we investigate the conditions that preserve the integrity of routines being transferred rather than the performance implication of the transfer for the recipient.

Based on the definition of routines adopted in this chapter (see below), three sets of distinct but interdependent conditions conducive to routine replication are spelled out. First, replication is more likely to succeed when organizational members leave as a group, and even more so if they have worked together for an extended time. Second, organizational members have more freedom in replicating routines when leaving and starting a new venture than joining an incumbent already endowed with a well-ingrained set of routines. Finally, successful replication is a function of the co-location of the two firms as routines embody both organization- and context-specific characteristics. As successful replication increases the interdependence between organizations, this study sheds light on the competitive implication of routine replication due to inter-firm mobility.

As the concern is with the competitive implications for the donor organization of higher-order routine replication due to inter-firm mobility, we focus on the departure of so-called 'key' members, that is, members with decision-making authority (for example, members of the board of directors, or senior partners). Following previous research on inter-firm routine transfer as a function of departing individuals' position or rank in the origin firm (Phillips, 2002), we track the departure of partners, disregarding exits of other members, such as associates, whose participation in the creation of higher order routines is much less critical. Other forms of turnover, including death, retirement or transfer to a non-rival firm are rather inconsequential in competitive terms. Such turnover is unlikely to engender replication of organizational routines in rival firms, which is the focus of this chapter.

THEORETICAL BACKGROUND

We start with the premise that inter-firm mobility may produce a transformation of a firm's competitive surroundings. Previous studies showed how personnel mobility might increase similarity of both routines and resources across organizations (Boeker, 1997; Sørensen, 1999b; Phillips, 2002) and their competitive interdependence. We concern ourselves only with the competitive implications occasioned by organizational routines replication resulting from inter-firm mobility. The focus is on routines because resources such as human and social capital are typically attached to individuals. Even when resources are firm-specific and therefore less valuable in a different context, members may bring them along as they move from firm to firm.

By contrast, successful replication of firm-entrenched routines is a less obvious outcome of inter-firm mobility. Routines usually originate from repeated interaction among multiple actors inside and/or outside the firm over an extended period of time, which render them less sticky to single individuals. As a result, the odds of success at replicating them are contingent on a much broader range of conditions to be satisfied. Previous research showed how existing routines are more effectively transferred between a firm and its offspring or progeny (Phillips, 2002; Klepper, 2001). But this is just one condition facilitating their replication that requires us to elaborate on the mechanisms that allow preservation of their integrity and value in a different context than the one in which they originally developed. The present chapter moves beyond existing research on the competitive implications of inter-firm mobility, precisely because it provides an effort to embrace a whole set of interdependent conditions rooted in the definition of routines.

Routines are hierarchical in their configuration. Their categorization has followed an ordering from operational to meta-routines (Cyert and March, 1963; Nelson and Winter, 1982). While the former dictate day-to-day firm behavior, the latter refer to the managerial discretion to coordinate, integrate and deploy resources throughout the organization (see Knott, 2001). Higher-order routines 'govern' the use, combination or recalibration of lower-order ones (Nelson and Winter, 1982; Teece et al., 1997). This integrative role renders higher-order routines readily transferable when moved by groups rather than individuals. Such a view is in line with Nelson and Winter (1982: 105) who underscored that '[T]o view organizational memory as reducible to individual member memories is to overlook, or undervalue, the linking of those individual memories by shared experience in the past, experiences that have established the extremely detailed and communication system that underlies routine performance.' When people migrate to other firms, therefore, the propensity to replicate routines will be higher as they move with peers who have experienced similar histories and display equivalent cognitive dispositions.

We claim that three conditions significantly affect the efficacy of higher-order routine replication and its impact on the donor's performance. First, it is important to distinguish between solitary versus group migrations of members. Next, since existing organizations soon after their birth become imprinted with high-order routines that are unlikely to be modified during their existence (see Baron et al., 1996), we should examine how the classification of the destination firm – established or entrepreneurial – impedes or facilitates that routine transfer. Finally, as a partial 'replica' of the donor firm, the competitive fallout will be more intensive if that replica resides in the same environment. That is because the firm with reproduced template is more likely to secure resources (for example, funding, employees, goodwill) that mirror those of the donor.

Inter-firm Mobility: Individual versus Collective Replication

Following Cohen and Bacdayan (1994: 555), routines can be defined as 'patterned sequences of learned behavior involving multiple actors who are linked by relations of communication and/or authority'. For instance, landing a commercial aircraft is a highly standardized but complex task, involving multiple actors performing interconnected subtasks requiring proper coordination. One cannot fully understand how that routine actually works by examining only the pilot's part (Cohen and Bacdayan, 1994: 555). Routines depend on 'the connections, the stitching together of multiple participants and their actions to form a pattern that people can recognize and talk about as a routine' (Pentland and Feldman, 2005: 6). They are, therefore, anchored in the context or social network of actors, whether internal or external to the firm, whose behavior they govern.

Replication varies depending on whether routines are operational or meta-routines. This view fits that of Cyert and March (1963) and Nelson and Winter (1982) who elaborated on a dual routines perspective, where organizational behavior stems from two sets of hierarchically ordered routines: a set of operational routines that control day-to-day actions and a set of meta-routines that govern operational routines (see Knott, 2001). Meta-routines or higher-order routines lie at the core of managerial intervention. They entail learned sequences of conduct regarding governance, and idiosyncratic procedural knowledge of the competitive environment and organization of work flows – in short, the arrangement and coordination of firm activities (Teece et al., 1997; Henderson and Cockburn, 1994). Their directive role and involvement of people and processes permeate the behavior of the entire organization. In this respect, higher-order routines are holistic in their use and are harder to replicate than atomistic or modular routines such as those associated with operational tasks like sales, production and other functional activities. Furthermore, higher-order routines are inherently social and success of replication hinges on retention of their integrity.

Being socially constructed, higher-order routines transcend individual skills. That is why several authors (for example, Kogut and Zander, 1992; Levitt and March, 1988; Nelson and Winter, 1982) have argued that turnover does not necessarily compromise the integrity of existing routines and firm performance, on the premise that organizational routines are independent from individuals (but for a more comprehensive review see Felin and Foss, 2004). Empirical research has likewise shown that routines are strongly embedded in the behavior and cognition of organizational members (Song et al., 2003): when migrating elsewhere, those very individuals could replicate previously developed routines. Therefore, inter-firm mobility may lower the donor firm's performance through the leakage of proprietary routines as a result of the migration of members who have internalized the donor firm's legacy. Successful transfer of routines to another firm is also a function of the position or rank of a departing individual in the origin firm. As Phillips (2002: 476) puts it, the 'more critical the potential founder's position is, the more likely that the parent organization's resources and routines will be affected as that founder exits to entrepreneurship'.

However, since routines usually involve multiple actors, whether internal or external to the firm, their replication in other firms depends on preserving existing patterns of interaction among those actors (Nelson and Winter, 1982). The ability to preserve their integrity, and thereby their successful replication, is diminished when organizational members leave alone. This also accords with the finding from a study showing that surgeons' performance declines when they try to move their individual skill sets towards other hospitals (so-called 'splitting' of membership): existing surgical routines combine with hospital-specific cultural and institutional elements to produce well-integrated operation room teams of medical personnel (Huckman and Pisano, 2006). When imported to other organizations, those routines become dislodged and produce comparatively inferior postoperative results – that is, higher patient mortality.

Yet, when groups rather than individuals export their routines, the tacit coordination and alignment of any replication is more readily attained (see Edmondson et al., 2001). Individuals are only partially engaged in the firm's bundle of routines because their skills are complementary with those of their colleagues. In contrast, collective departure is more conducive to holistic replication since pre-existing systems of coordinated roles can be maintained. Successful replication of routines therefore is contingent on whether mobility entails groups or single individuals. If a group of members departs together for a new firm, its routines can be transferred with greater integrity and at greater risk to the source firm. Accordingly, we hypothesize:

Hypothesis 9.1   The risk of organizational dissolution is higher when key members leave collectively rather than individually.

Although collective movements engender successful replication, not all groups are homogeneous. Groups vary along dimensions that affect successful routine transfer across organizational boundaries. Member homogeneity hinges on shared internalization of routines among individual members. The accumulation of a common mindset is subject to time compression diseconomies as compliance with or attachment to certain routines depends on the amount of time spent together. As Groysberg et al. (2006: 94) have recently shown, similar considerations hold even in the case of an executive's mobility because 'individual manager's effectiveness can be attributed to his experience working with colleagues or as part of a team'. Central to the present perspective is both the notion of repeated interaction among actors and the idea that this interaction must unfold over an extended period of time.

As members have gravitated towards a common mindset, they will have preserved their stock of routines and therefore stand a better chance at replicating them. The longer the departing members have kept company the more likely they are to subscribe to a common logic and a well-institutionalized template. This argument is consistent with empirical research on the relevance of team cohesiveness in building group coordination and trust. For example, in their study on start-ups in the semiconductor industry, Eisenhardt and Schoonhoven (1990: 509) argue that '[E]xecutives who have a history together have probably learned how to get along and communicate with each other'. Ruef et al. (2003) similarly found that trust and familiarity are more critical to founding team composition than are complementary skillsets. The implication is that under conditions of collective out-migration, members having spent a significant amount of time together manifest better odds of successful replication. We thus hypothesize:

Hypothesis 9.1a   The risk of organizational dissolution due to collective exit is higher the longer departing members have spent time together before turning over.

Member Exit and Firm Destination: Start-ups versus Incumbents

Research has shown that individuals formerly employed by established firms often start new ventures (Freeman, 1986; Burton et al., 2002). This phenomenon is common to both high-tech (Braum and MacDonald, 1978; Klepper and Sleeper, 2000; Agarwal et al., 2004) and service (Phillips, 2002) industries. Replication of routines in a start-up typically results in a more reliable and authentic copy of routines than replication in an existing firm. Departing members enjoy less leeway in transferring existing routines from other firms when they join an incumbent with an established set of routines. The competitive implications of replication of routines are bound to be more harmful when the source firm is new and not yet endowed with such institutionalized practices. The reason is that high-order routines become imprinted during the early stages of the organizational life-cycle and shape future actions and behaviors (see, for example, Baron et al., 1996).

Knowledge stored in individual memories is 'meaningful and effective only in some context' (Nelson and Winter, 1982: 105). Lacking the conditions that prompted the emergence of certain routines, the replication of routines might be severely compromised. Using a genealogical framework, Phillips (2002) showed how members who leave an existing organization (parent) to found a new venture (progeny) within the same population are more likely to transfer resources and to replicate routines from their former employer. As they are not constrained by pre-existing patterns of interaction in the destination firm, those members enjoy more latitude in creating conditions similar to those of the source firm. As a result, the parent organization's blueprint will 'carry over to the new organization through the career experiences of the offspring's founders' (Phillips, 2002: 474). Similarly, the literature on spin-offs (for example, Bhide, 2000; Agarwal et al., 2004; Klepper and Sleeper, 2005) has shed new insights into the role of departing members for the build-up of a new firm. Since spin-offs exploit their parents' knowledge to offer products or services similar to those of their parents they are competitively more threatening. As Agarwal et al. (2004: 501) noted, '[S]pin-outs pose a special threat to incumbents since they can capitalize on knowledge gained from discoveries made during the course of their founders' employment in the incumbent firm.'

Unlike start-ups, established firms already exhibit an array of routines. As routines – especially higher-order ones – become imprinted in organizations early on (Stinchcombe, 1965), any incumbent recipient exhibits a pattern of interaction producing resistance against the import of extramural routines. Internal resistance is likely to ensue because transferring routines from another firm might jeopardize the functioning of routines in the destination firm by questioning what Nelson and Winter (1982) call the 'truce' – that is, the presence of an implicit understanding reducing the conflict between the divergent interests among organizational members. Attempts at replicating routines from another source may undermine the truce and require new processes and objectives, together with re-establishing a political equilibrium among the membership. In the case of newly founded firms, no truce is under threat and the replication of routines does not face any internal resistance. It is therefore plausible to expect successful transfer of existing routines to be more likely if the host organization is an entrepreneurial rather than an incumbent firm – and by implication to expect greater harm to the source firm. We thus hypothesize:

Hypothesis 9.2   The risk of organizational dissolution due to key members' inter-firm mobility is higher when the recipient firm is a newly founded rather than an incumbent firm.

Member Exit and Spatial Routines Replication

Collective turnover and start-ups as destination are conditions conducive to routine replication. The departure of organizational members however takes on a rather different significance depending on whether or not the source and the destination firms are co-located. Replication is context-dependent in that the actors whose conduct reflects the enactment of routines are institutionally embedded. As Nelson and Winter (1982: 125) put it, '[A] routine may involve extensive direct interactions with the organization's environment and the making of numerous "choices" that are contingent both upon the state of the environment and the state of the organization itself.' While geographical proximity is recognized as an important condition for routine replication, it becomes relevant only if proximity implies similarity in the broader organizational context. To put it differently, it is not physical distance per se that matters, but whether that distance corresponds to historical socio-economic and institutional differences. Previous research has showed the existence of significant historical socio-economic and institutional differences across spatially proximate locations (see for example, Putnam, 1996; Linz and de Miguel, 1966).

As this stream of research suggests, the replication of routines due to inter-firm mobility among co-located firms is more likely to succeed when they share the same context. This line of reasoning is consistent with Stinchcombe's (1965) original insights. As Lounsbury and Ventresca (2002: 21) recognized, 'Stinchcombe focuses on the capacity for new organizations to develop new roles and routines that vary based on the distribution of generalized skills outside an organization, the initiative of employees in the labor force, the degree of trust among workers based on competence in work roles.' Because we defined routines as sequences of learned behavior involving multiple actors both internal and external to the firm, we expect institutions, customers and competitors to significantly shape them. When actors share the very same context, existing patterns of interaction, including relations of communication and/or authority relations, among such actors become geographically embedded.

The connection between routines and their context has been emphasized in theorizing on the origins of organizational capabilities, defined as high-level or meta-routines (Winter, 2000). In elaborating on capability learning, for instance, Winter (2000: 982) asserted that meta-routines are meaningful only 'in relation to a particular competitive context' and 'are wired directly to the environment' (Winter, 2000: 983). This line of reasoning seems also to be consistent with the insights of ecological research (Hannan and Freeman, 1977; Hannan and Freeman, 1984) whose framing of inertia implies a close correspondence between the organizational routines and the broader institutional and historical, not merely competitive, context. The same bundle of routines which enhances the fit between one organization and its external environment might prove of little value when applied to a different organization. The implication is that successful replication, and its associated competitive threat, is contingent on whether or not the donor and recipient organizations share the same context. Accordingly, we hypothesize:

Hypothesis 9.3 The risk of organizational dissolution due to key members' outbound movement is higher when they migrate to co-located competitors.

These three dimensions – collective vs. individual, start-up vs. incumbent, same vs. different context – can generate diverse survival consequences for the donor. For instance, while the movement of groups of key members harms survival, this effect varies with the destination firm being new or established, or sharing the same environment. A complete appreciation of the survival consequences of inter-firm mobility requires considering all three conditions jointly.

Inter-firm mobility should have greater competitive implications for the donor when the departure of members amounts to a collective rather than an individual act and results in an entrepreneurial rival residing in the same competitive environment. Groups of members that move to newly founded firms exhibit substantial discretion in replicating previously acquired routines, especially within the same context. With any other combination of these three dimensions (for example, the rival is located in a different environment, or is an established firm, or the departure involves a single member), the competitive effects of inter-firm mobility diminish. We thus hypothesize:

Hypothesis 9.4 The risk of organizational dissolution due to inter-firm mobility is highest when key members leave in groups to start a new firm in the same context.

EMPIRICAL SETTING

In line with chapters 7 and 8 we divided the overall population of accounting firms into 11 sub-populations, each corresponding to a different province. Our rationale is that each province represents a distinct selection environment. We argue that the same factors and geographical boundaries are critical for the likelihood of replicability of existing routines across organizations. As organizations and their routines are designed to match a specific environment, successful replication is contingent on whether or not the origin and the destination environments are the same. The idiosyncratic historical path to industrialization which Dutch provinces took has generated a distinctive pattern of regulating social groups which continues to influence the evolution of individual firms as well as entire industries. We believe that several reasons justify our choice of mapping the geographical dimension along a dichotomous indicator (within/outside province) rather than using a continuous measure (that is, distance in kilometers).

Data

For the specific analyses of this chapter we eliminated single proprietor-ships from our risk set, ending up with a population of 676 organizations. As usual, the larger gaps in data challenged our mapping of the effects of inter-firm mobility on organizational dissolution. However, as explained below in the model section, in our analyses we controlled for the variance in interval length by creating a variable accounting for diverse time spans. We reconstructed the histories of individual organizations by first aggregating individual-level data to the firm level.

As in Chapter 8, we define dissolution as exit from the market without distinguishing between bankruptcy and merger or acquisition. Our choice is motivated by the fact that 'failure, in the sense of bankruptcy, cannot be observed in the audit industry and therefore, cannot be distinguished from other types of exit' (Boone et al., 2000: 368). Thus, organizational dissolution encompasses different types of exit, ranging from the case in which a firm disappears because its owners are no longer listed in the Certified Professional Accountant directories, to the case of dissolution by acquisition or merger. In all such cases, we coded our dichotomous dependent variable as 1 and removed the firm from the risk set. Since the industry became more concentrated in the late 1960s in the wake of intense M&A activity, we checked whether our results might be affected by our broad notion of dissolution. We conducted a sensitivity analysis including only the data up to and including 1966. The results obtained are similar to those presented here.

Accounting firms are stratified, consisting of partners and associates. In the analysis we investigated the inter-firm mobility events involving only partners because they usually possess superior replication potential (if only because they have been around longer and have successfully completed the tournament to partnership). The competitive effects of higher-order routine replication should therefore be higher when departure of organizational members involves partners rather than associates. Within accounting firms, partners serve as producer-managers by actively participating in the business as key production workers (Maister, 1993). Unlike shareholders of large corporations, partners are also responsible for the overall management. Their decision-making power extends to the task of building/changing routines, such as those dealing with hiring and firing policies, procuring work and deploying junior professionals, differentiation (that is, to hedge against market shrinkage), investment, personal financial planning, and liability insurance premium decisions (for more details see Maister, 1993). Being owners, partners enjoy more latitude in the transfer of organizational routines. This latitude of freedom is much larger in newly founded firms because partnership agreements strictly define the criteria of succession (for example, setting the voting rights of partners for the transition) and the principles behind the successor's management.

Qualitative Evidence

The present study draws from archival sources and subjects the data to an econometric analysis exposing relationships between variables that defy comprehensive efforts at triangulation with other data – most notably qualitative observations. The replication of routines, which is central to this study, remains an unobserved phenomenon. As we argued before, the migration of senior members to peer firms harms the donor firm particularly because, under certain conditions, they can successfully replicate higher-order routines. To obtain a more intuitive understanding, three informants were consulted: one was a former partner in a Swedish accounting firm (he retired in January 2006), one is still affiliated with a Dutch accounting firm, and a third one is no longer active as CPA but currently heads a major Dutch consulting company to accounting firms. Although our study period ends in 1986, only one of them began to work as a CPA prior to that year. Since they all are or were partners of large accounting firms, we had the opportunity to ask them specific questions regarding different classes of routines (which in the chapter we labelled as higher-order and operating routines), their stickiness to individuals and their replication due to inter-firm mobility. The interviews were semi-structured and lasted from one to three hours each.

According to one senior CPA, it is important to distinguish between what he calls 'technically' and 'commercially' proficient CPAs because different types of routines are involved in the performance of their task. The technical routines that are usually relevant in activities such as auditing and sampling are highly portable and therefore more easily separable from professionals. By contrast, on the commercial side, routines can only be transferred when people move. The commercial routines play a critical role when it comes to recruiting, coaching and retaining junior professionals to ensure their loyalty. Professionals can take with them these higher-order routines as they leave to join or create another firm. Higher-order routines are in fact strongly attached to professionals and their career profiles.

A second CPA hinted at the difference between outbound movements towards a new versus an incumbent firm. He suggested that the management style of partners renders a firm consistent in its governance. For instance, he referred to changes in the rules of governance after the completion of a merger when the treatment of billable hours was revised and partners' discretionary allocation was suddenly curtailed – as were the smiles on their face. This scenario is contrasted with a peer firm where changes in firm climate do not occur each time a 'new wind blows through the land', but rather 'they stick to their ways of doing things'. In that firm, as our informant noted, no '*tussensprints*' are observed – a Tour de France metaphor for an intermittent and opportunistic acceleration.

Both CPAs objected to the view that partner mobility produces mobility among clients as well. They point to 'anti-competition clauses' as part of partnership agreements. Since clients too are legally expected to abide by such clauses, the transfer of a professional to a peer firm does not result in a concomitant transfer of clients. Reputation damage to the professional and firm would exacerbate the ill-advised appropriation of such clients. If anything gets transferred, it is governance practices that migrate with the partner to a peer firm. The competitive damage due to partner turnover, thus, can be hardly attributed to a loss of clients.

Finally, when probing on individual versus collective departure, one CPA hinted at the major advantage of collective transfer to form a new firm: 'They can leverage their governance skills when departing as a team, are no longer distracted by "atmospheric frictions," personality clashes, person–culture misfits, in short they start with a clean slate and do not become distracted politically.' Recruitment and retention of people working well together far exceeds any other success-factor in accountancy. The competitive advantage derives from getting professionals rather than clients.

Although such observations are limited in validating the econometric results to be reported, they nevertheless shed light on the meaning of higher-order routines in our setting and their replication as a result of inter-firm mobility. Moreover, the implicit triangulation resulting from combining archival data with interview data, in conjunction with key informants' review of our study, also helped us to overcome the limitations of each separate source and to reduce construct-validity problems (see Yin, 1994).

Independent Variables

We tested our hypotheses by distinguishing inter-firm mobility according to the three dimensions suggested by our theory: (i) joint group experience, (ii) type of destination: incumbent or a newly founded organization, (iii) location of destination: same province or different province. The conditions under which they pose a competitive threat to the donor firm, however, are likely to vary. Our theoretical reasoning suggests that inter-firm mobility affects the source firm's survival chances more strongly when partners leave collectively (Hypothesis 9.1). We thus created two dummy variables flagging whether the event under study involved vidual (*Individual-Exit*) or collective (*Group-Exit*) cases of inter-firm mobility.[1] We defined a group as consisting of two or more partners who leave their employer and wind up working together for another firm, whether an incumbent or a start-up.

We carried out the test concerning the potential of the group to replicate existing routines by counting the average number of years that the departing members spent together before their exit. Our choice of this variable is rooted in existing research that shows how joint experience improves cohesion, trust and efficacy of communication among team members (Eisenhardt and Schoonhoven, 2000; Zenger and Lawrence, 1989; Groysberg et al., 2006). While in any given interval a firm might lose several partners who exit individually, we typically observe only one collective departure in any given year. For each firm, our data do not display two or more groups of defecting partners during the same year, but more than one partner may leave to start up a new venture or join a competitor. Since higher-order routines typically involve multiple actors linked by patterns of communications and interaction, the ability to preserve their integrity as well as replicate them in a different context is diminished when a partner leaves alone. Although the number of partners leaving individually also represents a loss of valuable human and social capital for the focal firm (and we control for this effect in the analysis), our theory suggests that the degree of competition faced by the donor is proportional to the stock of experience shared by the defecting members.

Following this logic, we tested Hypothesis 9.1a by creating a measure of the (logged) average joint experience of defecting members. We also ran the analysis using the minimum number of years organizational members spent together before leaving as a group. The average might fail to distinguish between a group where a few members had worked together for a long time while others had been part of the group for only a few years, and a group in which all group members had worked together for a long time. Thus, although the average joint experience could be the same in both cases, the situation would of course be significantly different: in the latter case group members most likely contributed to the creation of (and therefore would be sharing) the same bundle of routines. Since in our data groups typically consist of partners who worked together most of the time before leaving, the results do not depend on whether we use the average or the minimum number of years.

The average joint experience was then disaggregated in several ways to test the remaining hypotheses. To test Hypothesis 9.2 we distinguished between the average experience of departing members founding a new venture (*Average-Joint-Experience-To-New-Firm*) and the average experience of departing members joining an existing firm (*Average-Joint-Experience-To-Incumbent*). As before, since we presume that the effect of the joint experience of departing members increases organizational dissolution at a decreasing rate, we log-transformed each member exit variable. To test Hypothesis 9.3 we distinguished between the (logged) average joint experience of partners moving to a firm located within the same province as the source firm (*Average-Joint-Experience-To-Local-Firm*) or a different one (*Average-Joint-Experience-To-Non-Local-Firm*).

The ultimate question to be addressed, however, is how these three forces jointly shape organizational survival. We predicted that the competitive effects of inter-firm mobility are stronger when collective rather than individual departures lead to a new venture in a geographical area similar to that of the source firm. Accordingly, we sorted the average experience of departing members along four different combinations to test Hypothesis 9.4. In particular, we distinguished between (i) the (logged) average joint experience of organizational members leaving as a group to found a new venture located within the same (*Average-Joint-Experience-To-Local-New-Firm*) or a different (*Average-Joint-Experience-To-Non-Local-New-Firm*) province; and (ii) the (logged) average joint experience of organizational members leaving as a group to work for an incumbent firm located within the same (*Average-Joint-Experience-To-Local-Incumbent*) or a different (*Average-Joint-Experience-To-Non-Local-Incumbent*) province. Because all the above variables can take on the value of zero we log-transformed them after adding 1 to their base value. Finally, to reinforce our causal inferences, we lagged all the independent variables by one observation period.

Control Variables

In the final model we included several control variables – at the organizational, historical, and provincial levels – to rule out a number of competing hypotheses.

Organizational controls A crucial alternative hypothesis concerns internal disruption. Since internal disruption of routines should take place in the presence of any type of turnover, we controlled for turnover events (for example, death, retirement or joining a non-accounting firm such as a client organization) that represent exit from the sector by creating the (logged) variable *Other-than-Inter-firm-Mobility*. Our theory suggests that the replication of higher-order routines is a distinct phenomenon arising from the transfer of (human and) social capital as a result of inter-firm mobility. As in previous research (for example, Phillips, 2002; Rao and Drazin, 2002) we did not directly measure routines. However, unlike this research we tried to tease apart the effect of routines' replication from the potentially confounding consequences of losing social capital, by creating the variable *Social Capital Loss*, which measures the change in the stock (in years) of province-specific experience due to inter-firm mobility. While this variable may also account for human capital features, we rely on our robustness checks – see model section on the individual level analyses – to rule out the existence of selectivity on exiting partners' human and social capital. We also ruled out the impact of any 'Diaspora effect' by adding a control that adjusts for the percentage of partners leaving in a specific year relative to the total number of partners at the company level the year before an inter-firm mobility event (*Percentage-of-partners-exiting*). Additionally, instead of measuring the ratio of partners to associates, we followed Phillips (2002) by taking the (logged) number of associates, while controlling for the (logged) number of partners. A dummy variable was coded as 1 to indicate a very *Small firm* – that is, size of 2 – as much more fragile and exposed to a higher risk of failure. We finally controlled for the number of years elapsed since the founding of an organization by creating the variable *Age*. Following Petersen (1991), we coded the variable by taking the midpoint of each period.

Historical controls   The history of the Dutch accounting industry has been marked by important historical events that might well account for organization dissolution in specific years. Several controls were added. We created two dummies for the governmental regulations dealing with *World War I* conditions (1 if during 1914–18, 0 otherwise) and the occurrence of *World War II* (1 if during 1941–46, 0 otherwise). Another institutional event was the emergence of a *Single Association* (or NIvRA), which represented the collective interests of all Dutch accounting organizations and was established in 1966 (1 if year > 1966, 0 otherwise). The effect of regulatory changes enforced in 1971 and 1984 that significantly heightened the demand for audit services was captured by two dummy variables, *Regulation of 1971* (1 if year > 1971) and *Regulation of 1984* (1 if year > 1984). We used the rate of unemployment (*Unemployment*), a time-varying variable measured at the national level, to control for some of the circumstances under which the migration of professional accountants is more/less frequently observed.

Provincial controls   We tried to estimate the extent to which more general ecological phenomena affect the risk of organizational dissolution with the inclusion of the linear and quadratic effects of density measures at the provincial level: *Province Density* and *Province Density2* (that is, density squared). To control for the impact that the number of organizations populating the industry has on organization dissolution we also included *C4*, a measure of the level of concentration of the industry given by the total market share of the top four firms. The risk of dissolution might also be influenced by how many firms were created or disappeared each year, which reflects not only the degree of munificence of the environment, but also the extent to which ecological conditions affect inter-organizational mobility by creating/destroying new job opportunities. Thus, we included two variables, *Birth Province* and *Death Province*, to control for the number of firms founded and dissolved during the previous year within a given province. We also included the variable *Province Density at Founding* to account for any imprinting effect. Finally, to capture variations in carrying capacity (number of potential clients) over time, we controlled for *Provincial Inhabitants*, the number of inhabitants in each province for each year. Table 9.1 reports the correlation values for the variables we used in the analysis.

MODEL AND METHODS

In creating the dataset, we treated the year in which the organization appeared for the first time on the Register of Accountants as the founding year and the last year of appearance as the year of dissolution. After excluding single proprietorships, the final dataset includes the life of 676 firms divided into 5404 year-segments, for a total of 518 exits.

For the analysis we used event history techniques. We adopted a discrete-time formulation similar to that used in chapters 5 and 8. A well-known complication in using this procedure is due to the presence of crude observation points. The data structure challenges the use of a logit model. As Yamaguchi (1991) noted, logit model approaches can be interpreted as a ratio of two odds and such a ratio approaches the ratio of two rates only if the interval between observations is sufficiently small. A valid alternative is a continuous-time data specification which can be used to derive a model for data grouped into intervals (Allison, 1995). A complementary log-log specification resembles a piecewise specification with the difference that the hazard of failure is not forced to remain constant across intervals, but is allowed to fluctuate in various ways so long as the assumption of proportionality within each of them is satisfied. As in Chapter 4, we set those intervals equal to the time gaps in our data and controlled for firm age – that is, a curvilinear effect of duration.

Table 9.1 Pairwise correlations

Variables	1	2	3	4	5	6	7	8	9	10	11	12	13	14	15
1. Age	1.00														
2. World War I	-0.06	1.00													
3. World War II	0.20	-0.05	1.00												
4. Single Association	-0.28	-0.10	-0.18	1.00											
5. Regulation 1971	-0.24	-0.08	-0.15	0.83	1.00										
6. Regulation 1984	-0.18	-0.06	-0.11	0.63	0.75	1.00									
7. Province Inhabitants	-0.02	-0.15	-0.03	0.27	0.23	0.17	1.00								
8. C4	-0.26	-0.08	-0.19	0.85	0.85	0.63	0.22	1.00							
9. Birth Province	0.04	-0.06	0.10	0.17	0.10	0.17	0.35	0.08	1.00						
10. Death Province	0.00	-0.13	-0.08	0.18	0.19	0.21	0.48	0.18	0.45	1.00					
11. Provincial Density at Founding	-0.26	-0.13	0.00	-0.07	-0.10	-0.12	0.62	-0.12	0.29	0.41	1.00				
12. Provincial Density	0.21	-0.11	0.09	-0.41	-0.38	-0.31	0.50	-0.44	0.20	0.35	0.69	1.00			
13. Provincial Density Squared	0.23	-0.14	0.06	-0.47	-0.42	-0.34	0.40	-0.48	0.09	0.29	0.64	0.97	1.00		
14. Unemployment	0.06	0.02	0.17	-0.14	-0.04	0.07	-0.17	-0.20	0.15	0.08	-0.09	0.12	0.12	1.00	
15. Small Firm	-0.08	0.09	-0.01	-0.11	-0.10	-0.10	-0.07	-0.10	-0.06	-0.06	0.02	-0.02	-0.02	0.05	1.00
16. No. of Partners (log)	0.10	-0.02	-0.03	0.17	0.16	0.14	0.09	0.17	0.14	0.14	0.01	0.02	-0.01	-0.02	-0.56
17. No. of Associates (log)	0.11	-0.11	0.02	0.12	0.13	0.13	0.21	0.12	0.08	0.15	0.11	0.10	0.10	-0.13	-0.47
18. Other-Than-Inter-firm-Exits	0.07	0.01	-0.04	0.02	0.01	-0.01	0.00	0.02	-0.01	0.07	0.04	0.05	0.05	-0.02	-0.19

19. Social Capital Loss	0.09	−0.02	−0.03	0.03	0.05	0.05	0.01	0.04	0.06	0.03	0.00	0.00	0.00	−0.04	−0.10
20. Percentage-partners-leaving	0.10	0.01	−0.02	−0.03	−0.02	−0.02	−0.02	−0.02	−0.05	−0.03	−0.03	0.01	0.02	−0.06	0.00
21. Group-exit-dummy	−0.02	−0.05	−0.07	0.17	0.11	0.05	0.10	0.15	0.01	0.11	0.04	−0.03	−0.03	−0.14	−0.15
22. Individual-exit-dummy	0.05	0.06	0.02	−0.14	−0.12	−0.10	−0.11	−0.15	−0.04	−0.02	−0.02	0.05	0.05	0.09	−0.03
23. Group-avg-joint-exp-to-any	0.01	−0.02	−0.04	0.12	0.13	0.13	0.05	0.12	0.02	0.05	0.01	−0.03	−0.04	−0.05	−0.10
24. Group-avg-joint-exp-to-new	0.00	0.00	−0.03	0.11	0.09	0.11	0.04	0.10	0.03	0.02	0.00	−0.03	−0.04	−0.01	−0.05
25. Group-avg-joint-exp-to-inc	0.02	−0.03	−0.04	0.08	0.10	0.07	0.04	0.09	−0.01	0.05	0.01	−0.02	−0.02	−0.07	−0.10
26. Group-avg-joint-exp-to-same-pr	−0.01	0.01	−0.03	0.10	0.10	0.12	0.02	0.09	0.03	0.02	−0.01	−0.03	−0.04	0.00	−0.05
27. Group-avg-joint-exp-to-diff-pr	0.05	−0.02	−0.03	0.06	0.05	0.02	0.04	0.06	−0.01	0.03	0.01	−0.02	−0.01	−0.07	−0.09
28. Group-avg-joint-exp-to-inc-same-pr	−0.04	−0.02	−0.03	0.09	0.11	0.12	0.04	0.09	0.02	0.05	0.01	−0.02	−0.02	−0.02	−0.05
29. Group-avg-joint-exp-to-new-same-pr	0.01	0.01	−0.02	0.08	0.08	0.10	0.01	0.07	0.03	0.01	−0.01	−0.03	−0.04	0.01	−0.04
30. Group-avg-joint-exp-to-inc-diff-pr	0.06	−0.02	−0.02	0.03	0.03	0.01	0.02	0.03	−0.01	0.03	0.01	−0.01	0.00	−0.07	−0.08
31. Group-avg-joint-exp-to-new-diff-pr	−0.01	−0.01	−0.02	0.07	0.05	0.04	0.04	0.07	0.00	0.02	0.02	−0.02	−0.02	−0.02	−0.04

Table 9.1 (continued)

Variables	16	17	18	19	20	21	22	23	24	25	26	27	28	29	30	31
1. Age																
2. World War I																
3. World War II																
4. Single Association																
5. Regulation 1971																
6. Regulation 1984																
7. Province Inhabitants																
8. C4																
9. Birth Province																
10. Death Province																
11. Provincial Density at Founding																
12. Provincial Density																
13. Provincial Density Squared																
14. Unemployment																
15. Small Firm																
16. No. of Partners (log)	1.00															
17. No. of Associates (log)	0.49	1.00														
18. Other-Than-Inter-firm-Exits	0.39	0.21	1.00													

232

	16	17	18	19	20	21	22	23	24	25	26	27	28	29	30	31
19. Social Capital Loss	0.22	0.18	0.38	1.00												
20. Percentage-partners-leaving	−0.01	0.01	0.08	0.06	1.00											
21. Group-exit-dummy	0.20	0.09	0.26	0.15	0.06	1.00										
22. Individual-exit-dummy	0.08	−0.04	0.52	0.25	0.09	0.06	1.00									
23. Group-avg-joint-exp-to-any	0.17	0.11	0.20	0.25	0.05	0.32	0.07	1.00								
24. Group-avg-joint-exp-to-new	0.13	0.09	0.17	0.24	0.04	0.14	0.07	0.61	1.00							
25. Group-avg-joint-exp-to-inc	0.13	0.07	0.15	0.15	0.04	0.33	0.04	0.80	0.04	1.00						
26. Group-avg-joint-exp-to-same-pr	0.10	0.08	0.13	0.22	0.02	0.13	0.07	0.58	0.80	0.12	1.00					
27. Group-avg-joint-exp-to-diff-pr	0.15	0.08	0.20	0.17	0.05	0.31	0.04	0.70	0.32	0.70	0.02	1.00				
28. Group-avg-joint-exp-to-inc-same-pr	0.06	0.03	0.04	0.08	0.01	0.14	0.01	0.49	−0.01	0.61	0.16	0.00	1.00			
29. Group-avg-joint-exp-to-new-same-pr	0.09	0.08	0.12	0.21	0.02	0.10	0.07	0.51	0.80	0.01	0.98	0.02	−0.01	1.00		
30. Group-avg-joint-exp-to-inc-diff-pr	0.11	0.07	0.15	0.13	0.03	0.28	0.04	0.64	0.05	0.78	0.02	0.88	0.00	0.02	1.00	
31. Group-avg-joint-exp-to-new-diff-pr	0.09	0.05	0.12	0.13	0.04	0.09	0.02	0.35	0.58	0.05	0.01	0.51	−0.01	0.00	0.07	1.00

Further potential problems in our analysis concern the direction of causality and endogeneity. Inter-firm mobility might be an effect rather than a cause of organizational dissolution; individuals are more likely to quit when their firm is performing poorly and 'death is sneaking around the corner' (see Wagner, 1999). We addressed this concern in different ways. First, we lagged the variables by one period. Since in our data a 'period' ranges from a one- to a five-year interval, for 84 per cent of the firms in our database a one-period lag corresponds to 1 to 2 years and for 16 per cent to 3 to 5 years. But endogeneity may be due to systematic differences across exiting individuals. High profile partners (that is, with high quality human capital), for instance, are more likely to leave the company to join an incumbent or to found their own venture. In a similar vein, the inclination to remain in the same area may also be higher for individuals with a high stock of human and social capital. This potential scenario renders endogenous any donation to organizations located in similar geographical areas, potentially biasing the values of the estimated coefficients.

We then double-checked the robustness of our findings in several ways. The spurious effect of poor performance on inter-firm mobility might be ruled out by controlling for a lagged accounting measure of performance. Since we could not obtain accounting data on firm performance (for example, financial data), we opted for a different solution. Because size growth represents an often-used proxy for organizational success (for example, see Sørensen, 1999), the lagged rate of *Size Growth* can be construed as lagged performance, under the assumption that firms expand their ranks when they perform well. Size is easily observed by the firm's membership, and growth in membership suggests success and long-term viability. If performance is what motivates members to stay or quit, the harmful effects of turnover should be weaker in well performing organizations. We examined this possibility by creating an interaction term between size growth and our most relevant measures of inter-firm mobility – that is, group average experience transferred to newly founded firms within the same province. The results of this robustness check are reported in the last column of Table 9.2 below.

Second, we checked the existence of any underlying correlation between the partners' human/social capital and geographical destination by running a set of analyses at the individual level. More specifically, we reconstructed the history of all the accountants in our database and measured the probability of remaining within the same province against that of moving to a different province upon the realization of an inter-firm mobility event. After excluding the single proprietorships and all the non-mobility events (that is, other than inter-firm mobility cases such as death and retirement) we ended up with a sample of 867 cases of partner mobility, 62 per cent of which involved movements within the same province and 38 per cent across provinces. We proxied the quality of the human capital involved in the transfer by measuring the relative time-to-promotion of each partner – that is, the number of years needed to complete the tournament and to move from associate to partner (for a discussion of the relevance of this measure see Maister, 1993). The results (obtained with a complementary log-log specification, coding 1 the event of remaining within the same province, and 0 all the shifts to a different province) reassured us that human capital randomly distributes across geographical space upon an inter-firm mobility event: the estimates of the coefficients associated with human and social capital (proxied by local experience) were positive but far from being statistically significant. Again, the same coefficients turned out to be statistically insignificant when we estimated the impact of social and human capital on the decision to found a new company (65 per cent of the cases) versus joining an incumbent (35 per cent) upon exiting.

We further checked the existence of any systematic difference across firms due to unobserved effects by running a random effects complementary log-log model.[2] Since no evidence of any unobserved effect was found, we present the results adopting a more parsimonious specification. The analyses presented below, however, are controlling for fixed effects at the province level (not reported in Table 9.2) to account for unobserved systematic geographical differences across provinces. The statistically significant improvement in the fit of the model due to the addition of provincial fixed effects points to the existence of different selection environments. All the estimates were obtained using STATA 8.

RESULTS

Table 9.3 presents the estimates of the complementary log-log models for organizational dissolution. Model 1 includes all the control variables. In model 2, we tested Hypothesis 9.1 by adding our measures of individual and group-related mobility. In model 3, a measure of the (logged) average time spent together by the groups leaving is used to test Hypothesis 9.1a. In model 4, we juxtaposed the average joint experience of group migrations within and across provinces to test Hypothesis 9.2. To test Hypothesis 9.3, in model 5 we looked at the effect of average joint experience of groups moving to newly founded firms and incumbents (located both inside and outside the focal province). In model 6 we tested Hypothesis 9.4 by considering the three dimensions simultaneously. Model 7 reports the coefficient estimates after we included the interaction term between the size growth variable and the measure of 'group exit' which is central to our theoretical reasoning.

Table 9.2 Complementary log-log models for the dissolution rate of Dutch accounting firms, 1880–1986

Variables	Model 1	Std. Err.	Model 2	Std. Err.	Model 3	Std. Err.	Model 4	Std. Err.	Model 5	Std. Err.	Model 6	Std. Err.	Model 7	Std. Err.
Time gap 2 years	1.510	0.095**	1.275	0.114**	1.501	0.095**	1.503	0.096**	1.509	0.095**	1.502	0.096**	1.513	0.096**
Time gap 3 years	-2.134	1.006**	-1.952	1.019*	-2.125	1.006**	-2.123	1.006**	-2.128	1.006**	-2.126	1.006**	-2.121	1.006**
Time gap 4 years	3.422	0.182**	3.002	0.210**	3.382	0.183**	3.386	0.182**	3.406	0.183**	3.369	0.184**	3.386	0.185**
Time gap 5 years	2.652	0.559**	2.515	0.535**	2.604	0.561**	2.618	0.560**	2.641	0.559**	2.617	0.560**	2.634	0.560**
Age	-0.087	0.012**	-0.091	0.013**	-0.088	0.012**	-0.088	0.012**	-0.088	0.012**	-0.089	0.012**	-0.089	0.012**
Age 2	0.002	0.0002**	0.002	0.0002**	0.002	0.0002**	0.002	0.0002**	0.002	0.0002**	0.002	0.0002**	0.002	0.0002**
World War I	-0.078	0.607	0.051	0.618	-0.074	0.608	-0.073	0.608	-0.075	0.608	-0.073	0.608	-0.091	0.608
World War II	-0.536	0.398	-0.362	0.389	-0.498	0.398	-0.500	0.398	-0.517	0.398	-0.492	0.398	-0.517	0.402
Single Association	1.195	0.280**	1.174	0.316**	1.190	0.278**	1.185	0.277**	1.187	0.279**	1.179	0.276**	1.165	0.277**
Regulation 1971	-0.016	0.281	0.118	0.258	-0.009	0.280	-0.001	0.280	-0.001	0.281	0.008	0.282	0.045	0.284
Regulation 1984	-1.680	0.222**	-1.450	0.237**	-1.694	0.222**	-1.690	0.222**	-1.693	0.222**	-1.705	0.223**	-1.713	0.223**
Province Inhabitants (in millions)	0.02	0.03	0.02	0.03	0.02	0.03	0.02	0.03	0.02	0.03	0.02	0.03	0.02	0.03
C4	1.151	1.141	0.590	1.124	1.105	1.131	1.081	1.135	1.098	1.140	1.082	1.136	0.994	1.141
Birth Province	-0.021	0.007**	-0.025	0.007**	-0.021	0.007**	-0.021	0.007**	-0.021	0.007**	-0.021	0.007**	-0.020	0.007**
Death Province	0.059	0.006**	0.058	0.006**	0.059	0.006**	0.059	0.006**	0.059	0.006**	0.059	0.006**	0.059	0.006**
Provincial Density at Founding	0.006	0.003**	0.007	0.003**	0.006	0.003**	0.006	0.003**	0.006	0.003**	0.006	0.003**	0.006	0.003**
Provincial Density	-0.030	0.014**	-0.024	0.015	-0.027	0.014*	-0.017	0.014	-0.026	0.014*	-0.027	0.014*	-0.026	0.014*
Provincial Density Squared	0.0002	0.0001**	0.0002	0.0001**	0.0002	0.0001**	0.0002	0.0001**	0.0002	0.0001**	0.0002	0.0001**	0.0002	0.0001**
Unemployment	-0.063	0.017**	-0.039	0.016**	-0.063	0.017**	-0.063	0.017**	-0.063	0.017**	-0.063	0.017**	-0.063	0.017**
Small Firm	0.047	0.115	0.528	0.128**	0.057	0.115	0.054	0.115	0.045	0.115	0.060	0.115	0.109	0.118
No. of Partners (log)	-0.007	0.075	-0.335	0.083**	-0.028	0.076	-0.028	0.076	-0.017	0.077	-0.024	0.075	0.048	0.080
No. of Associates (log)	-0.067	0.034*	0.070	0.039*	-0.066	0.034*	-0.067	0.034*	-0.069	0.034**	-0.066	0.034*	-0.038	0.035**
Other-Than-Inter-firm-Exits	0.011	0.026	-0.094	0.031**	0.008	0.027	0.007	0.027	0.008	0.027	0.011	0.027	0.004	0.028
Social Capital Loss	0.157	0.065**	0.116	0.069*	0.115	0.063*	0.112	0.064**	0.126	0.062**	0.117	0.063**	0.073	0.077

236

Percentage-partners-leaving	0.252 0.102**	0.213 0.128*	0.256 0.102**	0.256 0.102**	0.254 0.102**	0.255 0.102**	0.287 0.101**
Group-exit-dummy (Ha9.1)		2.628 0.135**					
Individual-exit-dummy (Ha9.1)		0.070 0.145					
Group-avg-joint-exp-to-any (Ha9.1a)			0.215 0.079**				
Group-avg-joint-exp-to-new (Ha9.2)				0.167 0.081**			
Group-avg-joint-exp-to-inc (Ha9.2)				0.107 0.074			
Group-avg-joint-exp-to-same-pr (Ha9.3)					0.036 0.017**		
Group-avg-joint-exp-to-diff-pr (Ha9.3)					0.019 0.072		
Group-avg-joint-exp-to-inc-same-pr (Ha9.4)						0.203 0.165	0.241 0.164
Group-avg-joint-exp-to-new-same-pr (Ha9.4)						0.455 0.113**	0.383 0.115**
Group-avg-joint-exp-to-inc-diff-pr (Ha9.4)						0.032 0.151	0.026 0.149
Group-avg-joint-exp-to-new-diff-pr (Ha9.4)						0.245 0.153	0.239 0.152
Size Growth							-0.032 0.013**
Size Growth*Group-avg-exp-to-new-same-pr							0.006 0.008
Constant	-2.535 0.497**	-2.595 0.510**	-2.288 0.501**	-1.316 0.683**	-2.214 0.584**	-1.583 0.600**	-1.592 0.594**
Log Likelihood	-1257.62	-1254.78	-1254.54	-1254.53	-1255.18	-1251.99	-1247.19

Notes: Provincial fixed effects included: 518 events; ** $p < 0.05$; * $p < 0.10$. Two-tails tests.

237

The baseline model (model 1) reports the control variables. Again, the pattern of the *Age* variable suggests the existence of a curvilinear effect. The coefficients measuring the impact of ecological dynamics on failure rates – *Birth Province*, *Death Province*, *Provincial Density at Founding*, *Provincial Density* and *Provincial Density2* – are all in the expected direction and statistically significant. These results confirm that the survival chances of the focal firm are mainly dependent on the evolutionary dynamics of local populations.[3] Although the coefficient estimating the effect of exits that do not involve inter-firm mobility is positive, it does not reach statistical significance. On the contrary, the coefficient estimate of the variable measuring the impact of losing social capital is positive and statistically significant.

Model 2 presents the estimates measuring the competitive effects of inter-firm mobility after we distinguished between individual versus group movements. The risk of organizational dissolution is statistically significant when inter-firm mobility involves a group of partners rather than single individuals. Model 3 refines this finding by replacing the group dummy with a measure of average joint experience of departing members. The positive and statistically significant estimate of the variable *Group-avg-joint-exp-to-any* provides support to our Hypothesis 9.1a. We then disaggregated this measure according to the nature of the destination firm (incumbent or newly founded) and to its geographical location (within the same province or a different one). Model 4 compares the findings depending on whether the recipient firm is an incumbent or an entrepreneurial firm. Only the coefficient for newly founded organizations is statistically significant, so confirming Hypothesis 9.2. Model 5 reports the estimates across geographical space. Similarly, the estimates seem to confirm Hypothesis 9.3: the coefficient of the variable capturing movements within the same province is the only one that is statistically significant.[4]

In the previous models the three dimensions (individual vs. group, incumbent vs. start-up, same vs. different geographical context) were treated as independent. Thus, they do not inform us about how those dimensions jointly affect organizational survival. Model 6 is meant to aggregate these three dimensions. The coefficient estimates reported in model 6 suggest a few considerations. First, the effect of migration as a group is stronger than that of individual movement. Second, the strongest effects of inter-firm mobility on dissolution are related to movements within the same geographical area. Third, for each case the risk of organizational dissolution is much higher when partners leave the focal organization to found a new rival rather than to join an existing rival. In line with Hypothesis 9.4, the hazard of dissolution is the highest when groups depart to found a new firm located in the same province as the source firm.

Model 7 further corroborates these findings by combining *Size Growth* (lagged) – a proxy for good performance – with the *Group-avg-joint-exp-to-new-diff-pr* variable presented in model 6. Since this interaction term turned out to be non-significant, we interpreted this result as an indication that the competitive impact of routines replication is independent of the donor's firm health.

DISCUSSION AND CONCLUSIONS

The analysis of the effects of member exit on organizational survival has spun-off into research on the antecedents and the consequences of this event. The present study pushes this inquiry by investigating the competitive consequences for the donor firm of inter-firm mobility. We limited our theorizing to those exit cases in which a member departs to a peer firm, while controlling for other scenarios representing complete departure from the sector. Being a study of partnerships, we focused on partners, that is, key members who participate in the governance of their firm. Their exit was framed in terms of higher-order routines replication. Since these routines govern processes of resource acquisition and allocation, focusing on the conditions facilitating their replication is critical to understand when inter-firm mobility increases competitive interdependence among organizations.

Recent research has begun to investigate how such mobility affects the performance of the source firm (Sørensen, 1999b), the destination firm (Agarwal et al., 2004; Rao and Drazin, 2002; Wezel and Saka, 2006), or both simultaneously (Phillips, 2002), under the assumption that inter-firm mobility entails the transfer of routines but without further qualifying the conditions facilitating their replication. We contribute to this body of research in three ways. First, special attention is drawn to the scenario where inter-firm mobility translates into the transfer of higher-order routines across organizations, such that the different effect of individual versus collective migrations is exposed. Second, this chapter demonstrates how migrations to incumbents are less likely to affect the long-term performance of the donor than are migrations to newly founded firms. Third, this study shows the relevance of the same historical, socio-economic and institutional environment in facilitating successful replication of existing routines (see Stinchcombe, 1965 and for a comprehensive review of this article, Lounsbury and Ventresca, 2002) and therefore increasing the competitive effects of inter-firm mobility. Altogether, this chapter builds on the insights of research into the behavior of spin-offs (Agarwal et al., 2004; Phillips, 2002; Ruef, 2005; Burton et al., 2002; Klepper and Sleeper, 2005) to uncover conditions under which the spillover of proprietary routines exposes the source firm to unfavorable survival prospects. The loss of proprietary organizational routines occurs most ominously when senior members depart collectively, and especially so when they have spent many years together before leaving.

This chapter is concerned with the competitive consequences occasioned by routine replication due to outbound movements, while controlling for the loss of human and social capital. Unlike previous research that does not distinguish between resources and routines, we believe such a distinction to be important both theoretically and empirically. The thrust of the argument is that resources such as social capital are usually attached to individuals and therefore more likely to be transferred when those individuals move from firm to firm. Moreover, as our qualitative evidence suggests, the presence of 'anti-competitive clauses' significantly constrains the extent to which individuals' social capital can be transferred, especially when it involves clients who should contractually abide by such clauses. The competitive damage due to partner turnover, thus, cannot be primarily attributed to a loss of clients.

By contrast, routines are not bound to single individuals: since they originate from repeated interaction among multiple actors inside and/or outside the firm, their successful replication is a more complex and uncertain phenomenon necessitating that a much broader set of conditions must hold. Even though routines are unobserved, and in this chapter – as in the kindred papers of Phillips (2002) and Klepper and Sleeper (2005) – we do not measure replication as such, we attempted to measure the impact thereof, net of the effect of losing human/social capital. Needless to say, further empirical research, using more fine-grained data, is needed to validate our claims. Better measures should properly account for the spillover effects due to the loss of human and social capital. Our proxy captures such effects only indirectly. With respect to human capital, we found self-selection not to be at work even though our analysis remains silent about the specific characteristics (for example, education, skills or expertise) of departing individuals. While the findings concerning social capital are consistent with existing literature, the way we operationalize this construct only proxies for the effect of external ties (for example, relations with clients) disregarding that of internal ties – that is, repeated interaction among partners which stimulates communications and cohesion. Our measure of average joint experience partly captures this effect because it accounts for defecting members' dynamic patterns of interaction. Whether higher-order routine replication or the transfer of internal social capital between firms is responsible for the findings observed is a matter of debate. In our opinion, however, it remains unclear why the transfer of internal social capital should harm the donor's performance – especially when controlling for possible causes of internal disruption. We interpret the findings as pointing to routine replication as the critical mechanism responsible for donor's mortality. Regardless of the specific mechanism at work, a study on the conditions favoring the portability of skills, resources and routines across organizations should move beyond the individual level of analysis to embrace group dynamics as well.

Our focus on higher-order routine replication also sheds light on the reason why inter-firm mobility can be viewed as a source of competitive interdependence. Unlike operating routines, which usually attend to an organization's daily activities, higher-order routines govern the processes by which resources are allocated throughout the organization. It is their successful replication – not that of operating routines – that ultimately increases the degree of similarity between the donor and the recipient firms. Studying the conditions facilitating higher-order routine replication, there-fore, helps understand when inter-firm mobility produces competitive con-sequences. In this respect, it should be noted that the replication of proprietary routines under investigation in this chapter is typically not premeditated, even though 'poaching' is usually driven by competitive motives. Spin-offs are frequently due to inadvertent turnover of employees who seek an organizational setting outside the parent firm. The presump-tion is that voluntary (as in the case of partners) out-movement produces consequences quite different from those turnover events brought about by intended and intentional 'human resources' strategies. For example, many firms maintain elaborate job rotation systems as one of the means of delib-erate routine transfer. As for such transfers, consider that many firms – for example, Home Depot, Kinko's, Toyota, Carrefour – base their strategic intentions on routine replication, usually well-articulated and explicit orga-nizational routines (see Winter and Szulanski, 2001). Intentional transfer occurs also between firms through strategic alliances, outsourcing, guest engineers, and so on. We believe that our study emphasizes theoretically how such non-premeditated events involving key players reveal competitive externalities.

In its present form, the study suffers from several limitations. Each limi-tation, however, can be associated with a specific direction for future research. The contextually-dependent replication of routines involves knowledge-intensive firms. Similar mobility consequences can be observed in high-tech industries (for example, software, biotech, semiconductors – see Klepper and Sleeper, 2005) where spin-offs occasion spatial replication of routines. Further research should spell out the mobility implications for manufacturing versus service firms. Partnerships differ from incorporated firms with various levels of limited liability and family-owned or single pro-prietorships (which we omitted from the present analysis). How do such varying classes of organizations and their legal or institutional traditions affect the absorption of new higher-order routines? Apart from variations among sectors, within-sector heterogeneity among firms differently exposed to the routine replication risk was observed as well. The present chapter does not address this question and treats organizations in a dichotomous way: a newly founded firm or an incumbent. This distinction is premised on the idea that incumbents are already saddled with legacies of routines, that is, endowed with institutionalized patterns of interaction that are unlike those having an extramural provenance. Accordingly, in the analysis we compared these two classes of firms as a dichotomy. Yet existing firms differ along several dimensions that shape their susceptibility to absorption of extramural routines. Accounting for those dimensions amounts to an important refinement and further elaborates on the conduciveness of routine replication across firms. Consider dimensions such as firm size, aspects of organizational demography such as diversity in experience or skillsets and firm performance prior to outbound movements. Such inquiries push the frontiers of knowledge regarding migration of firm proprietary routines and related spillovers to new levels but are beyond the scope of this study.

The finding that the effects of inter-firm mobility are very much regional hints at geographic niches harboring organizational routines. The exit of professionals often precipitates jolts, upheavals and other forms of organizational change and discontinuity. We argued that the equivalence of geographic embeddedness for mobility-based replication is critical, and that one should spell out the nature of location equivalence. We have shown that the effects of mobility and routine replication are most observable if they occur within the same environment – that is, when donor and destination firms are co-located. Historical, socio-economic and institutional differences in the location of the donor and the destination firms matter more than geographical distance per se. Additional specification of the nature of geographic units such as SMSAs and industrial districts should improve the explanatory power of geography and co-location.

Finally, access to individual motivation and cognition for inter-firm mobility remains elusive. We have been agnostic about motives that induce individual or collective career-related action. We exposed effects of individual conduct shaping firm and sector-level externalities, even if we did not find any evidence of selectivity among events involving individuals endowed with significant human or social capital (fast-trackers or partners ranking high in their level of industry experience). Yet the motives of individuals to leave and thus to significantly affect local competition suggest drawing the individual level of analysis more centrally into an inquiry of inter-firm competition. Additional multi-level information about this issue might thus contribute to a more comprehensive understanding of the implications of inter-firm mobility, routines replication and organizational survival.

NOTES

1. We opted for this measurement of the construct to keep the test as simple as possible and to show how the loss of a team of partners – rather than that associated to individual mobility – reduces the donor's survival chances independently from its intensity and characteristics, which we further qualify by using other measures. The test carried out by using continuous measures provides, however, comparable results. Since one possible concern has to do with the underlying size distribution, we re-ran the analysis after controlling for the number of members involved in the event. Moreover, to reduce the impact of outliers, we did so only for those cases in which up to three members exited together (accounting for 68 per cent of all the team events). These additional checks did not alter the findings reported here.
2. A more complex solution to this problem is to create instruments for all the variables of theoretical interest. This procedure entails the estimation of a survival model where the eight inter-firm variables are replaced with the estimated number of events obtained through eight count models – that is, instrumented variables. As we found no evident sign of endogeneity while running our robustness checks, we decided not to use this technical correction.
3. Analyses not reported here demonstrate that the local ecological effects dominate national effects.
4. Hypotheses 9.2 and 9.3 might be linked to arguments regarding age and structure based on the argument that if the donor and the recipient firms were age equivalent they would also be structurally equivalent and therefore routine transfer between them would be more likely. Such a coincidence was examined by constructing a variable measuring the age difference between donor and recipient firms at the time of an inter-firm mobility event. The findings obtained point to an increasing and independent impact of age distance on mortality. In other words, the larger the donor spin-off age divergence, the stronger the competitive effect of inter-firm mobility. Adding this variable to the estimation did not affect the findings' robustness. A peculiar complication involves the donor's age when the recipient firm is a start-up, an issue that we resolved by adding a dummy variable flagging those transfers involving newly founded firms and interacting this variable with the age-difference measure. None of the coefficients however turned out to be statistically significant. The same procedure was repeated for the case of geographical destination – that is, by adding an interaction term between age-difference and a dummy variable indicating whether the transfer took place within the same province or a different province. In this case, the dummy suggested the existence of a positive effect on mortality of transfers taking place between equally aged and proximate pairs of firms. The robustness of these results was further tested by adding geographically-split measures. This addition canceled out the previous results, supporting a dichotomous rather than continuous difference between newly founded firms and incumbents in the presence of routines replication. The implication is that high-order routines become imprinted during the early stages of the organizational life cycle (for example, Baron et al., 1996) rendering incumbents, whatever their age, less amenable to the injection of new (high-order) routines.

10. In conclusion: micro behaviors as inducements for firm and sector evolution

In the foregoing chapters, we have explored organizational strategies and structures that are conditioned by individual actions. We have been able to trace changes in competitive positioning, behavior and structure that are triggered by the actions of the firm's membership. Members engage in behaviors that have repercussions at the level of their firm but also at higher levels including the local and sector-wide environment and taking in the competitive arena within which the firm competes.

Two sets of empirical studies were included in this volume. The first set, examined in Part II, looked at intangible assets among human-intensive organizations as distinct from organizations in general. Obviously, as human-intensive firms become increasingly important in Western societies and agricultural, manufacturing and mining firms recede into the background, the nature of such firms should accord a prominent place to their membership. After all the skills and capabilities that reside in the membership represent the primary source of their competitive advantage.

The prominence of membership in human asset-intensive firms is also evident in the second collection of chapters, in Part III, dealing with individual mobility within and between firms. Recently, the recognition that firms often face a retention dilemma (for example, Coff, 1997) has highlighted a major managerial factor in attracting, retaining and integrating human resources. Unlike mining and numerous manufacturing firms which are endowed with significant physical assets, the assets in services firms like those covered in this volume are largely intangible. Inflows and outflows of members occasion shifts in organizational behavior and long-term performance.

After a review of micro behavior and organizational evolution and a contrast between partnerships and private/public corporations, Chapter 4 set the tone for this volume by contrasting personnel, structural and sector-level aspects of this knowledge-intensive industry. The personnel-related aspects, such as the firms' human and social capital, stood out in relation to firm-level aspects, such as their leverage (for example, owner–employee ratio), and sector-level attributes, including density or competitiveness inferred from amount of crowding. At least in a sector such as professional accounting, the membership as carriers of intangible assets represents an important performance factor even when contrasted with ecological variables such as industry density. Human and social capital represents a critical asset in most firms, but particularly in those that are human asset-intensive. In knowledge-intensive industries such as the one that forms the basis of the studies reported in this volume, firms derive their competitive advantage from such resources and capabilities. One could add that in the twenty-first century, even manufacturing firms have become more human asset-intensive and likewise derive their competitive advantage from human rather than physical capital. *The Economist* (Hindle, 2006) views 'the modern firm' mostly in such terms. Partnerships in professional services sectors are evidently the embodiment of 'modern'.

The importance of human and social capital was also borne out in our inquiry of mergers and acquisitions. Typically M&A is understood to be motivated by ex ante conditions such as whether or not two firms are related in terms of their strategic dispositions – for example whether they originate from the same industry or market segments. That concern with strategic, external market positioning shifted recently to the post-M&A integration processes with a greater internal focus on strengthening a firm's capabilities. At present we enjoy a better understanding of the success and failure of M&A due to the management of the fit between the two firms. The benefits of an optimal merger accrue to the merging new firm, either at the onset of the merger as due diligence is carried out or during its aftermath when the firms bundle and consolidate their resources, especially the intangible kind such as capabilities and knowledge. The findings in this volume serve to bridge the two strands of inquiry in that results point to the importance of ex ante conditions such as the similarity and compatibility of the two firms involved. However, by abstaining from the conventional inquiry into abnormal returns and exploring the survival probability of the newly emerging firm, this book's results also illustrate the importance of the process of completing the deal beyond the initial decision to merge. The congruence of human and social capital among merging partnerships that we consider in Chapter 6 shows in another way the importance of multi-level research in dealing with questions that are traditionally examined at the firm or industry level of analysis.

In Part II, in addition to ecological regularities, we also examined institutional developments. In Chapter 5 the role of members in accounting for growing uniformity of firm governance was presented. The diffusion of the vertical differentiation among members into owners and employees began to unfold in the mid-1920s. Increasingly these professional services firms adopted a structural innovation in terms of whether partnerships consisted of owners only or whether they moved towards a bifurcation of owners and employees. The rise of the partner-associate structure (PA-structure) surfaced around 1925 and became increasingly common towards the twenty-first century. The results in this volume demonstrated the importance of membership and the migration of members among their firms; in fact the migrating members demonstrate that the embeddedness of individuals significantly accounts for the spread of new organizational forms. Likewise, at still a higher level of analysis we observed that networking among the competing firms, together with their propensity to innovate, produced changes at the sector level of analysis. The aggregate feedback among innovators versus non-innovators helped us in identifying trends in the industry towards a growing acceptance of the partner–associate structure. The diffusion of new governance forms is thus both a function of the migration of members whose behavior produces a tipping point that far exceeds the presumed importance of their individual conduct and a function of inter-firm networking, occasioned by inter-firm mobility and the ensuing spread of information and conformity that serves to explain that tipping point.

In Part III, we explored in detail the organizational and strategic shifts among firms in relation to the conduct of individual members. In these chapters we also included a geographic aspect. In chapters 7 to 9 we traced the movement of individuals between firms that were proximate in terms of either market or geography. The role of human agency is even more evident here. In chapters 7 and 9 we examined the effect of inflows and outflows of members respectively. Additionally, in Chapter 8 we discovered that organizational demography due to member migration does not only affect the internal heterogeneity of a focal firm, but also the compositional heterogeneity between firms. Internal diversity is harmful, while between-firm differences in demography are beneficial in that they drive competitors into different strategic directions – a result that is particularly compelling when competition is geographically localized. We obtained a causal understanding of the diversity–performance link by regressing survival on shifts in the demographic diversity within and between firms. Much of the research to date has been cross-sectional but the inclusion of member actions and the subsequent upturns or downturns of within- and between-organizational heterogeneity permits us to consider the implications in a temporal, causal context.

Personnel mobility is a critical conduit for organizational learning (Argote, 1993), institutional change and knowledge transfer across organizations. When observed at the organizational level, the recruitment of new personnel amounts to the formation and the renewal of inter-organizational networks, and contributes to the timely and rich knowledge dissemination between them. Newcomers, however, are likely to inject fresh ideas into the organization and elicit new solutions to existing problems. The introduction of less socialized people 'increases exploration, and thereby improves aggregate knowledge' (March, 1991: 79). Member entry might also attenuate the drawbacks of organizational learning. While deemed beneficial, learning pushes a firm towards and even beyond the asymptotic stage of the learning curve and its associated rigid, stale platform of skills. Since learning is a self-reinforcing process, organizations often 'become increasingly removed from other bases of experience and knowledge and more vulnerable to change in their environments' (Levinthal and March, 1993: 102). By indulging in local search, they risk falling into competency traps or developing core rigidities (Leonard-Barton, 1992). As 'every other process within organizations promotes homogeneity' (Staw, 1980: 264), personnel inflows generate variation and thereby creativity and serendipity – a situation that is crucial when markets and technology change and the development of new capabilities is called for. New members facilitate changes in the recipient firm's knowledge base by bringing in new knowledge. Furthermore, recruits endow an organization with new social relations (Galanter and Palay, 1991).

However, when exploring the consequences of inter-firm mobility at the population level, it becomes clear that it represents a powerful mechanism reducing differences among organizations and ultimately increasing niche overlap. Personnel mobility plays a critical role in consolidating institutional changes through the diffusion of isomorphic behaviors (Kraatz and Moore, 2002). Since executives significantly shape organizational behavior (for example, Hambrick and Mason, 1984) and tend to replicate their choices across firms (for example, Fligstein, 1990), the migration of key personnel raises the level of similarity among organizations. As Phillips (2002) has recently pointed out, the parent–progeny transfer of existing organizational practices and routines enhances the degree of similarity between the parent and the offspring and, in consequence, the likelihood that they might directly compete. As a result of heightened homogeneity, ecological competition between recipient and donor firms intensifies. Sørensen (1999a) has shown how recruiting managers from competitors – either directly or indirectly – triggers competition between them, resulting in lower growth rates. Further elaborating on the idea of localized competition, Sørensen (1999b) has argued that tenure overlap between competing organizations significantly exacerbates competition, thereby depressing growth rates. Part III of this book advances this inquiry and thoroughly discusses the 'across-level' consequences of individual choice (that is, voluntary mobility) for the diffusion of organizational forms (Chapter 7) and for triggering ecological competition with specific reference to organizational dissolution (chapters 8 and 9).

Several theoretical implications derived from the above-mentioned rationale are introduced and discussed in each chapter. We expect that the evidence reported here will stimulate further intellectual debate among macro-organizational theorists on the role of individuals for firm and sector evolution. In particular, we hope that the findings presented here will draw more attention to the considerable leverage individuals (at least key ones or upper echelons) have in their conduct. The individuals in these multi-level studies enjoy latitude in career paths within a single profession but not infrequently across different firms, and trigger competitive trends that far outweigh what they could achieve individually. As members of a professional group they have become socialized into a social environment with distinct boundaries and stringent screening and advancement hurdles. Yet as professionals, they readily migrate between firms, whether alone or as part of a merger or acquisition, and contribute to competitive, ecological and institutional shifts. So, a further insight from the studies presented here can be read in the term 'dynamic embeddedness'. Networks of people and firms evolve, enter and exit firms and their markets. As volitional actors, they manifest changes in social and geographic locations; but shifts in location may destroy existing networks or behaviors, even while forging new ones, at the firm level, as well as at lower and higher levels of analysis.

A final consideration regards ecological and institutional theory. Ecological and institutional approaches have been criticized as relying on an underdeveloped theory of agency (for a discussion on institutional theory see DiMaggio, 1988) because of their tendency to aggregate events (for example, foundings, new adoptions) and, by so doing, implicitly attributing homogeneity to the lower levels of analysis. These macro-organizational theories, in fact, remain rather silent on the role of individual actions, goals and intents in triggering innovation and entrepreneurship or in stimulating the revision of institutionalized patterns of change (for an interesting discussion on these issues see Thornton, 1999 and Aldrich and Wiedenmayer, 1993). This is not to argue for the primacy of individual action for firm and industry evolution. We rather aim at stimulating some reflections among organizational theorists and strategic management scholars on a middle ground between 'structuralistic' and 'individualistic' approaches to the study of organizations, how they learn and develop their capabilities, in the strategy literature – compare Grant (1996) with Kogut and Zander (1996).

We agree with Felin and Hesterly (2007) in conceiving organizations as repositories of knowledge and values, which may become upgraded and modified through the actions of individuals. Their structures, practices, and routines as stock or as changes in the stock are constantly subject to the influence of individuals and what they import or remove from their firm. Aldrich recently likewise asserted that 'if we truly focused on routines, competencies, practices and so on, we would not follow people anymore in our research. Instead we would follow how competencies are spread, replicate and insinuate themselves into organizations. People would disappear from our equations' (Murmann et al., 2003: 27). The studies in this volume have explored individual mobility as a vehicle for information and knowledge diffusion accross firms and examined their nested heterogeneity to isolate spillovers of intangible assets – all this with a concern for firm performance and long-term survival. New data (even more fine-grained that those analyzed here) are now available to researchers, allowing them to further push the envelope of multi-level theory and research, encompassing the individual, the firm and the industry. The challenge of developing new theories and insights from studying the dynamics of complex systems is open. This book aims to initiate the trend that will see individual choice and behavior becoming an increasingly prominent area of macro-organizational research.

References

Abrahamson, E. (1997), 'The emergence and prevalence of employee management rhetorics: the effects of long wave, labor unions, and turnover, 1875 to 1992', *Academy of Management Journal*, 40: 491–533.

Abrahamson, E. and G. Fairchild (1999), 'Management fashion: lifecycles, triggers, and collective learning processes', *Administrative Science Quarterly*, 44: 708–40.

Acevado, M., E.M. Basualdo and M. Khavisse (1990), *Quien as quien?: Los duenos del poder economico (Argentina 1973–1987)*, Buenos Aires: Editora.

Adams, J.S. (1976), 'The structure and dynamics of behavior in organizational boundary roles', in M.D. Dunette (ed.), *Handbook of Industrial and Organizational Psychology*, Chicago: Rand McNally, pp. 1175–99.

Adner, R. and C.E. Helfat (2003), 'Corporate effects and dynamic managerial capabilities', *Strategic Management Journal*, 24(10): 1011–25.

Agarwal, R., R. Echambadi, A. Franco and M.B. Sarkar (2004), 'Knowledge transfer through inheritance: spin-out generation, development, and survival', *Academy of Management Journal*, 47(4): 501–22.

Ahuja, G. (1998), 'Collaboration networks, structural holes and innovation: a longitudinal study', *Best Paper Proceedings*, Academy of Management Convention, San Diego.

Alchian, A.A. (1950), 'Uncertainty, evolution, and economic theory', *Journal of Political Economy*, 58: 211–21.

Aldrich, H.E. and C.M. Fiol (1994), 'Fools rush in? The institutional context of industry creation', *Academy of Management Review*, 19: 645–70.

Aldrich, H.E. and J. Pfeffer (1976), 'Environments of organizations', *Annual Review of Sociology*, 2: 79–105.

Aldrich, H.E. and G. Wiedenmayer (1993), 'From traits to rates: an ecological perspective on organizational foundings', in J. Katz and R.H. Brockhouse (eds), *Advances in Entrepreneurship, Firm Emergence, and Growth, Vol. I*, Greenwich, CT: JAI Press.

Allison, G.T. (1971), *Essence of Decision*, Boston, MA: Little Brown.

Allison, P.D. (1982), 'Discrete-time methods for the analysis of event histories', in S. Leinhardt (ed.), *Sociological Methodology*, San Francisco: Jossey-Bass, pp. 61–98.

Allison, P.D. (1995), *Survival Analysis using the SAS System*, Cary, NC: SAS Institute.

Allport, F.H. (1933), *Institutional Behavior*, Chapel Hill, NC: University of North Carolina Press.

Almedia, P. and B. Kogut (1999), 'Localization of knowledge and the mobility of engineers in regional networks', *Management Science*, 45(7): 905–18.

Alpert, S. and D. Whetten (1985), 'Organizational identity', in B.M. Staw and L.L. Cummings (eds), *Research in Organizational Behavior*, Greenwich, CT: JAI Press, pp. 263–96.

Amburgey, T.L. and A.S. Miner (1992), 'Strategic momentum: the effects of repetitive, positional, and contextual momentum on merger activity', *Strategic Management Journal*, 13: 335–48.

Amsden, P.H. (1989), *Asia's Next Giant: South Korea and Late Industrialization*, New York: Oxford University Press.

Ancona, D.G. and D.F. Caldwell (1992), 'Bridging the boundary: external activity and performance in organizational teams', *Administrative Science Quarterly*, 37: 634–65.

Argote, L. (1993), 'Group and organizational learning curves: individual system and environmental components', *British Journal of Social Psychology*, 32: 31–51.

Argote, L. (1999), *Organizational Learning. Creating, Retaining and Transferring Knowledge*, Norwell, MA: Kluwer Academic Publishers.

Armour, N.O. and D.J. Teece (1978), 'Organization structure and economic performance: a test of the multidivisional hypothesis', *Bell Journal of Economics*, 9: 106–22.

Arrow, K.J. (1962), 'The economic implications of learning by doing', *Review of Economic Studies*, 29: 155–73.

Arrow, K.J. (1973), 'Higher education as a filter', *Journal of Public Economics*, 2: 193–216.

Audretsch, D.B. and P.E. Stephan (1996), 'Company–scientist locational links: the case of biotechnology', *American Economic Review*, 86: 641–52.

Bailey, N.T. (1976), *The Mathematical Theory of Infectious Diseases and Applications*, New York: Hafner.

Bala, V. and S. Goyal (1998), 'Learning from neighbours', *Review of Economic Studies*, 65(3): 595–621.

Baldwin, C.Y. and K. Clark (2000), *Design Rules: The Power of Modularity*, vol. 1, Cambridge, MA: MIT Press.

Bantel, K. and S. Jackson (1989), 'Top management and innovation in banking: does the composition of the top team make a difference?', *Strategic Management Journal*, 10: 107–24.

Barefield, R.M., J.J. Gaver and T.B. O'Keefe (1993), 'Additional evidence on the economics of attest: extending results from the audit market to the market for compilations and reviews', *Auditing: A Journal of Practice and Theory*, 12: 76–87.

Barley, S.R. and P.S. Tolbert (1997), 'Institutionalization and structuration: studying the links between action and institution', *Organization Studies*, 18: 93–117.

Barnard, C. (1939), *The Functions of the Executive*, Cambridge, MA: Harvard University Press.

Barnett, W.P., A.N. Swanson and O. Sorenson (2002), 'Asymmetric selection from organizational founding to survival', Annual meeting of the Nagymaros group, Wassenaar, The Netherlands.

Barney, J.B. (1991), 'Firm resources and sustained competitive advantage', *Journal of Management*, 17: 99–120.

Baron, J.N., M.D. Burton and M.T. Hannan (1996), 'The road taken: origins and early evolution of employment systems in emerging companies', *Industrial and Corporate Change*, 5: 239–75.

Barsade, S.G., A.J. Ward, J.D.F. Turner and J.A. Sonnenfeld (2000), 'To your hearts content: a model of affective diversity in top management teams', *Administrative Science Quarterly*, 45: 802–36.

Bates, T. (1990), 'Entrepreneurial human capital inputs and small business longevity', *Review of Economics and Statistics*, 72: 551–9.

Baum, J.A.C. (1995), 'The changing basis of competition in organizational populations: the Manhattan hotel industry, 1887–1990', *Social Forces*, 74: 177–205.

Baum, J.A.C. (1996), 'Organizational ecology', in S.R. Clegg, C. Hardy and W.R. Nord (eds), *Handbook of Organization Studies*, London: Sage Publications, pp. 77–114.

Baum, J.A.C. and T. Amburgey (2002), 'Organizational ecology', in J.A.C. Baum (ed.), *Companion to Organizations*, Oxford: Blackwell, pp. 304–26.

Baum, J.A.C. and T.K. Lant (2003), 'Hits and misses: managers' (mis)categorization of competitors in the Manhattan hotel industry', in J.A.C. Baum and O. Sorenson (eds), *Advances in Strategic Management: Geography and Strategy*, Oxford: JAI/Elsevier, pp. 119–58.

Baum, J.A.C. and S. Mezias (1992), 'Localized competition and organizational failure in the Manhattan hotel industry, 1898–1990', *Administrative Science Quarterly*, 37: 580–604.

Baum, J.A.C. and W.W. Powell (1995), 'Cultivating an institutional ecology of organizations: comment on Hannan, Carroll, Dundon, and Torres', *American Sociological Review*, 60: 529–38.

Baum, J.A.C. and J.V. Singh (1994), *Evolutionary Dynamics of Organizations*, New York: Oxford University Press.

Becker, G.S. (1964), *Human Capital*, New York: Columbia University Press.

Becker, G.S. (1975), *Human Capital: A Theoretical and Empirical Analysis with Special Reference to Education*, New York: Columbia University Press.

Belzil, C. (2001), 'Unemployment insurance and subsequent job duration: job matching versus unobserved heterogeneity', *Journal of Applied Econometrics*, 16(5): 619–36.

Benjamin, B.A. and J.M. Podolny (1999), 'Status, quality, and social order in the California wine industry', *Administrative Science Quarterly*, 44: 563–89.

Ben-Porath, Y. (1980), 'The F-connection: families, friends, and firms and the organization of exchange', *Population and Development Review*, 6: 1–30.

Benston, G.J. (1985), 'The market for public accounting services: demand, supply and regulation', *Journal of Accounting and Public Policy*, 4: 33–79.

Berger, P.L. and T. Luckmann (1967), *The Social Construction of Reality*, New York: Doubleday Anchor.

Berglov, E. (1994), 'Ownership of equity and corporate governance – the case of Sweden', in T. Baums, R.M. Buxbaum and K.J. Hopt (eds), *Institutional Investors and Corporate Governance*, Berlin: Walter de Gruyter.

Berle, A.A. and G.C. Means (1932), *The Modern Corporation and Private Property*, New York: Macmillan.

Bhide, A. (1992), 'McKinsey and Company, (A): 1956', *Harvard Business School Cases*, No. 9: 303–66.

Bhide, A.V. (1994), 'How entrepreneurs craft strategies that work', *Harvard Business Review*, March–April.

Bhide, A.V. (2000), *The Origin and Evolution of New Businesses*, Oxford: Oxford University Press.

Bigelow, L., G.R. Carroll, M. Seidel and L. Tsai (1997), 'Legitimation, geographical scale, and organizational density: regional pattern of foundings of American automobile producers, 1885–1981', *Social Science Research*, 26: 377–98.

Birch, D. (1981), *Firm Behavior as a Determinant of Economic Change*, Cambridge, MA: MIT Press.

Black, J.A. and K.B. Boal (1994), 'Strategic resources: traits, configurations and paths to sustainable competitive advantage', *Strategic Management Journal*, 15: 131–48.

Blau, P.M. (1977), *Inequality and Heterogeneity*, New York: Free Press.

Blau, P.M. and R.W. Scott (1962), *Formal Organizations, a Comparative Approach*, San Francisco: Chandler Publishing Co.

Blondel, C., N. Rowell and L. Van der Heyden (2002), *Prevalence of Patrimonial Firms in the SBF 250: Evolution from 1993 to 1998*, INSEAD, Fontainebleau, France, Research Report.

Boeker, W. (1989), 'The development and institutionalization of sub-unit power in organizations', *Administrative Science Quarterly*, 34: 388–410.

Boeker, W. (1997), 'Executive migration and strategic change: the effect of top manager movement on product market entry', *Administrative Science Quarterly*, 42: 213–36.

Boone, C.A.J.J., B. de Brabander and A. van Witteloostuijn (1996), 'CEO locus of control and small business performance: an integrative framework and empirical test', *Journal of Management Studies*, 33: 667–99.

Boone, C., V. Bröcheler and G.R. Carroll (2000), 'Custom service: application and tests of resource-partitioning theory among Dutch auditing firms from 1896 to 1992', *Organization Studies*, 21: 355–81.

Boone, C.A.J.J., G.R. Carroll and A. van Witteloostuijn (2002), 'Environmental resource distributions and market partitioning: Dutch daily newspaper organizations from 1968 to 1994', *American Sociological Review*, 67(3): 408–31.

Boone, C., B. de Brabander, W. van Olffen and A. van Witteloostuijn (2004), 'The genesis of top management team diversity', *Academy of Management Journal*, 47: 633–56.

Boone, C., F.C. Wezel and A. van Witteloostuijn (2006), 'Top management team composition and organizational ecology', in J.A.C. Baum, S. Dobrev and A. van Witteloostuijn (eds), *Ecology and Strategy: 23 (Advances in Strategic Management)*, Greenwich, CT: JAI Press, pp. 103–35.

Bornstein, G. and M. Ben-Yossef (1994), 'Cooperation in intergroup and single-group social dilemmas', *Journal of Experimental Social Psychology*, 30: 52–67.

Bourdieu, P. (1980), 'Le capital social: note provisoires', *Actes des recherche en sciences sociales*, 3: 2–3.

Bourdieu, P. (1994), *Raisons politiques: Sur la theorie de l'action*, Paris: Editions du Seuil.

Boxman, E.A.W., P.M. De Graaf and H.D. Flap (1991), 'The impact of social and human capital on the income attainment of Dutch managers', *Social Networks*, 13: 51–73.

Boyd, R. and P.J. Richerson (1985), *Culture and the Evolutionary Process*, Chicago: University of Chicago Press.

Bradach, J.L. and R.G. Eccles (1989), 'Markets versus hierarchies: from ideal types to plural forms', in W.R. Scott (ed.), *Annual Review of Sociology*, 15, Palo Alto, CA: Annual Reviews Inc, pp. 97–118.

Brown, B. (2003), *The History of the Corporation*, Sumas, WA: BF Communications Inc.

Brown, J.S. and J.P. Duguid (1997), 'Organizing knowledge', Paper presented at the First Berkeley Forum, UC Berkeley.

Brüderl, J., P. Preisendörfer and R. Ziegler (1992), 'Survival chances of newly founded business organizations', *American Sociological Review*, 57: 227–42.

Bruton, G.D., B.M. Oviatt and M.A. White (1994), 'Performance of acquisitions of distressed firm', *Academy of Management Journal*, 37: 972–89.

Buono, A.F. and J.L. Bowditch (1989), *The Human Side of Mergers and Acquisitions: Managing Collisions between People, Cultures, and Organizations*, San Francisco: Jossey-Bass.

Buono, A.F., J.L. Bowditch and J.W. Lewis III (1985), 'When cultures collide: the anatomy of a merger', *Human Relations*, 38: 477–500.

Burckhard, M., F. Panunzi and A. Schleifer (2003), 'Family firms', *Journal of Finance*, 53: 2167–205.

Burke, P.J. and D.C. Reitzes (1981), 'The link between identity and role performance', *Social Psychology Quarterly*, 44: 83–92.

Burns, T. and G.M. Stalker (1962), *The Management of Motivation*, Chicago: Quadrangle Books.

Burt, R.S. (1992), *Structural Holes*, Cambridge, MA: Harvard University Press.

Burt, R.S. (1997), 'The contingent value of social capital', *Administrative Science Quarterly*, 42(2): 339–65.

Burt, R.S. and D. Ronchi (1990), 'Contested control in a large manufacturing plant', in J. Weesie and H.D. Flap (eds), *Social Networks through Time*, Utrecht: Isor, pp. 121–57.

Burton, M.D., J.B. Sorensen and C.M. Beckman (2002), 'Coming from good stock: career histories and new venture formation', in M. Lounsbury and M.J. Ventresca (eds), *Research in the Sociology of Organizations*, New York: Elsevier Science, pp. 229–62.

Campbell, D.T. (1974), 'Downward causation in hierarchically organized biological systems', in F.J. Ayala and F. Dobzhansky (eds), *Studies in the Philosophy of Biology*, Berkeley, CA: University of California Press, pp. 179–86.

Campbell, D.T. (1994), 'How individual and face-to-face group selection undermine firm selection in organizational evolution', in J.A.C. Baum and J. Singh (eds), *Evolutionary Dynamics of Organizations*, New York: Oxford University Press, pp. 23–38.

Carpenter, M.A. and J.W. Fredrickson (2001), 'Top management teams global strategies posture and the moderating role of uncertainty', *Academy of Management Journal*, 44(3): 533–45.

Carpenter, M.A., W.G. Sanders and M.A. Geletkanycz (2004), 'The upper echelons revisited: the antecedents, elements, and consequences of TMT composition', *Journal of Management*, 30: 749–78.

Carroll, G.R. (1985), 'Concentration and specialization: dynamics of niche width in populations of organizations', *American Journal of Sociology*, 90: 1262–83.

Carroll, G.R. and M.T. Hannan (1989), 'Density dependence in the evolution of populations of newspaper organizations', *American Sociological Review*, 54: 524–48.

Carroll, G.R. and M.T. Hannan (2000), *The Demography of Corporations and Industries*, Princeton, NJ: Princeton University Press.

Carroll, G.R. and J.R. Harrison (1998), 'Organizational demography and culture: insights from a formal model and simulation', *Administrative Science Quarterly*, 43(3): 637–67.

Carroll, G.R. and J. Wade (1991), 'Density dependence in the organizational evolution of the American brewing industry across different levels of analysis', *Social Science Research*, 20: 217–302.

Carroll, G.R., H.A. Haveman and A. Swaminathan (1992), 'Careers in organizations: an ecological perspective', in David Featherman, Richard Lerner and Marion Perlmutter (eds), *Life-span Development and Behavior*, Hillsdale, NJ: Lawrence Erlbaum Associates, pp. 112–44.

Cattani, G., J.M. Pennings and F.C. Wezel (2003), 'Spatial and temporal heterogeneity in founding patterns', *Organization Science*, 14(6): 670–85.

Caves, R.E. and R.M. Bradburd (1988), 'The empirical determinants of vertical integration', *Journal of Economic Behavior and Organization*, 9: 265–79.

Centraal Bureau Statistiek (2002), 'Ministerie van Binnelandse Zaken', Bevolking der Gemeenten van Nederland [Population of Communities of the Netherlands].

Chan, D. (1998), 'Functional relations among constructs in the same content domain at different levels of analysis: a typology of composition models', *Journal of Applied Psychology*, 83: 234–46.

Chatterjee, S. (1986), 'Types of synergy and economic value: the impact of acquisitions on merging and rival firms', *Strategic Management Journal*, 7: 119–39.

Chatterjee, S., M.H. Lubatkin, D.M. Schweiger and Y. Weber (1992), 'Cultural differences and shareholder value in related mergers: linking equity and human capital', *Strategic Management Journal*, 13: 319–34.

Cheng, D.C., B.E. Gup and L.D. Wall (1989), 'Financial determinants of bank takeovers', *Journal of Money, Credit and Banking*, 21: 524–36.

Cho, D.S., S. Nam and L. Tung (1998), *Korean Chaebols*, New York: Oxford University Press.

Christensen, C. (1997), *The Innovator's Dilemma*, Boston, MA: Harvard Business School Press.

Chung, S. (1996), 'Performance effects of cooperative strategies among investement banking firms: a log-linear analysis of organizational exchange networks', *Social Networks*, 18: 121–48.

Chung, S., H. Singh and K. Lee (1999), 'Comparative capabilities and reputational capital as drivers of strategic alliance formation', *Strategic Management Journal*, **21**(1), 1–22.

Clark, K. and T. Fujimoto (1991), *Product Development Performance: Strategy, Organization and Management in the World Auto Industry*, Boston: Harvard Business School Press.

Cliff, A.D., P. Haggett, J.K. Ord and G.R. Versey (1981), *Spatial Diffusion. An Historical Geography of Epidemics in an Island Community*, New York: Cambridge University Press.

Coff, R. (1997), 'Human assets and management dilemmas: coping with hazards on the road to resource-based theory', *Academy of Management Review*, 22: 374–402.

Cohen, M. and P. Bacdayan (1994), 'Organizational routines are stored as procedural memory', *Organization Science*, 5: 554–68.

Cohen, M.D., J.G. March and J.P. Olsen (1972), 'A garbage can model of organizational choice', *Administrative Science Quarterly*, 17: 1–25.

Coleman, J.S. (1988), 'Social capital in the creation of social capital', *American Journal of Sociology*, 94: S95–S120.

Coleman, J.S. (1990), *Foundations of Social Theory*, Cambridge, MA: Harvard University Press.

Coleman, J.S., E. Katz and H. Menzel (1966), *Medical Innovation*, New York: Bobbs-Merrill.

Colyvas, J. and W.W. Powell (2006), 'Roads to institutionalization', *Research in Organizational Behavior*, 27: 305–53, Greenwich, CT: JAI Press.

Copeland, T.E. and J.F. Weston (1988), *Financial Theory and Corporate Policy* (3rd edn), Reading, MA: Addison-Wesley.

Cox, D.R. and D. Oakes (1984), *Analysis of Survival Data*, London: Chapman and Hall.

Cyert, R. and J.G. March (1963), *A Behavioral Theory of the Firm*, Englewood Cliffs, NJ: Prentice Hall.

Datta, D.K. (1991), 'Organizational fit and acquisition performance: effects of post-acquisition integration', *Strategic Management Journal*, 12: 281–97.

Davis, G.F. (1991), 'Agent without principles? The spread of poison pill through the intercorporate network', *Administrative Science Quarterly*, 36: 583–613.

Davis, G.F. and H.R. Greve (1997), 'Corporate elite networks and governance changes in the 1980s', *American Journal of Sociology*, 103: 1–37.

De Pree, J.C.I. (1997), *Grenzen aan Verandering: Reorganisatie en structuurprincipes van het binnenlands bestuur* [Borders [or limits] to change: The relationship between reorganization and structural attributes of interior governance], The Hague: Wetenschappelijke Raad voor het Regeringsbeleid.

Dendrinos, D. and M. Sonis (1990), 'Chaos and socio-spatial dynamics', New York: Springer Verlag.

DiMaggio, P.J. (1988), 'Interest and agency in institutional theory', in L.G. Zucker (ed.), *Institutional Patterns and Organizations: Culture and Environment*, Cambridge, MA: Ballinger, pp. 3–21.

DiMaggio, P.J. (1991), 'Constructing an organizational field as a professional project: US art museums, 1920–1940', in W.W. Powell and P.J. DiMaggio (eds), *The New Institutionalism in Organizational Analysis*, Chicago and London: University of Chicago Press, pp. 267–92.

DiMaggio, P.J. and W.W. Powell (1983), 'The iron cage revisited: institutional isomorphism and collective rationality in organizational fields', *American Sociological Review*, 48: 147–60.

Dobbin, F.R., L. Edelman, J.W. Meyer, W.R. Scott and A. Swidler (1988), 'The expansion of due process in organizations', in L.G. Zucker (ed.), *Institutional Patterns and Organizations: Culture and Environment*, Cambridge, MA: Ballinger, pp. 71–100.

Dobrev, S.D., T.Y. Kim and M.T. Hannan (2001), 'Dynamics of niche width and resource partitioning', *American Journal of Sociology*, 106: 1299–337.

Dore, R. (1983), 'Goodwill and the spirit of market capitalism', *British Journal of Sociology*, 34: 459–82.

Dosi, G., R.R. Nelson and S.G. Winter (2000), *The Nature and Dynamics of Organizational Capabilities*, Oxford: Oxford University Press.

Durkheim, E. ([1897] 1933), *The Division of Labor in Society*, Glencoe, IL: Free Press.

Dyer, J. (1996), 'Specialized supplier networks as a source of competitive advantage: evidence from the auto industry', *Strategic Management Journal*, 17: 271–91.

The Economist (1995), 'Accountancy firms: a glimmer of hope', 1 April, 62–3.

Edelman, L. (1990), 'Legal environments and organizational governance: the expansion of due process in the American workplace', *American Journal of Sociology*, 95: 1401–40.

Edmondson, A., R. Bohmer and G. Pisano (2001), 'Disrupted routines:

group learning and new technology implementation in hospitals', *Administrative Science Quarterly*, 46: 685–716.

Eisenhardt, K.M. (1988), 'Agency- and institutional-theory explanations: the case of retail sales compensation', *Academy of Management Journal*, 31: 488–511.

Eisenhardt, K.M. and C.B. Schoonhoven (1990), 'Organizational growth: linking founding team, strategy, environment, and growth among U.S. semiconductor ventures, 1978–1988', *Administrative Science Quarterly*, 35: 504–29.

Fama, E. and M. Jensen (1980), 'Separation of ownership and control', *Journal of Political Economy*, 88, 288–309.

Felin, T. and N.J. Foss (2004), 'Organizational routines: a sceptical look', DRUID working paper No. 04-13.

Felin, T. and W.S. Hesterly (2007), 'The knowledge-based view, heterogeneity, and new value creation: philosophical considerations on the locus of knowledge', *Academy of Management Review*, 32(1): 195–218.

Festinger, L. (1953), 'Informal social communication', *Psychology Review*, LVII: 271–92.

Fiegenbaum, A. and H. Thomas (1995), 'Strategic groups as reference groups', *Strategic Management Journal*, 16: 461–76.

Finkelstein, S. and D. Hambrick (1990), 'Top-management-team tenure and organizational outcomes: the moderating role of managerial discretion', *Administrative Science Quarterly*, 35: 484–503.

Finkelstein, S. and D.C. Hambrick (1996), *Strategic Leadership: Top Executives and their Effects on Organizations*, St Paul, MN: West Publishing Company.

Firth, M. (1993), 'Price setting and the value of a strong brand name', *International Journal of Research in Marketing*, 10(4): 381–6.

Fligstein, N. (1985), 'The spread of multidivisional form among large firms, 1919–1979', *American Sociological Review*, 50: 377–91.

Fligstein, N. (1990), *Transformation of Corporate Control*, Cambridge, MA: Harvard University Press.

Fligstein, N. (1991), 'The structural transformation of American industry: an institutional account of the causes of diversification in the largest firms, 1919–1979', in W.W. Powell and P.J. DiMaggio (eds), *The New Institutionalism in Organizational Analysis*, Chicago: University of Chicago Press, pp. 311–36.

Fombrun, C. and E. Zajac (1987), 'Structural and perceptual influences of intra-industry stratification', *Academy of Management Journal*, 30: 33–50.

Foote, N.N. (1951), 'Identification as the basis for a theory of motivation', *American Sociological Review*, 26: 14–21.

Foss, N.J. (2003), 'Selective intervention and internal hybrids: interpreting and learning from the rise and decline of the Ozicon Spaghetti Organization', *Organization Science*, 14: 331–49.

Fowler, K.L. and D.R. Schmidt (1989), 'Determinants of tender offer post-acquisition financial performance', *Strategic Management Journal*, 10: 339–50.

Francis, J.R. and D.T. Simon (1987), 'A test of audit pricing in the small-client segment of the US audit market', *Accounting Review*, 62: 145–57.

Freeman, J.H. (1986), 'Entrepreneurs as organizational products: semiconductor firms and venture capital firms', in G. Libecap (ed.), *Advances in the Study of Entrepreneurial Innovation*, Greenwich, CT: JAI Press, pp. 33–58.

Freeman, J. and M.T. Hannan (1983), 'Niche width and the dynamics of organizational populations', *American Journal of Sociology*, 88: 1116–45.

Freeman, J. and A. Lomi (1994), 'Resource partitioning and the founding of banking cooperatives in Italy', in J.A.C. Baum and J. Singh (eds), *Evolutionary Dynamics of Organizations*, New York: Oxford University Press, pp. 269–93.

Fujiwara-Greve, T. and H.R. Greve (2000), 'Organizational ecology and job mobility', *Social Forces*, 79: 547–68.

Galanter, M. and T. Palay (1991), *Tournament of Lawyers. The Transformation of the Big Law Firm*, Chicago: University of Chicago Press.

Galaskiewicz, J. and S. Wasserman (1989), 'Mimetic processes within an interorganizational field: an empirical test', *Administrative Science Quarterly*, 34: 454–79.

Gerlach, M.L. (1987), 'Business alliances and the strategy of the Japanese firm', in G. Carroll and C. Vogel (eds), *Organizational Approaches to Strategy*, Berkeley: University of Califiornia Press.

Gerlach, M.L. (1992), 'Twilight of the keiretzu: a critical assessment', *Journal of Japanese Studies*, 18(1): 79–118.

Geroski, P.A. (2000), 'Models of technology diffusion', *Research Policy*, 29: 603–25.

Giddens, A. (1971), *Capitalism and Modern Social Theory: An Analysis of the Writings of Marx, Durkheim, and Weber*, Cambridge: Cambridge University Press.

Gilson, R.J. and R.H. Mnookin (1989), 'Coming of age in a corporate law firm: the economics of associate career patterns', *Stanford Law Review*, 41: 567–95.

Gould, R.V. (1995), *Insurgent Identities: Class, Commune, and Protest in Paris from 1848 to the Commune*, Chicago: University of Chicago Press.

Granstrand, O. and S. Sjolander (1990), 'The acquisition of technology and small firms by large firms', *Journal of Economic Behavior and Organization*, 13: 367–86.

Granovetter, M.S. (1974), *Getting a Job*, Cambridge, MA: Harvard University Press.

Granovetter, M.S. (1985), 'Economic action and social structure: the problem of embeddedness', *American Journal of Sociology*, 91: 481–510.

Grant, R.M. (1996), 'Toward a knowledge-based theory of the firm', *Strategic Management Journal*, 17: 109–22.

Greene, W.H. (2000), *Econometric Analysis* (4th edn), Upper Saddle River, NJ: Prentice Hall.

Greenwood, R. and L. Empson (2003), 'The professional partnership: relic or exemplary form of governance?' *Organization Studies*, 24(6): 909–33.

Greenwood, R., C.R. Hinings and J.L. Brown (1990), 'The P²-form of strategic management: corporate practices in the professional partnership', *Academy of Management Journal*, 33: 725–55.

Greenwood, R., C.R. Hinings and J.L. Brown (1994), 'Merging professional service firms', *Organization Science*, 5: 239–57.

Greve, H.R. (1994), 'Industry diversity effects on job mobility', *Acta Sociologica*, 37: 119–40.

Greve, H. (2002), 'An ecological theory of spatial evolution: local density dependence in Tokyo banking, 1894–1936', *Social Forces*, 80(3): 847–79.

Greve, H.R. (2003), *Organizational Learning from Performance Feedback: A Behavioral Perspective on Innovation and Change*, Cambridge: Cambridge University Press.

Groysberg, B. (2001), 'Can they take it with them? The portability of star knowledge workers performance: myth or reality?' Unpublished doctoral dissertation, Harvard Business School.

Groysberg, B. and A. Nanda (2002), 'Does stardom affect job mobility? Evidence from analyst turnover in investment banks', Harvard Business School Division of Research Working Paper series 02-029.

Groysberg, B., S. Matthews, A. Nanda and M. Salter (1999), 'The Goldman Sachs IPO', Harvard Business School Cases No. 9: 800-016.

Groysberg, B., A.N. McLean and N. Nohria (2006), 'Are leaders portable?' *Harvard Business Review*, 84: 92–101.

Guillen, M.F. (1997), 'Business groups in economic development', *Best Papers Proceedings*, Academy of Management, Annual Meeting, Boston, pp. 170–4.

Guzzo, R.A. and M.W. Dickson (1996), 'Teams in organizations: recent research on performance and effectiveness', *Annual Review of Psychology*, 47: 307–38.

Hachen, D. (1992), 'Industrial characteristics and job mobility rates', *American Sociological Review*, 57: 39–55.

Hagedoorn, J. and J. Schakenraad (1994), 'The effect of strategic technology alliances on company performance', *Strategic Management Journal*, 15: 291–309.

Hägerstrand, T. (1953/1969), *Innovation Diffusion as a Spatial Process*, Chicago: University of Chicago Press.

Hakanson, H. and J. Johanson (1993), 'The network as a governance structure: interfirm cooperation beyond markets and hierarchies', in F. Grabber (ed.), *The Embedded Firm*, London: Routledge.

Hambrick, D.C. and R.A. D'Aveni (1988), 'Large corporate failures as downward spirals', *Administrative Science Quarterly*, 33: 1–23.

Hambrick, D.C. and R.A. D'Aveni (1992), 'Top team deterioration as part of the downward spiral of large corporate bankruptcies', *Management Science*, 38(10): 1445–66.

Hambrick, D.C. and P.A. Mason (1984), 'Upper echelons: the organization as a reflection of its top management', *Academy of Management Journal*, 9(2): 193–206.

Hambrick, D.C., M.A. Geletkancyz and J.W. Fredrickson (1993), 'Top executive commitment to the status quo', *Strategic Management Journal*, 14: 401–18.

Hambrick, D.C., T. Cho and M. Chen (1996), 'The influence of top management team heterogeneity on firms competitive moves', *Administrative Science Quarterly*, 41: 659–84.

Hammer, J. and J. Champy (1993), *Reengineering the Corporation*, New York: Harper Collins.

Han, S. (1994), 'Mimetic isomorphism and its effect on the audit services market', *Social Forces*, 73: 637–64.

Hannan, M.T. (1986), 'Competitive and institutional processes in organizational ecology', Tech. Rep. 86-13, Cornell University, Department of Sociology, Ithaca, NY.

Hannan, M.T. (1988), 'Social change, organizational diversity, and individual careers', in N. Smelser and D. Gerstein (eds), *Social and Behavioral Sciences: Discoveries over Fifty Years*, Washington, DC: National Academy Press, pp. 73–86.

Hannan, M.T. (1997), 'Inertia, density and structure of organizational populations: entries in European automobile industries, 1886–1981', *Organization Studies*, 18: 193–228.

Hannan, Michael T. and Glenn R. Carroll (1992), *Dynamics of Organizational Populations*, New York: Oxford University Press.

Hannan, M.T. and J.H. Freeman (1977), 'The population ecology of organizations', *American Journal of Sociology*, 83: 929–84.

Hannan, M.T. and J.H. Freeman (1984), 'Structural inertia and organizational change', *American Sociological Review*, 49: 149–64.

Hannan, M.T. and J.K. Freeman (1986), 'Where do organizational forms come from?', *Sociological Forum*, 1: 50–72.

Hannan, M.T. and J.H. Freeman (1987), 'The ecology of organizational founding: American labor unions, 1836–1985', *American Journal of Sociology*, 92: 910–43.

Hannan, M.T. and J. Freeman (1989), *Organizational Ecology*, Cambridge, MA: Harvard University Press.

Hannan, M.T., G.R. Carroll, E.A. Dundon and J.C. Torres (1995), 'Organizational evolution in a multinational context: entries of automobile manufacturers in Belgium, Britain, France, Germany, and Italy', *American Sociological Review*, 60: 509–28.

Hannan, M.T., G.R. Carroll, S.D. Dobrev, J. Han and J.C. Torres (1998), 'Organizational mortality in European and American automobile industry. Part II: coupled clocks', *European Sociological Review*, 14: 303–13.

Hansen, M.T. (1997), 'Integrating knowledge through the intra-company network: implications for product development time', working paper, Harvard Business School.

Hansen, M.T. (1999), 'Search-transfer problem: the role of weak ties in transferring knowledge across organization subunits', *Administrative Science Quarterly*, 44: 82–111.

Harris, D. and C. Helfat (1997), 'Specificity of CEO human capital and compensation', *Strategic Management Journal*, 18: 895–920.

Harrison, D.A., K.H. Price, J.H. Gavin and A.T. Florey (2002), 'Time, teams, and task performance: changing effects of diversity on group functioning', *Academy of Management Journal*, 45: 1029–45.

Hart, O. and J. Moore (1990), 'Property rights and the nature of the firm', *Journal of Political Economy*, 96(6): 1119–58.

Haunschild, P.R. (1993), 'Interorganizational imitation: the impact of interlocks on corporate acquisition activity', *Administrative Science Quarterly*, 38: 564–92.

Haunschild, P.R. and C.M. Beckman (1998), 'When do interlocks matter? Alternative sources of information and interlock influence', *Administrative Science Quarterly*, 43: 815–44.

Haunschild, P.R. and A.S. Miner (1997), 'Modes of interorganizational imitation: the effects of outcome salience and uncertainty', *Administrative Science Quarterly*, 42: 472–500.

Hausman, J.B., H. Hall and Z. Griliches (1984), 'Econometric models for count data with an application to the patents–R&D relationship', *Econometrica*, 52(4): 909–38.

Haveman, H.A. (1993), 'Follow the leader: mimetic isomorphism and entry into new markets', *Administrative Science Quarterly*, 38: 593–627.

Haveman, H.A. (1995), 'The demographic metabolism of organizations: industry dynamics, turnover, and tenure distributions', *Administrative Science Quarterly*, 40: 586–618.

Haveman, H.A. and L.E. Cohen (1994), 'The ecological dynamics of careers: the impact of organizational founding, dissolution, and merger on job mobility', *American Journal of Sociology*, 100: 104–52.

Hawley, A.H. (1950), *Human Ecology. A Theory of Community Structure*, New York: Ronald Press.

Heckman, J. (1979), 'Sample selection bias as a specification error', *Econometrica*, 47: 153–61.

Hedström, P. (1994), 'Contagious collectives: on the spatial diffusion of Swedish trade unions, 1890–1940', *American Journal of Sociology*, 99: 1157–79.

Hedström, P., R. Sandell and C. Stern (2000), 'Mesolevel networks and the diffusion of social movements: the case of the Swedish social democratic party', *American Journal of Sociology*, 106: 145–72.

Henderson, R. and I. Cockburn (1994), 'Measuring competence: exploring firm effects in pharmaceutical research', *Strategic Management Journal*, 15: 63–84.

Hinings, C.R., J.L. Brown and R. Greenwood (1991), 'Change in an autonomous professional organization', *Journal of Management Studies*, 28: 375–93.

Hofstede, G.H. (1980), *Culture's Consequences*, Beverly Hills, CA: Sage.

Homans, G.C. (1950), *The Human Group*, New York: Harcourt, Brace and World.

Horwitz, Morton (1977), *The Transformation of American Law, 1780–1860*, Cambridge, MA: MIT Press.

Huckman, R.S. and G.P. Pisano (2006), 'The firm specificity of individual performance: evidence from cardiac surgery', *Management Science*, 52: 473–88.

Ingram, P. (2002), 'International learning', in J.A.C. Baum (ed.), *Companion to Organizations*, Oxford: Blackwell, pp. 642–63.

Ingram, P. and J.A.C. Baum (1997), 'Opportunity and constraint: organizations' learning from the operating and competitive experience of industries', *Strategic Management Journal*, 18 (summer special issue): 75–98.

Jaffe, A.B., M. Trajtenberg and R.M. Henderson (1993), 'Geographical localization of knowledge spillovers, as evidenced by patent citations', *Quarterly Journal of Economics*, 108: 577–98.

Jehn, K.A., G.B. Northcraft and M.A. Neale (1999), 'Why differences make a difference: a field study of diversity conflict and performance in workgroups', *Administrative Science Quarterly*, 44: 741–63.

Jensen, M.C. and W.H. Meckling (1976), 'Theory of the firm: managerial behavior, agency costs and ownership structure', *Journal of Financial Economics*, 3: 305–60.

Jovanovic, B. (1979), 'Job matching and the theory of turnover', *Journal of Political Economy*, 87(5): 972–90.

Kanter, R.M. (1977), *Men and Women of the Corporation*, New York: Basic Books.

Kaplan, R. and D. Norton (1992), 'The balanced scorecard: measures that drive performance', *Harvard Business Review*, January–February, 71–9.

Keck, S.L. and M.L. Tushman (1993), 'Environmental and organizational context and executive team structure', *Academy of Management Journal*, 36: 1314–44.

Kiesler, S. and L. Sproull (1982), 'Managerial response to changing environments: perspectives on problem sensing from social cognition', *Administrative Science Quarterly*, 27: 548–70.

Kilduff, M., R. Angelmar and A. Merha (2000), 'Top management-team diversity and firm performance: examining the role of cognitions', *Organization Science*, 11(1): 21–34.

Kim, D. (2007), 'The next best thing to getting married: partnerships among the jewellery manufacturers in the Providence/Attleboro Area during the nineteenth century', *Enterprise Society*, 8: 106–35.

Kim, E.U. (1997), '*Big Business, Strong State: Collusion and Conflict in South Korean Development, 1960–1990*', Albany, NY: SUNY Press.

Kim, Y.H. (1989), *Kwangwon Kyongje T'ukhye Kyongje* [*State led economy, preferential treatment economy*], Seoul: Ch'ung Am.

Kimberly, J.R. (1976), 'Organizational size and the structural perspective: a review, critique, and proposal', *Administrative Science Quarterly*, 21: 571–97.

Klepper, S. (2001), 'Employee startups in high-tech industries', *Industrial and Corporate Change*, 10: 639–74.

Klepper, S. and S.D. Sleeper (2005), 'Entry by spinoffs', *Management Science*, 51(8): 1291–306.

Knight, D., C.L. Pearce, K.G. Smith, J.D. Olian, H.P. Sims, K.A. Smith and P. Flood (1999), 'Top management team diversity, group process, and strategic consensus', *Strategic Management Journal*, 20: 445–65.

Knott, A.M. (2001), 'The dynamic value of hierarchy', *Management Science*, 47(3): 430–48.

Kogut, B. and U. Zander (1992), 'Knowledge of the firm, combinative capabilities, and the replication of technology', *Organization Science*, 3: 383–97.

Kogut, B. and U. Zander (1996), 'What firms do? Coordination, identity, and learning', *Organization Science*, 7(5): 502–18.

Kraatz, M. (1998), 'Learning by association? Interorganizational networks and adaptation to environmental change', *Academy of Management Journal*, 41: 621–43.

Kraatz, M. and D. Moore (2002), 'Executive migration and institutional change', *Academy of Management Journal*, 45: 120–43.

Lamoreaux, N.R. (1995), 'Constructing firms, partnerships and alternative contractual arrangements in the early-nineteenth-century American business', *Business and Economic History*, 24(2): 43–71.

Lamoreaux, N.R. (1998), 'Partnerships, corporations and the theory of the firm', *American Economic Review*, 88(2): 66–71.

Langedijk, H.P. (1990), 'Wisseling van accountantskantoor: een fata morgana in de toekomst?' *Maandblad voor Accountancy en Bedrijfseconomie*, 64: 264–70.

Lant, T.K., F.J. Milliken and B. Batra (1992), 'The role of managerial learning and interpretation in strategic persistence and reorientation: an empirical exploration', *Strategic Management Journal*, 13: 585–608.

Laumann, E.O., P.V. Marsden and D. Prensky (1989), 'The boundary specification problem in network analysis', in L.C. Freeman, D.R. White and A.K. Romny (eds), *Research Methods in Social Network Analysis*, Fairfax, VA: George Mason University Press, pp. 61–87.

Lawrence, B. (1997), 'The black box of organizational demography', *Organization Science*, 8: 1–22.

Lawrence, R.Z. (1991), 'Efficient or exclusionist? The import behavior of Japanese corporate groups', *Brookings Papers on Economic Activity*, 1: 311–14.

Lazarsfeld, P.F. and R.K. Merton (1954), 'Friendship as a social process: a substantive and methodological analysis', in M. Berger, T. Abel and C.H. Page (eds), *Freedom and Control in Modern Society*, New York: Van Nostrand, pp. 18–66.

Lazega, E. (1999), 'Generalized exchange and environmental performance outcomes: social embeddedness of labor contracts in a corporate law firm', in Roger Leenders and Shaul Gabbay (eds), *Corporate, Social Capital and Liabilities*, Boston, MA: Kluwer, pp. 237–65.

Lazega, E. (2001), *The Collegial Phenomenon: The Social Mechanisms of Cooperation among Peers in a Contemporary Law Partnership*. Oxford: Oxford University Press.

Leblebici, H., G.R. Salancik, A. Copay and T. King (1991), 'Institutional change and the transformation of interorganizational fields: an organizational history of the US radio broadcasting industry', *Administrative Science Quarterly*, 36: 333–63.

Lee, C., K. Lee and J.M. Pennings (2001), 'Internal capabilities, external linkages, and performance: a study on technology-based ventures', *Strategic Management Journal*, Special Issue, 22(6/7): 615–40.

Lee, K. and J.M. Pennings (2002), 'Mimicry and the market', *Academy of Management Journal*, 45(1): 144–62.

Leonard-Barton, D. (1992), 'Core capabilities and core rigidities: a paradox in new product development', *Strategic Management Journal*, 13: 111–26.

Lev, B. (2001), *Intangibles: Management, Measurement, and Reporting*, Oxford: Oxford University Press.

Levin, S.A. (1989), 'Challenges in the development of a theory of community and ecosystem structure and function', in J. Roughgarden, R.M. May and S.A. Levin (eds), *Perspectives on Ecological Theory*, Princeton, NJ: Princeton University Press, pp. 242–55.

Levine, J.H. (1972), 'The sphere of influence', *American Sociological Review*, 37: 14–27.

Levins, R. (1968), *Evolution in Changing Environments*, Princeton, NJ: Princeton University Press.

Levinthal, D.A. and J.G. March (1993), 'The myopia of learning', *Strategic Management Journal*, 14: 95–112.

Levitt, B. and J.G. March (1988), 'Organizational learning', *Annual Review of Sociology*, 14: 314–40.

Likert, R. (1961), *The Human Organization*, New York: Wiley.

Lin, N., W.M. Ensel and J.C. Vaughn (1981), 'Social resources and strength of ties', *American Sociological Review*, 46: 393–405.

Lincoln, J.R., C.L. Ahmadjian and E. Mason (1998), 'Organizational learning and purchase-supply relations in Japan: Hitachi, Matsushita and Toyota compared', *California Management Review*, 40(3): 241–64.

Linz, J.J. and A. de Miguel (1966), 'Within-nation differences and comparisons: the eight Spains', in R.L. Merritt and S. Rokkan (eds), *Comparing Nations: The Use of Quantitative Data in Cross-National Research*, New Haven, CT: Yale University Press.

Lomi, A. (1995), 'The population ecology of organizational founding: location dependence and unobserved heterogeneity', *Administrative Science Quarterly*, 40: 111–45.

Lomi, A. (2000), 'Density dependence and spatial duality in organizational founding rates: Danish commercial banks, 1846–1989', *Organization Studies*, 21(2): 433–61.

Lomi, A. and E.R. Larsen (1996), 'Interacting locally and evolving globally: a computational approach to the dynamics of organizational populations', *Academy of Management Journal*, 39(5): 1287–321.

Lomi, A., E.R. Larsen and J.H. Freeman (2005), 'Things change: dynamic resource constraints and systems-dependent selection in the evolution of organizational populations', *Management Science*, 51: 882–903.

Lorenzoni, G. and A. Lipparini (1997), 'Leveraging internal and external competencies in boundary shifting strategies. A longitudinal approach', working paper, Department of Management, Economics Faculty, University of Bologna.

Lounsbury, M. and M.J. Ventresca (2002), 'Social structure and organizations revisited', in M. Lounsbury and M.J. Ventresca (eds), *Research in the Sociology of Organizations*, Greenwich, CT: JAI Press, pp. 3–36.

Lowendal, B. (1997), *Strategic Management of Profesional Firms*, Copenhagen: Handelshojskolens Forlag.

Lubatkin, M. (1983), 'Mergers and the performance of the acquiring firm', *Academy of Management Review*, 8: 218–25.

Lubatkin, M. (1987), 'Merger strategies and stockholder value', *Strategic Management Journal*, 8: 39–53.

Lubatkin, M. and H.M. O'Neill (1987), 'Merger strategies and capital market risk', *Academy of Management Journal*, 30: 665–84.

Luhmann, N. (1979), *Trust and Power*, New York: Wiley.

Madsen, T.L., E. Mosakowski and S. Zaheer (2003), 'Knowledge retention and personnel mobility: the non-disruptive effects of inflows of experience', *Organization Science*, 14: 173–91.

Maijoor, S. and A. van Witteloostuijn (1996), 'An empirical test of the resource based theory: strategic regulation in the Dutch audit industry', *Strategic Management Journal*, 17: 549–70.

Maister, D.H. (1993), *Managing the Professional Service Firm*, New York: Free Press.

March, J.G. (1991), 'Exploration and exploitation in organizational learning', *Organizational Science*, 2(1): 71–87.

March, J.G. (1994), *A Primer on Decision Making*, New York: Free Press.

March, J.G. and H.A. Simon (1958), *Organizations*, New York: Wiley.

Marshall, A. (1922), *Principles of Economics* (8th edn), London: Macmillan.

Matsusaka, J.G. (1993), 'Takeover motives during the conglomerate merger wave', *RAND Journal of Economics*, 24: 357–79.

Mayer, R.C., J.H. Davis and F.D. Schoorman (1995), 'An integrative model of organizational trust', *Academy of Management Review*, 20: 709–34.

McDonald, Duff (2005), 'Please sir, I want some more: how Goldman Sachs is carving up its $11 billion pie', *New York Metro*, 21 December.

McFadden, D. (1974), 'Conditional logit analysis of qualitative choice behavior', in P. Zaremka (ed.), *Frontiers in Econometrics*, New York: Academy Press.

McKelvey, B. (1982), *Organizational Systematics: Taxonomy, Evolution and Classification*, Berkeley, CA: University of California Press.

McKenzie, R.D. (1968), *On Human Ecology*, Chicago: University of Chicago Press.

McPherson, J.M. (1983), 'An ecology of affiliation', *American Sociological Review*, 48: 519–32.

McPherson, J.M. and J.R. Ranger-Moore (1991), 'Evolution on a dancing landscape: organizations and networks in dynamic Blau space', *Social Forces*, 70: 19–42.

McPherson, J.M. and T. Rotolo (1996), 'Testing a dynamic model of social composition: diversity and change in voluntary groups', *American Sociological Review*, 61: 179–202.

McPherson, J.M. and L. Smith-Lovin (1987), 'Homophily in voluntary organizations: status distance and the composition of face-to-face groups', *American Sociological Review*, 52: 370–79.

McPherson, J.M., P.A. Popielarz and S. Drobnic (1992), 'Social networks and organizational dynamics', *American Sociological Review*, 57: 153–70.

McPherson, J.M., L. Smith-Lovin and J.M. Cook (2001), 'Birds of a feather: homophily in social networks', *Annual Review of Sociology*, 27: 415–44.

McVey, Henry and Jason Draho (2005), 'US family-run companies – they may be better than you think', *Journal of Applied Corporate Finance*, 17(4): 134–43.

Meyer, J.W. (1994), 'Rationalized environments', in W.R. Scott and J.W. Meyer (eds), *Institutional Environments and Organizations: Structural Complexity and Individualism*, Thousand Oaks, CA: Sage, pp. 28–54.

Meyer, J.W. and B. Rowan (1977), 'Institutionalized organizations: formal structure as myth and ceremony', *American Journal of Sociology*, 83: 340–63.

Meyer, J.W. and W.R. Scott (1983), *Organizational Environments: Rituals and Rationality*, Beverly Hills, CA: Sage.

Meyer, M.W. and V. Gupta (1994), 'The performance paradox', in L.L. Cummings and B.M. Staw (eds), *Research in Organizational Behavior*, Greenwich, CT: JAI Press, pp. 309–69.

Michel, J. and D.C. Hambrick (1992), 'Diversification posture and the characteristics of the top management team', *Academy of Management Journal*, 35: 9–37.

Michels, R. (1915), *Political Parties; a Sociological Study of the Oligarchical Tendencies of Modern Democracy*, Glencoe, USA: Free Press.

Milgrom, P. and J. Roberts (1992), *Economics, Organization and Management*, Englewood Cliffs, NJ: Prentice Hall.

Mincer, J. (1974), *Schooling, Experience, and Earnings*, New York: Columbia University Press.

Miner, A. (1994), 'Seeking adaptive advantage: evolutionary theory and managerial action', in J.A.C. Baum and J.V. Singh (eds), *Evolutionary Dynamics of Organizations*, New York: Oxford University Press, pp. 76–89.

Mitchell, E.J. (1969), 'Some econometrics of the Huk rebellion', *American Political Science Review*, 63(4): 1159–71.

Mizruchi, M.S. (1993), 'Cohesion, equivalence, and similarity of behavior: a theoretical and empirical assessment', *Social Networks*, 15: 275–307.

Moore, J. and M.S. Kraatz (2007), 'Governance form and organizational adaptation: lessons from the savings and loan industry in the 1980s', *Working Paper*, College of Business UIUC.

Morgan, S. (2005), *A Family Portrait*, New York: Morgan Stanley Equity Report, North America.

Mozier, P. and S. Turley (1993), 'The audit expectation gap in Britain: an empirical investigation', *Accounting and Business Research*, 23(91A): 395–411.

Murmann, J., H. Aldrich, D. Levinthal and S. Winter (2003), 'Evolutionary thought in management and organization theory at the beginning of the new millennium', *Journal of Management Inquiry*, 12: 22–40.

Nakatani, I. (1984), 'The economic role of financial corporate grouping', in M. Aoki (ed.), *The Economic Analysis of Japanese Firm*, New York: North-Holland, pp. 227–58.

Napier, N.K. (1989), 'Mergers and acquisitions, human resource issues and outcomes: a review and suggested typology', *Journal of Management Studies*, 26: 271–90.

Nelson, R.R. and S.G. Winter (1982), *An Evolutionary Theory of Economic Change*, Cambridge, MA: Harvard University Press.

Newcomb, T.M. (1943), *Personality and Social Change*, New York: Holt, Rinehart and Winston.

Nishiyama, T. (1982), 'The structure of managerial control: who owns and controls Japanese businesses', *Japanese Economic Studies*, Fall: 37–77.

Nobeoka, K. and J.H. Dyer (1998), 'The influence of customer scope on supplier learning and performance in the Japanese automobile industry', working paper, The Wharton School, University of Pennsylvania, Philadelphia.

Nonaka, T. and H. Takeuchi (1995), *The Knowledge Creating Company*, Oxford: Oxford University Press.

North, D. (1981), *Structure and Change in Economic History*, New York: Norton.

North, D. (1990), *Institution, Institutional Change and Economic Performance*, Cambridge: Cambridge University Press.

Noteboom, B. (1999), 'The triangle: roles of the go-between', in Roger

Leenders and Shaul Gabbay (eds), *Corporate Social Capital and Liabilities*, Boston, MA: Kluwer.

O'Reilly, C.A., D. Caldwell and W. Barnett (1989), 'Work group demography social integration and turnover', *Administrative Science Quarterly*, 34: 21–37.

Palmer, D.P., D. Jennings and X. Zhou (1993), 'Late adoption of the multidivisional form by large US corporations: institutional, political, and economic accounts', *Administrative Science Quarterly*, 38: 100–131.

Park, R.E. (1926), 'The urban community as a spatial pattern and a moral order', in E.W. Burgess (ed.), *The Urban Community*, Chicago: University of Chicago Press, pp. 3–18.

Pegels C.C., Y.I. Song and B. Yang (2000), 'Management heterogeneity, competitive interaction groups and firm performance', *Strategic Management Journal*, 21(9): 911–23.

Pennings, J.M. (1980), *Interlocking Directorates*, San Francisco: Jossey Bass.

Pennings, J.M. (1982), 'Organizational birth frequencies: an empirical investigation', *Administrative Science Quarterly*, 27: 120–45.

Pennings, J.M. and F. Harianto (1992), 'The diffusion of technological innovation in the commercial banking industry', *Strategic Management Journal*, 13(1): 29–46.

Pennings, J.M. and K. Lee (1999), 'Social capital of organizations: level of analysis, conceptualization and performance implications', in S. Gabbay and R. Leenders (eds), *Corporate Social Capital*, New York: Addison-Wesley, pp. 43–67.

Pennings, J.M., H. Barkema and S. Douma (1994), 'Organizational learning and diversification', *Academy of Management Journal*, 37: 608–40.

Pennings J.M., K. Lee and A. van Witteloostuijn (1998), 'Human capital, social capital and firm survival', *Academy of Management Journal*, 41(4): 425–40.

Penrose, E.T. (1959), *The Theory of the Growth of the Firm*, Oxford: Blackwell.

Pentland, B.T. and M.S. Feldman (2005), 'Organizational routines as a unit of analysis', *Industrial and Corporate Change*, 14(5): 793–81.

Peteraf, M. and M. Shanley (1997), 'Getting to know you: a theory of strategic group identity', *Strategic Management Journal*, 18: 165–86.

Peters, T.J. and R.H. Waterman, Jr (1982), *In Search of Excellence*, New York: Harper and Row.

Petersen, T. (1991), 'Time aggregation bias in continuous-time hazard-rate models', in P.V. Marsden (ed.), *Sociological Methodology*, Oxford: Blackwell, pp. 263–90.

Petersen, T. and K.W. Koput (1991), 'Density dependence in organizational mortality: legitimacy or unobserved heterogeneity?', *American Sociological Review*, 56: 399–409.

Petersen, T. and K.W. Koput (1992), 'Time-aggregation bias in hazard-rate models with covariates', *Sociological Methods and Research*, 21: 25–51.

Pettigrew, A. (1974), *The Politics of Organization Decision Making*. London: Tavistock.

Pfeffer, J. (1983), 'Organizational demography', in L.L. Cummings and B.M. Staw (eds), *Research in Organizational Behavior*, Greenwich, CT: JAI Press, pp. 299–357.

Pfeffer, J. (1994), *Competitive Advantage through People*, Boston, MA: Harvard Business School Press.

Pfeffer, J. and H. Leblebici (1973), 'Executive recruitment and the development of interfirm organization', *Administrative Science Quarterly*, 18: 449–61.

Pfeffer, J. and G.R. Salancik (1978), *The External Control of Organizations: A Resource Dependence Perspective*, New York: Harper and Row.

Phillips, D.J. (2002), 'A genealogical approach to organizational life chances: the parent-progeny transfer and Silicon Valley law firms, 1946–1996', *Administrative Science Quarterly*, 47: 474–506.

Phillips, M.E. (1994), 'Industry mindsets: exploring the cultures of two macro-organizational settings', *Organization Science*, 5(3): 384–402.

Pil, F.K. and J.P. MacDuffie (1996), 'The adoption of high-involvement work practices', *Industrial Relations*, 35: 423–55.

Podolny, J.M. (1993), 'A status-based model of market competition', *American Journal of Sociology*, 98: 829–72.

Podolny, J. and J. Baron (1997), 'Resources and relationships: social networks and mobility in the workplace', *American Sociological Review*, 62: 673–93.

Podolny, J.M. and F. Castelluci (1999), 'Choosing ties from inside the prison', in Roger Leenders and Shaul Gabbay (eds), *Corporate Social Capital and Liabilities*, Boston, MA: Kluwer.

Podolny, J.M. and A. Shepard (1996), 'When are technological spillovers local?' mimeo, Stanford Business School, Stanford, CA.

Podolny, J.M., T. Stuart and M.T. Hannan (1996), 'Networks, knowledge, and niches: competition in the worldwide semiconductor industry, 1984–1991', *American Journal of Sociology*, 102: 659–89.

Polanyi, M. (1967), *The Tacit Dimension*, Garden City, New York: Doubleday Anchor.

Polanyi, M. (1974), *Personal Knowledge: Towards a Post-Critical Philosophy*, Chicago: University of Chicago Press.

Pólos, L., M.T. Hannan and G.R. Carroll (2002), 'Foundations of a theory of social forms', *Industrial and Corporate Change*, 11: 85–116.

Polzer, J.T., L.P. Milton and W.B. Swann Jr (2002), 'Capitalizing on diversity: interpersonal congruence in small work groups', *Administrative Science Quarterly*, 47: 296–324.

Popielarz, P.A. and J.M. McPherson (1995), 'On the edge or in between: niche position, niche overlap, and the duration of voluntary association memberships', *American Journal of Sociology*, 101: 698–720.

Porac, J. and H. Thomas (1990), 'Taxonomic mental models in competitor definition', *Academy of Management Review*, 15: 224–40.

Porac, J.F., H. Thomas and C. Baden-Fuller (1989), 'Industries as cognitive communities: The case of Scottish knitwear manufacturers', *Journal of Management Studies*, 26: 397–416.

Porter, K.W. (1937), *The Jacksons and the Lees: Two Generations of Massachusetts Merchants*, Cambridge, MA: Harvard University Press.

Porter, M.E. (1980), *Competitive Strategy*, New York: Free Press.

Powell, W.W. (1988), 'Institutional effects on organizational structure and performance', in L.G. Zucker (ed.), *Institutional Patterns and Organizations: Culture and Environment*, Cambridge, MA: Ballinger, pp. 115–36.

Powell, W.W. (1990), 'Neither market nor hierarchy: network forms of organization', in B.M. Staw and L.L. Cummings (eds), *Research in Organizational Behavior*, Greenwich, CT: JAI Press, pp. 295–336.

Powell, W.W. (1991), 'Expanding the scope of institutional analysis', in W.W. Powell and P.J. DiMaggio (eds), *The New Institutionalism in Organizational Analysis*, Chicago: University of Chicago Press, pp. 183–203.

Powell, W.W. and P. Brantley (1992), 'Competitive cooperation in biotechnology: learning through networks', in N. Nohria and R.G. Eccles (eds), *Networks and Organizations*, Boston, MA: Harvard Business School Press, pp. 366–94.

Powell, W.W. and P.J. DiMaggio (1991), *The New Institutionalism in Organizational Analysis*, Chicago: University of Chicago Press.

Public Accounting Report (1994), Exclusive Ranking of America's Largest Public Accounting Firms, Strafford Publications, Atlanta.

Puranam, P., H. Singh and M. Zollo (2006), 'Organizing for innovation: managing the coordination–autonomy dilemma in technology acquisition', *Academy of Management Jounarl*, 49: 263–80.

Putnam, R.D. (1996), 'The strange disappearance of civic America', *The American Prospect*, 7(24): 34–8.

Putman, R.D. (2000), *Bowling Alone: America's Declining Social Capital*, New York: Simon and Schuster.

Quinn, L.R. (1988), 'The mangled mergers of banking', *Bankers Monthly*, 105(4): 17–24.

Rao, H. and R. Drazin (2002), 'Overcoming resource constraints on product innovation by recruiting talent from rivals: a study of the mutual fund industry 1986–1994', *Academy of Management Journal*, 45(3): 491–507.

Rao, H. and J.V. Singh (1999), 'Types of variation in organizational populations: the speciation of new organizational forms', in J.A.C. Baum and B. McKelvey (eds), *Variations in Organization Science: In Honor of Donald T. Campbell*, Thousand Oaks, CA: Sage Publications, pp. 63–77.

Rao, H., C. Morill and M. Zald (2000), 'Power plays: how social movements and collective action create new organizational form', in Barry Staw and Robert Sutton (eds), *Research in Organizational Behavior*, Greenwich, CT: JAI Press, pp. 237–82.

Rao, H., H. Greve and G.F. Davis (2001), 'Fool's gold: social proof in the initiation and abandonment of coverage by Wall Street analysts', *Administrative Science Quarterly*, 46(3): 502–27.

Ravenscraft, David, J. and F.M. Scherer (1991), 'Divisional sell-off: a hazard function analysis', *Managerial and Decision Economics*, 12: 429–38.

Reger, R.K. (1987), 'Competitive positioning in the Chicago banking market: mapping the mind of the strategist', unpublished doctoral dissertation, University of Illinois at Urbana-Champaign.

Reger R.K. and A.S. Huff (1993), 'Strategic groups: a cognitive perspective', *Strategic Management Journal*, 14(2): 103–23.

Ridley, M. (1999), *Evolution* (2nd edn), Cambridge, MA: Blackwell Science.

Roberts, J. (2004), *The Modern Firm*, Oxford: Oxford University Press.

Rogers, E. (1962), *Diffusion of Innovations*, New York: Free Press.

Rogers, E.M. (1995), *Diffusion of Innovations* (4th edn), New York: Free Press.

Romer, P.M. (1986), 'Increasing returns and long-run growth', *Journal of Political Economy*, 94: 1002–37.

Rosenkopf, L. and P. Almeida (2003), 'Overcoming local search through alliances and mobility', *Management Science*, 49: 751–66.

Rotolo, T. and J.M. McPherson (2001), 'The system of occupations: modeling the competition of occupations in sociodemographic dimensions', *Social Forces*, 79: 1095–130.

Ruef, M. (2005), 'Origins of organizations: the entrepreneurial process', in L. Keister (ed.), *Research in the Sociology of Work*, Amsterdam: JAI Press, pp. 63–100.

Ruef, M. and W.R. Scott (1998), 'A multidimensional model of organizational legitimacy: hospital survival in changing institutional environments', *Administrative Science Quarterly*, 43: 877–904.

Ruef, M., H.E. Aldrich and N. Carter (2003), 'The structure of organizational founding teams: homophily, strong ties, and isolation among US entrepreneurs', *American Sociological Review*, 68: 195–222.

Rumelt, R.P. (1974), *Strategy, Structure and Economic Performance*, Cambridge, MA: Harvard University Press.

Rumelt, R.P., D. Schendel and D.J. Teece (1991), 'Strategic management and economics', *Strategic Management Journal*, 12 (Winter): 5–29.

Russell, R. (1985), 'Employee ownership and internal governance', *Journal of Economic Behavior and Organizations*, 6: 217–41.

Sabel, C. (1989), 'Flexible specialization and the re-emergence of regional economies', in P. Hirst and J. Zeitlin (eds), *Reversing Industrial Decline? Industrial Structure and Policy in Britain and her Competitors*, Oxford: Berg, pp. 17–70.

Saka, A. and F.C. Wezel (2006), 'The moderating impact of organizational status for the adoption of new institutional rules', working paper, Tilburg University.

Salancik, G.R. and J. Pfeffer (1978), 'A social informationa processing approach to job attitudes and task design', *Administrative Science Quarterly*, 23: 224–53.

Sales, A.L. and P.H. Mirvis (1984), 'When cultures collide: issues in acquisition', in J.R. Kimberly and R.E. Quinn (eds), *Managing Organizational Transitions*, Homewood, IL: Irwin, pp. 107–33.

Salter, M.S. and W.A. Weinhold (1979), *Diversification through Acquisition: Strategies for Creating Economic Value*, New York: Free Press.

Sanders, W.M. and M.A. Carpenter (1998), 'Internationalization and firm governance: the roles of CEO compensation, top team composition and board structure', *Academy of Management Journal*, 41(2): 158–78.

Saxenian, A. (1994), *Regional Advantage: Culture and Competition in Silicon Valley and Route 128*, Cambridge, MA: Harvard University Press.

Schelling, T.C. (1978), *Micromotives and Macrobehavior*, New York: W.W. Norton and Company.

Scherer, F.M. (1984), *Invention and Growth: Schumpeterian Perspectives*, Cambridge, MA: MIT Press.

Schluter, D. (2000), *The Ecology of Adaptive Radiation*, New York: Oxford University Press.

Schmalensee, R. (1985), 'Do markets differ much?' *American Economic Review*, 75: 341–51.

Schneider, B. (1987), 'The people make the place', *Personnel Psychology*, 40: 437–53.

Schultze, W.S., M.H. Lubatkin, R.N. Dino and A.K. Buchholtz (2001), 'Agency relationships in family firms: theory and evidence', *Organization Science*, 12(2): 99–116.

Scott, R. (1981), *Organizations, Rational, Natural and Open Systems*, Englewood Cliffs, NJ: Prentice-Hall.

Scott, W.R. (1987), 'The adolescence of institutional theory', *Administrative Science Quarterly*, 32: 493–511.

Scott, W.R. (1995), *Institutions and Organizations*, Thousand Oaks, CA: Sage.

Scott, W.R. (2001), *Institutions and Organizations* (2nd edn), Thousand Oaks, CA: Sage.

Scott, W.R. and J.W. Meyer (1991), 'The organization of social sectors: propositions and early evidence', in W.W. Powell and P.J. DiMaggio (eds), *The New Institutionalism in Organizational Analysis*, Chicago: University of Chicago Press, pp. 108–40.

Selznick, P. (1948), 'Foundations of the theory of organization', *American Sociological Review*, 13: 25–35.

Selznick, P. (1957), *Leadership in Administration*, Berkeley, CA: University of California Press.

Senge, P.M. (1990), *The Fifth Discipline*, New York: Doubleday/ Currency.

Seth, A. (1990), 'Value creation in acquisitions: a re-examination of performance issues', *Strategic Management Journal*, 11: 99–115.

Shapiro, D.L., B.H. Sheppard and L. Cheraskin (1992), 'In theory: business on a handshake', *Negotiation Journal*, 8: 365–77.

Shelton, L.M. (1988), 'Strategic business fits and corporate acquisition: empirical evidence', *Strategic Management Journal*, 9: 279–87.

Sherer, P.D. (1995), 'Leveraging human assets in law firms: human capital structure and organizational capabilities', *Industrial and Labor Relations Review*, 48: 671–91.

Sherif, M., O. Harvey, B. White, W. Hood and C. Sherif (1961), *Intergroup conflict and cooperation: The Robber's Cave experiment*, Norman, OK: Institute of Group Relationships, Oklahoma University.

Simmel, G. (1950), *Sociology of Georg Simmel*, Glencoe, USA: Free Press.

Simon, H.A. (1947), *Administrative Behavior: A Study of Decision-Making Processes in Administrative Organizations*, New York: Macmillan.

Simon, H.A. (1957), *Models of Man: Social and Rational: Mathematical Essays on Rational Human Behavior in Social Settings*, New York: Wiley.

Singh, J.V. (1993), 'Review essay: density dependence theory – current issues, future promise', *American Journal of Sociology*, 99: 464–73.

Singh J.V. and C.J. Lumsden (1990), 'Theory and research in organizational ecology', *Annual Review of Sociology*, 16: 161–95.

Singh, H. and C.A. Montgomery (1987), 'Corporate acquisition strategies and economic performance', *Strategic Management Journal*, 8: 377–86.

Singh, J.V., D.J. Tucker and R.J. House (1986), 'Organizational legitimacy and the liability of newness', *Administrative Science Quarterly*, 31: 171–93.

Skaggs, B.C. and M. Youndt (2004), 'Strategic positioning, human capital and performance in service organizations: a customer interaction approach', *Strategic Management Journal*, 25(1): 85–8.

Sluyterman, K.E. (1993), 'Moret: 110 Jaar van Accountancy naar Professionele Dienstverlening', Centrum voor Bedrijfsgeschiedenis: Erasmus University Rotterdam.

Smigel, E.O. (1969), *The Wall Street Lawyer, Professional Organization Man?* Bloomington: Indiana University Press.

Song, J., P. Almeida and G. Wu (2003), 'Learning-by-hiring: when is mobility more likely to facilitate interfirm knowledge transfer?' *Management Science*, 49: 351–65.

Sørensen, J.B. (1999a), 'The ecology of organizational demography: managerial tenure distributions and organizational competition', *Industrial and Corporate Change*, 8: 713–45.

Sørensen, J.B. (1999b), 'Executive migration and interorganizational competition', *Social Science Research*, 28: 289–315.

Sørensen, J.B. (2002), 'The use and misuse of the coefficient of variation in organizational demography research', *Sociological Methods and Research*, 30: 475–91.

Sørensen, O. (2000), 'The effect of population level learning on market entry: the American automobile industry', *Social Science Research*, 29(3): 307–26.

Sorenson, O. and P. Audia (2000), 'The social structure of entrepreneurial activity: geographic concentration of footwear production in the United States, 1940–1989', *American Journal of Sociology*, 106: 424–62.

Sorenson, O. and J.A.C. Baum (2003), 'Geography and strategy: the strategic management of space and place', in O. Sorenson and J.A.C. Baum (eds), *Advances in Strategic Management: Geography and Strategy*, Oxford: JAI/Elsevier.

Sorenson, O. and T.E. Stuart (2001), 'Syndication networks and the spatial distribution of venture capital investments', *American Journal of Sociology*, 106: 1546–88.

Spangler, E. (1984), *Lawyers for Hire: Salaried Professionals at Work*, New Haven, CT: Yale University Press.

Spangler, E. (1986), *Lawyers for Hire: Salaried Professionals at Work*, New Haven, CT: Yale University Press.

Spurr, S.J. (1987), 'How the market solves an assignment problem: the matching of lawyers with legal claims', *Journal of Labor Economics*, 5: 502–32.

Starbuck, W.H. (1992), 'Learning by knowledge-intensive firms', *Journal of Management Studies*, 29: 713–40.

Staw, B.M., L.E. Sandelands and J.E. Dutton (1981), 'Threat-rigidity effects in organizational behavior: a multi-level analysis', *Administrative Science Quarterly*, 26: 501–24.

Stearns, L.B. and K.D. Allan (1996), 'Economic behavior in institutional environments: the corporate merger wave of the 1980s', *American Sociological Review*, 61: 699–718.

Steers, R.M., Y.K. Shin and G.R. Ungson (1989), *The Chaebol*, New York: Harper and Row.

Stewart, I. and M. Golubitsky (1992), *Fearful Symmetry: Is God a Geometer?* Oxford: Blackwell.

Stewman, S. (1988), 'Organizational demography', *Annual Review of Sociology*, 14: 173–202.

Stinchcombe, A. (1965), 'Social structure and organizations', in J.G. March (ed.), *Handbook of Organizations*, Chicago: Rand McNally, pp. 142–93.

Stinchcombe, A. (1997), 'On the virtues of the old institutionalism', *Annual Review of Sociology*, 23: 1–18.

Stokman, F.N., R. Ziegler and J. Scott (1985), *Networks of Corporate Power*, Oxford: Polity Press.

Strang, D. and M.W. Macy (2001), 'In search of excellence: fad, success stories, and adaptive emulation', *American Journal of Sociology*, 107: 147–82.

Strang, D. and J.W. Meyer (1993), 'Institutional conditions for diffusion', *Theory and Society*, 22: 487–511.

Strang, D. and S.A. Soule (1998), 'Diffusion in organizations and social movements: from hybrid corn to poison pills', *Annual Review of Sociology*, 24: 265–90.

Strang, D. and N.B. Tuma (1993), 'Spatial and temporal heterogeneity in diffusion', *American Journal of Sociology*, 99: 614–39.

Straw, B.M. (1980), 'The consequences of turnover', *Journal of Occupational Behaviour*, 1: 253–73.

Stryker, S. (1968), 'Identity salience and role performance', *Journal of Marriage and Family*, 4: 558–64.

Stuart, T.E. (1999), 'Technological prestige and the accumulation of alliance capital', in Roger Leenders and Shaul Gabbay (eds), *Corporate Social Capital and Liabilities*, Boston, MA: Kluwer, pp. 376–89.

Stuart, T.E. and O. Sorenson (2002), 'Liquidity events and the geographic distribution of entrepreneurial activity', working paper, University of Chicago.

Stuart, T.E. and O. Sorenson (2003), 'The geography of opportunity: spatial heterogeneity in founding rates and the performance of biotechnology firms', *Research Policy*, 32: 229–53.

Stuart, T.E., H. Hoang and R.C. Hybels (1997), 'Interorganizational endorsements and the performance of entreptreneurial ventures', working paper, Graduate School of Business, University of Chicago.

Suchman, M.C. (1995), 'Managing legitimacy: strategic and institutional approaches', *Academy of Management Journal*, 20: 571–610.

Sundqvist, S.I. (1990), *Agarna och Markten I Sveriges Borsbolag 1986*, [Owners and Power in Sweden 1986], Stockholm: Dagens Nyheters Forlag.

Suzuki, S. and R.W. Wright (1985), 'Financial structure and bankruptcy risk in Japanese companies', *Journal of International Business Studies*, 16: 97–110.

Tam, S. (1990), 'Centrifugal and centripetal growth processes: contrasting ideal types for conceptualizing the developmental patterns of Chinese and Japanese firms', in S.R. Clegg and S.G. Redding (eds), *Capitalism in Contrasting Cultures*, New York: Walter de Gruyter, pp. 131–52.

Teece, D.J. (1986), 'Profiting from technological innovation: implications for integration, collaboration, licensing and public policy', *Research Policy*, 15(6): 285–305.

Teece, D.J. (1996), 'Firm organization, industrial structure and technological innovation', *Journal of Economic Behavior and Organization*, 31: 193–224.

Teece, D.J., G. Pisano and A. Shuen (1997), 'Dynamic capabilities and strategic management', *Strategic Management Journal*, 18(7): 509–33.

Thaler, P. (1997), 'A bridge lost – interethnicities along the German-Polish border', *International Migration Review*, 31: 694–703.

Thomas, H., S.M. Clark and D.A. Gioia (1993), 'Strategic sense making and organizational performance: linkages among scanning, interpretation, action, and outcomes', *Academy of Management Journal*, 36: 239–70.

Thompson, G. (1982), 'The firm as a dispersed social agency', *Economy and Society*, 11(3): 233–50.

Thompson, J.D. (1967), *Organizations in Action*, New York: McGraw Hill.

Thornton, P.H. (1999), 'The sociology of entrepreneurship', *Annual Review of Sociology*, 25: 19–46.

Tolbert, P.S. and L.G. Zucker (1983), 'Institutional sources of change in the formal structure of organizations: the diffusion of civil service reform, 1880–1935', *Administrative Science Quarterly*, 28: 22–39.

Tomczyk, S. and W.J. Read (1989), 'Direct measurement of supplier concentration in the market for audit services', *Auditing*, 9(1): 98–107.

Trautwein, F. (1990), 'Merger motives and merger prescriptions', *Strategic Management Journal*, 11: 283–95.

Tripsas, M. and G. Gavetti (2000), 'Capabilities cognition and inertia: evidence from digital imaging', *Strategic Management Journal*, 21(10–11): 1147–61.

Tsui, A. (1997), 'Where guanxi matters? Relational demography and guanxi in the Chinese context', *Work and Organizations*, 24: 56–79.

Tuma, N. and M.T. Hannan (1984), *Social Dynamics: Models and Methods*, Orlando: Academic Press.

Tushman, M.L. (1978), 'Task characteristics and technical communication in R&D', *Academy of Management Journal*, 21: 624–45.

Useem, M. and J. Karabel (1986), 'Pathways to corporate management', *American Sociological Review*, 51: 184–200.

Uzzi, B. (1996), 'The sources and consequences of embeddedness for the economic performance of organizations: the network effect', *American Sociological Review*, 61: 674–98.

Uzzi, B. (1997), 'Social structure and competition in inter-firm networks: the paradox of embeddedness', *Administrative Science Quarterly*, 42(1): 35–67.

Van de Ven, W. and B.M.S. Van Praag (1981), 'The demand for deductibles in private health insurance: a probit model with sample selection', *Journal of Econometrics*, 17: 229–52.

Wade, J.B., A. Swaminathan and M.S. Saxon (1998), 'Normative and resource flow consequences of local regulations in the American brewing industry, 1845–1918', *Administrative Science Quarterly*, 43(4): 905–35.

Wagner, J. (1999), 'The life history of exits from German manufacturing', *Small Business Economics*, 13: 71–9.

Walsh, J.P. (1995), 'Managerial and organizational cognition: notes from a trip down memory lane', *Organizational Science*, 6(3): 280–321.

Walton, E.J. (1986), 'Management prototypes of financial firms', *Journal of Management Studies*, 23: 679–98.

Walton, M. (1997), *Car: A Drama of the American Workplace*, New York: Norton.

Weber, M. (1947), *Theory of Economic and Social Organization [Wirtschaft und Gesellschaft]*, Glencoe: Free Press.

Weber, M. (1968), *Economy and Society*, New York: Bedminster Press.

Weick, K.E. (1979), *The Social Psychology of Organizing*, Reading: Addison Wesley.

Weidenbaum, M. and S. Hughes (1996), *The Bamboo Network*, New York: The Free Press.

Wernerfelt, B. (1984), 'A resource-based view of the firm', *Strategic Management Journal*, 5: 171–80.

Westphal, J.D., R. Gulati and S.M. Shortell (1997), 'Customization or conformity: an institutional and network perspective on the content and consequences of TQM adoption', *Administrative Science Quarterly*, 42: 161–83.

Wezel, F.C. (2002), 'Why do organizational populations die?' Working Paper No. 02G38, University of Groningen, The Netherlands.

Wezel, F.C. (2005), 'Location-dependence and industry evolution: founding rates in the United Kingdom motorcycle industry, 1895–1993', *Organization Studies*, 25: 729–54.

Wezel, F.C. and A. Lomi (2003), 'The organizational advantage of nations: an ecological perspective on the evolution of the motorcycle industry in Belgium, Italy and Japan, 1894–1993', in J.A.C. Baum and O. Sorenson (eds), *Geography and Strategy*, Advances in Strategic Management, Greenwich, CT: JAI Press, pp. 359–92.

Wezel, F.C. and A. Saka (2006), 'Antecedents and consequences of organizational change: "institutionalizing" the behavioral theory of the firm', *Organization Studies*, 27: 265–86.

Wezel, F.C. and A. van Witteloostuijn (2006), 'From scooters to choppers: product portfolio change and organizational failure', *Long Range Planning*, 39: 11–28.

Wezel, F.C., G. Cottani and J. Pennings (2006), 'Competitive complications of interfirm mobility', *Organizational Science*, **17**(6), 691–709.

White, H. (1970), *Chains of Opportunity: System Models of Mobility in Organizations*, Cambridge, MA: Harvard University Press.

Wholey, D.and L.R. Burns (1993), 'Adoption and abandonment of matrix management programs: effects of organizational characteristics and interorganizational networks', *Academy of Management Journal*, 36(1): 106–38.

Wiersema, M.A. and A. Bird (1993), 'Organizational demography in Japanese firms: group heterogeneity, individual dissimilarity and top management team turnover', *Academy of Management Journal*, 36: 996–1025.

Williams, C.R. (1999), 'Reward contingency, unemployment, and functional turnover', *Human Resource Management Review*, 9(4): 549–76.

Williams, K.Y. and C.A. O'Reilly III (1998), 'Demography and diversity in organizations: a review of 40 years of research', in L.L. Cummings and B.M. Staw (eds), *Research in Organizational Behavior*, Greenwich, CT: JAI Press, pp. 77–149.

Williamson, O.E. (1975), *Markets and Hierarchies*, New York: Free Press.

Williamson, O.E. (1996), *The Mechanisms of Governance*, New York: Oxford University Press.

Winter, S.G. (1987), 'Knowledge and competence as strategic assets', in D. Teece (ed.), *The Competitive Challenge*, Cambridge, MA: Ballinger, pp. 159–84.

Winter, S.G. (1990), 'Survival, selection, and inheritance in evolutionary theories of organization', in J.V. Singh (ed.), *Organizational Evolution: New Directions*, Newbury Park, CA: Sage, pp. 269–97.

Winter, S.G. (2000), 'The satisficing principle in capability learning', *Strategic Management Journal*, 21(Special Issue): 981–96.

Winter S.G. and G. Szulanski (2001), 'Replication as strategy', *Organization Science*, 12: 730–43.

Womack, J.P., D.T. Jones and D. Roos (1990), *The Machine that Changed the World*, New York: Rawson Associates.

Wrong, D.H. (1961), 'The oversocialized concept of man in modern sociology', *American Sociological Review*, 26: 183–93.

Wrong, D. (1977), 'The oversocialized conception of man in modern sociology', in D. Wrong, *Skeptical Sociology*, London: Heinemann, pp. 31–54.

Wulf, J. (2004), 'Do CEOs in mergers trade power for premium? Evidence from "mergers of equals" ', *Journal of Law, Economics and Organization*, 20(1): 60–101.

Yamaguchi, Y. (1991), *Event History Analysis*, Newbury Park, CA: Sage.

Yin, R. (1994), *Case Study Research: Design and Methods* (2nd edn), Beverly Hills, CA: Sage Publishing.

Yoffie, D.B. (1996), 'Competing in the age of digital convergence', *California Management Review*, 38(4): 31–53.

Yoshino, M.Y. and T.B. Lifson (1986), *The Invisible Link: Japan's Sogo Shosha and the Organization of Trade*, Cambridge, MA: MIT Press.

Young, G.J., M.P. Charns and S.M. Shortell (2001), 'Top manager and network effects on the adoption of innovative management practices: a study of TQM in a public hospital system', *Strategic Management Journal*, 22: 935–51.

Zajonc, R.L. (1968), 'Attitudinal effects of mere exposure', *Journal of Personality and Social Psychology*, 9(2): 1–27.

Zeff, S.A.F., F. Van der Wel and K. Camfferman (1992), *Company Financial Reporting: A Historical and Comparative Study of the Dutch Regulatory Process*, New York: North-Holland.

Zenger, T.R. and B.S. Lawrence (1989), 'Organizational demography: the differential effects of age and tenure distributions on technical communication', *Academy of Management Journal*, 32(2): 353–76.

Zenger, T. and J. Nickerson (2002), 'Being efficiently fickle: a dynamic theory of organizational choice', *Organization Science*, 13(5): 547–66.

Zollo, M. and S.G. Winter (2002), 'Deliberate learning and the evolution of dynamic capabilities', *Organization Science*, 13(3): 339–51.

Zucker, L.G. (1977), 'The role of institutionalization in cultural persistence', *American Sociological Review*, 42: 726–43.

Zucker, L.G. (1986), 'Production of trust: institutional sources of economic structure 1840–1920', in B.M. Staw and L.L. Cummings (eds), *Research in Organizational Behavior*, Greenwich, CT: JAI Press, pp. 53–111.

Zucker, L.G. (1989), 'Combining institutional theory and population ecology: no legitimacy, no history', *American Sociological Review*, 54: 542–5.

Index